# The
# Changing Life
## of the
# Corporate Wife

*By*
*Maryanne Vandervelde*

**WARNER BOOKS**

A Warner Communications Company

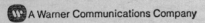

# THEY'RE ALL TALKING ABOUT THE CHANGING LIFE OF THE CORPORATE WIFE

"No subject is taboo—mental illness, alcoholism, even sex. . . . 'the corporate wife needs all the help she can get.' Like this book."

—*Baltimore Sun*

"Excellent . . . for all women."
—*The Fresno Bee*

"A keen analysis that not only questions the validity of such a lifestyle but provides important answers on resolving an identity crisis."

—*Booklist*

". . . should be helpful to both husbands and wives in resolving mutual adjustment problems that could come as a result of the husband's corporate position. But it should also be helpful to people in many other occupations as well."
—*Harmon Killebrew,* former major-league baseball player, now broadcaster and business executive; and *Elaine Killebrew,* artist and teacher; parents of five children.

# ABOUT THE AUTHOR

Maryanne Vandervelde received her A.B. in 1960 from Calvin College, her M.S.W. in 1962 from the University of California at Berkeley, and her Ph.D. in 1978 from the University of Washington. She has worked at a County hospital in California, Bellevue and Mt. Sinai Hospitals in New York, two hospitals in Fairfield County, Connecticut, and the University of Washington in Seattle. Her primary career interest is now administration, but she has maintained a small private practice of psychotherapy for many years. She has lectured at several universities, was co-founder of a Woman's Therapy Referral Service, has run workshops for N.O.W. and other women's groups, and has served as consultant to many organizations. She has had six articles published in professional journals, and is the author of a monograph titled "Management Preparation for Women." Dr. Vandervelde is listed in *Who's Who of American Women.*

*To Spencer and Ray*

# Foreword

It was Friday afternoon, almost three years ago. I was having my hair cut one last time in Connecticut, anticipating the move three thousand miles away and not knowing when I'd find another hairdresser this good—or another way of life this good, for that matter. I looked over to find my friend Rhoda Moss sitting in the next chair, and I began bitching to her about what it means to be a corporate wife. Her reaction was: "Why don't you write a book about it?"

Those words stayed in my head for several months—through periods of mild to moderate depression, through weeks of house hunting, through many disappointing job interviews, through several stages of adjustment, and then through a beginning search of the library.

I could find books about how to *look* good as a corporate wife, how to maintain the right image. I could find things on how to make nice parties, how to say the right thing at the right time, how to do all the "crap work" of a move, how to take complete charge of home and children because your husband is gone all the time. I found one book describing the problem of corporate wife casualties. But there was next to nothing about how a woman maintains her own identity, her own emotional stability and aliveness, her own sense of self, let alone her own career, while all the time functioning in the very prescribed and regimented role of corporate wife.

I had the personal perspective of sixteen years as a corporate wife—in four parts of the country, with three large *Fortune* 500 companies, with a husband in many positions from $7,200-a-year cost accountant to president of a company. I also had the professional perspective of a psychotherapist with fifteen years' working experience, the last seven of which had been in the affluent bedroom community of Fairfield County, Connecticut. I had been director of social work at a private psychiatric hospital there, which was full of corporate wives. Family therapy was an essential part of the treatment in that institution, and it had been fascinating to look into the inner workings of many corporate marriages. In addition, I have had for many years a small private practice, in which I have seen many corporate wives and couples.

But I also wanted some hard data. What are the current attitudes about corporate wives? Is there a prescribed role? What do women face from the corporation if they choose to be different? The chief executive officers of the *Fortune* 500 companies and their wives were selected as a target group—not because they are typical of all corporate couples, because they are not. They are older, more affluent, more powerful than most of us. But it is their opinions that affect every executive and every corporate wife in those companies. Futhermore, their opinions radiate to other, smaller companies, other kinds of businesses, and all kinds of peripheral people who deal with the *Fortune* 500 in any way. They are the thought leaders of the corporate world. Approximately a quarter of these thousand people (CEOs and their wives) completed my questionnaire, and of those, a substantial number were also interviewed subsequently.

With these three perspectives in place, this book began to evolve.

My experience thus far has indicated that men are as interested in this subject as women. Although the book is written primarily with the wife's perspective in mind, it is also meant for men—those who share some conflict about roles, those who want to understand their wives and their marital relationships better, and those who simply are curious about that woman to whom they are married. The epilogue, which my husband has written, is addressed more directly to men.

Although the focus is corporate wives, most of these points should be equally useful for wives of physicians, attorneys, clergymen, military officers, politicians, architects, small businessmen, and other men who pursue demanding and upwardly mobile careers. The unique things about corporate wives are the nature of corporate expectations, and perhaps the frequency and character of the moves they make. But many women other than corporate wives should recognize whereof I speak.

Thanks are due to many people who helped make this book a reality. I am indebted to the CEOs and their wives who took time from their busy schedules to complete the questionnaire, and especially to those who agreed to be interviewed. I am grateful to many friends and acquaintances who graciously submitted to questioning about their lives and roles. Most of the people I interviewed agreed to be quoted, and they were allowed to approve their quotes. To the many people all over the country who fed me information and critiqued parts of the manuscript: I couldn't have done it without you. To my family and friends, who weren't able to eat at my dining room table for a year, while various stages of the manuscript were strewn about: It's going to get better. And to four very special people—my husband and son, to whom this book is dedicated; my mother, Bertha W. Vandervelde, who was my example of an independent woman long before that was popular; and my brother David: love.

—M. V.

Mercer Island, Washington
February 1978

# Contents

# PART ONE

## Independent Woman Versus Versus Corporation Wife

# 1

# Contradiction, Confrontation, Compromise

The stereotype of the corporate wife is a woman whose own needs and happiness rank second to those of her husband, and probably third, fourth, fifth, and so on to those of her children. Her husband's career is of utmost importance in her life; her financial and emotional security come through his job; his success is the key to her contentment; and her sense of accomplishment comes in seeing him prosper.

When the corporation decides to move him to another location, she talks about the great opportunity, smiles bravely, takes care of the real estate problems and countless other onerous details, gets the family resettled, and mostly denies her feelings of loneliness, loss, isolation, fear, and depression. In fact, she would feel guilty if she admitted these reactions; her husband would most likely not understand, and she would generally be seen as hindering or impeding his career. She accepts gracefully the need to entertain people she often dislikes and has little in common with. She takes great pains to make a good impression on her husband's superiors, and would be most reluctant to express an opinion that is different from theirs. She accepts her husband's long hours and absences from home with a smile; her household is run like a branch office. She is willing to drop her old friends as he moves up, and she even tries to change her personality and habits, if necessary, to fit in with his job and associates. She may decide to take a job, but she would arrange her hours and vacations to fit in with her husband's, and she would find it impossible to put in the extra time and energy that a "career" versus a "job" requires.

In her most extreme—and some would say her most valuable—form, the corporate wife allows the company to get two employees for the price of one.

One graphic description of the corporate wife is this cartoon from the "Treadwells" series.

First, that she is in a serving position; she has his martini waiting when he arrives home. Second, she has a

THE TREADWELLS

"WELL, I ASKED HIM FOR THE RAISE, AS YOU TOLD ME TO, AND HE TURNED ME DOWN, AS *HIS* WIFE TOLD *HIM* TO."

tremendous investment in his career; she has given him advice and is waiting anxiously to hear its results. Third, she is both very powerful and very powerless; both of these men listened to and followed their wives' suggestions, but this wife has power only through her husband. She has no ability to act directly to get what she wants. In actuality, she may be more intelligent or more capable than her husband. She is pictured here as well dressed, composed, and emotionally stable, while he looks quite disheveled and distressed. Nevertheless, she must work through him and gain her satisfaction primarily through him. If she has a job, it is clear that she has made it home in time to greet him with a drink, and there is no indication that either of them is invested in her career. Last, but not least, this whole situation is subject matter for an assumedly funny cartoon.

A most extreme portrayal of corporate wives will be remembered by anyone who saw the movie "The Stepford Wives." The ideal wife there was pictured as a subservient automaton, a robot who met all her husband's physical needs while making no demands. Ira Levin wrote the script while he was in the process of a divorce, but many executives still joke about how nice it would be to have one of those Stepford Wives.

In contrast, an independent woman, whether or not she is married, is first and foremost *her own person*. She is free to have her own opinions, to pursue a career or any other interests, to experiment with various kinds of emotional and sexual relationships, to meet her own needs in ways she sees fit, to develop herself into as whole a person as possible. Volumes have been written about women's liberation and the women's movement, but more than anything else, the definitions of liberation stress *freedom* and *choice*. Psychologist Phyllis Chesler's definition of feminism is apt: the declaration that man as God on earth is dead.

Independent woman . . . corporation wife; these words conjure up pictures of opposite types of women. Until recently it would have been impossible to combine the two descriptions in the same person. Traditionally,

19

women have been forced to choose one role or the other. And there is still hard evidence that formidable forces are trying to keep the corporation wife in her place. But our social system is changing, and corporate wives are beginning to force changes in the lagging corporate structure as well. The struggle is important and worthwhile because there are tremendous benefits in being both an independent woman and a part of the American corporate scene. Indeed, there is no good reason why women should not be able to have the best of both worlds.

Corporate wives, then, perhaps a bit more slowly and tentatively than other women, are beginning to question all the prescriptions the world and the corporation have given them. They, like other American women, are having to ask themselves the difficult and serious question, "Who am I?"

For me, personally, the answers to this question are complex and often contradictory. As an independent woman, I am a psychotherapist and administrator, a Ph.D. candidate, the partner of a very special man, a proud and permissive mother, a nonathletic klutz (though my husband is a jock), a music and animal lover, and a person striving for fulfillment, getting pleasure from many different kinds of relationships. As the wife of a successful executive, I often feel restricted and confined by the demands made on my time and my attitudes. I am mindful of making the right impression on my husband's bosses; concerned about how much of "me" I can safely expose; delighted by the business trips I *decide* to go on; resentful of most of the trips I *have* to go on; accepting, even enjoying, some parts of the entertaining I do; hating entertaining when I'm pressed for time or the people are dull; relishing the benefits of his increasing salary; wishing I hadn't had to make the three-thousand-mile move that brought his last salary increase; trying to see the change in location in terms of new opportunities for both of us; missing terribly my friends and my job and the sense of security I had in the old location. My own often painful compromises and the equally joyful benefits that come from having feet in both worlds are unique to me, but they certainly are not atypical.

Many women these days are in some stage of struggle or conflict about roles. The corporate wife is certainly not alone, but that doesn't necessarily make her dilemma easier. Those who choose extreme independence often find that they must forgo family life. Those who choose the traditional corporate image often become empty inside—one-dimensional women whose identity is simply an extension or appendage of their husbands'. The traditional corporate wife works hard at her "job," but with all this effort, and with all the appearance of success in the corporate definition, she often seems half-alive. She is prone to moderate or severe depression, and she often feels terribly anxious, but she usually doesn't have the remotest idea of the cause. Certainly her life is the American dream; she should be happy.

And the problem does not belong only to women. Male executives are increasingly baffled by their wives' emotions, and upset that they are so unable to help. Most men have learned from childhood that if they provide well for their families in terms of money and status, everything will turn out all right. It follows then that somewhere in their guts they also feel responsible for the things that go wrong. They often feel the weighty burden of both financial and emotional support for their wives. If an executive's wife has given up all independent areas of her own life to help him up the success ladder, he had damn well better succeed. If his career falters or he experiences setbacks, he has certainly let his wife down as well as himself; it is natural for her to feel more disappointment than she would if her eggs were not all in one basket.

One corporate wife, now in her late thirties, said that when she married a brilliant young Harvard MBA just after he went to work for an automobile company in Detroit, she was absolutely sure that he would one day be president of General Motors. So she set about helping in every way possible to accomplish that goal. Although she herself had worked hard to get an education, she willingly gave up her own career after two years to be Supermom, become a gourmet cook, take care of her home, and entertain beautifully. Gradually, however, it dawned on her that her husband will never be president of GM. In fact, he has probably topped out at the department-head level. The anger at him, disappointment, loss, and frustration she felt almost ended their marriage and did send her into therapy. She gradually began to get back to her own career and became less dependent on him; but in the process she was amazed to hear from her husband what a heavy burden her expectations had been on him.

Men of good will may be aware of the changing attitudes about women; they may even think they are unbiased about roles for their wives. But they are finding, to their great frustration, that this is simply one area they cannot manage or control. Perhaps it is an area that they don't even understand very well.

## ATTITUDES THAT SHAPE THE ROLE

My questionnaire survey of the *Fortune* 500 companies' chief executive officers and their wives was designed to get an accurate picture of current attitudes about corporate wives—what is expected of them, what is the role or model into which they are expected to fit. The *Fortune* 500 CEOs and their wives were chosen for study because they, as people, and their attitudes, as policies, will affect every executive and every executive's wife associated with those companies. These men and women set the tone not only for their own companies—a wide range of America's largest industries—but they also greatly affect the practices of bankers, attorneys, suppliers and clients in smaller companies, trade associations, and many other people who come in contact with the *Fortune* 500.

The survey produced some fascinating information and some shocking statistics.

• Concern about her own identity is the least desirable characteristic of a corporate wife. The respondents were given five characteristics to list in order of im-

22

portance, and this one was consistently listed toward the end. In fact, 49 percent of the men and an amazing 72 percent of the women listed the identity characteristic last.

• Sense of humor is the most important quality of a good corporate wife to the chief executive officers of America's foremost companies. Seventy percent of the men and a proportionately high 65 percent of their wives said they would value this quality in a corporate wife. Does this mean that anyone who has a sense of humor and therefore a sense of perspective about her position can do a better job? Or does it mean that because the role of corporate wife is so demeaning, so comical, so ridiculous, only a woman who looks at it with a sense of humor can accomplish it well? Certainly, sense of humor in a corporate wife is more of an asset than a detriment. It is doubtful, however, that, if the *Fortune* 500 companies' chief executive officers were asked about the most important characteristics for their own positions, sense of humor would appear at the top of the list.

• Adaptability is the quality valued by the greatest number of wives, followed closely by graciousness. This is probably an accurate description of the "ideal" corporate wife. But would most people be satisfied with this epitaph: She/he was adaptable and gracious?

• Intelligence is important, but independence was near the bottom of the list (12 percent of the CEOs; 18 percent of their wives). Should this high intelligence be confined only to supportive activities and never used in independent pursuits? And what does it take to run a household and raise children essentially in the absence of the executive husband if not independence?

• Attitudes expressed about relationships are extremely moralistic, especially in sexual matters. Sexual conservatism is the norm. CEOs and their wives are overwhelmingly against open marriages, homosexuality or bisexuality, and extramarital affairs for themselves and others, although the old double standard is apparent in more sexual freedom for men than for women.

• Women see themselves doing considerably more

23

entertaining than their husbands acknowledge. It is possible that the women exaggerate the burdens of entertaining; it is more likely that husbands tend to ignore and underestimate this aspect of their careers.

• The average number of moves an executive and his family make is one every five years. This includes people in marketing, who would move more often, and people in finance, who would tend to move less often; but it adds up to a lot of disruption or change in a lifetime; and it is especially significant when compared to physicians or attorneys, who seldom make any geographical moves.

• Attitudes about corporate wives have not changed in the past few years, according to 85 percent of the men and 70 percent of the women. This is an astonishing finding indeed. With the rapidly changing consciousness about women and women's roles, this indicates a very unaware and/or unmoved group.

If she tries to break out of the mold, it is important that a corporate wife be aware of the climate, be tuned in to the people with whom she will be dealing, and be cognizant of some of the pressure and hostility she will face.


## THE SCHIZOPHRENOGENIC MESSAGE

The expected role of the corporate wife seems to have changed very little over the years, and it is propagated by both men and women. In her 1974 book, *How to Survive as a Corporate Wife,* Norma Upson explains what it means to be the wife of a salesman:

> Family living is different in the sales world. Erratic hours demand flexibility not needed in other homes. . . . [Entertaining] makes it mandatory for a wife to know how to cope with all types of personalities and situations diplomatically, graciously and expeditiously.
> Transfers are common. The trauma of leaving the familiar for the new, even though it means

24

promotion and a higher standard of living, can be overwhelming for the entire family. Knowing how to move, how to sell a home and choose a new one with an eye to happy living, convenience, and resale potential is a must.

A salesman's wife spends many hours alone. This creates a need for strength and inner resources not called upon in wives of men in other professions. Filling time productively and satisfactorily is a challenge.

Children of salesmen develop or diminish according to ways their particular problems (a father who travels, new environment, mother-dominated home, etc.) are handled.[1]

A complicated picture. But the advice to women is to accept it all and be strong:

Your real home is in your heart. Your best friends, your family, and your dearest loves are no farther than your memory. You can take life and mold it to suit your values. No outside force can warp you if you decide it cannot touch you. You must grow with life or it will leave you behind.[2]

And what if the little woman has some trouble doing all this? What if she has doubts about her role, or begins to feel a little crazy? How is she to deal with ambivalence?

There should be no conflict in the minds of women who prefer to spend their lives making safe and sane homes for their families. For if there is conflict, it must be in the mind rather than in choices we have made.[3]

Upson tells us we must not only cope with a multitude of problems, we must constantly show strength and growth, and through it all we have no right to feel conflict.

Another list of expectations, this time from Ninki

25

Hart Burger in *The Executive's Wife,* says that a corporate wife's role is:

> To help ease, perhaps even erase, some of the pressures on your husband, exposed each working day to the insane, inane, insistent, intense experiences of executive life.
> To control a home environment—a small revolving world within a great world—that allows your family and you to grow inwardly and yet share with each other.
> To view, not with alarm, but with understanding, the demands essential to your role as the wife of today's executive, and to perform with patience and sensitivity.
> To work to discover fuller, deeper enjoyment of your own life.[4]

One could not say that these objectives are wrong, but their priorities simply do not make sense for any woman who is concerned about her own identity. By the time any person accomplished the first three, there would be little time or energy for the last, and it is clearly the last one that has to be achieved in order to have any semblance of pleasure and security in oneself.

In her recent book, *Men and Women of the Corporation,* sociologist Rosabeth Moss Kanter has conceptualized the duality of the wife's position vis-à-vis the corporation. Corporate wives are both insiders and outsiders. They are at times directly involved with the company, at times involved only with and through their husbands, and at times totally uninvolved. At Indsco, the fictional name of the company Kanter studied, the "libertarian" position held that anything wives did was strictly voluntary, their own choice. Employees' private lives were supposedly their own business, and the company had no right to interfere. To think otherwise smacked of paternalism not in keeping with modern management practices. Yet this "libertarian" position was also used to avoid the issue of how much the company was already constraining employees' families; it helped evade any organizational responsibility.

> The most recurrent complaint from Indsco wives had to do with the limits of the role they were given to play: on the one hand, faced with strong demands to be gracious, charming hostesses and social creatures, supporting their husbands' careers and motivating their achievements, with the boundaries of their own life choices set by the company; but on the other hand, kept away from opportunities to see, understand, and even participate in their husbands' jobs. They simultaneously wanted to be left alone to live their own lives *and* to be more involved in their husbands'.[5]

A second school of thought at Indsco saw the wife's role as a source of marital tension and strain, which, in turn, had bearing on the man's work performance. These people supported the idea that more attention be given to work-family issues and that wives be considered "inside" company boundaries. The advocates of this point of view felt the company had a responsibility to wives—of what kind is not altogether clear.

Kanter does explicate clearly that the connection between the corporate wife role and the organization is not a simple matter. There are clear constraints within which the corporate wife must operate, and the corporation is central in the conduct of her life.

> The very ambivalence of corporations toward the "wife problem" (William Whyte's label) indicates a fundamental tension in social life between the demands of organization work and the pulls of family. . . . Is the wife a helper to be embraced or a danger to be minimized? Is she an unpaid worker, or a separate reality irrelevant to the organization—an independent person on whom the organization has no claims?[6]

It is important that women recognize the inconsistencies in the model and the conflicting demands placed on them. We must be loving, supportive, selfless, adaptable, and gracious. But we must also maintain good communication, be intelligent, and handle most family and household matters independently. The corporation sees us simultaneously as insiders and outsiders. It constrains our lives, but it does not compensate us in any way, and it sometimes considers us a nuisance. It expects us to be always available, but at the same time to live our own lives. Does this not make us feel crazy (if we can't do it all), or guilty (if we don't want to), or both? Doesn't it cause many of us to remain divided against ourselves? The message from both husband and corporation is: Be yourself, but cater to me first—a schizophrenogenic prescription if I ever heard one!

## PREPARATION

One of the biggest dilemmas is that very few young couples know when they marry what positions they will hold, what demands will be made on them, twenty or thirty years later. In the survey of the *Fortune* 500 companies' chief executive officers and their wives, it became blatantly clear that some wives are better suited to their leadership roles than others. To paraphrase Oliver Wendell Holmes's statement about Washington politicians and their wives: The corporate world is full of very interesting men and the women they married when they were very, very young.

Often a young executive thinks that a wife who serves him is in his best interests. Somewhere along the way, however, he may find that he wants something else. One CEO, a charming man who is head of a very large company, was divorced and remarried ten years ago. He described his first wife as a woman who did everything just the way he wanted, then said his second wife "is more difficult because she is into her own things and is not always available." He asked me not to use his name because it would be embarrassing to his ex-wife and grown children, but he summed up the difference between his current marriage and his first as "the difference between companionship and slavery." He says he never needed a slave, but he needs a companion very much and is very grateful finally to have one.

The problem of prediction is one that should be considered by both women and men. Asther Hayden Yogman, a bright, independent woman whose husband was chief executive officer of J. E. Seagram in New York and now is vice-chairman at Esquire, reminded me that she did not start out to be a top executive's wife: "I didn't marry an executive. I married a boy the day after he graduated. If I emphasize the importance of independence, intelligence, and resourcefulness, it is not for the corporation's sake, but my own. The corporate executive is never around for the crises of home and children, or even mere companionship. The wife is really alone with her kids. Unless you have lots of servants or send them away to school, you have to raise them alone." The Yogmans' daughter, Victoria, a delightful college sophomore, echoed her mother's sentiments. She said she admires her father but "I often feel like I was brought up by a widowed mother." They both suggested that many executives are totally involved in their careers; "they are fathers by accident."

Mrs. Yogman's ideas are typical of many other introspective, honest executives' wives who feel they might do it differently today: "My daughter's generation is more wise; my kind is largely about to be over. People like Vicky are going to have a career of their own; all of her friends are career oriented. If Vicky knows the pitfalls beforehand, she can plan differently than I did. If I had a career I could follow, I would work. But I have no intention of working as a secretary, and it's a little late for me to go back to school. I have volunteered for twenty-five years and could list three pages of board memberships where I was always a working member, but that could never make for a fulfilling life." Mrs. Yogman is available for conven-

29

tions and entertaining as necessary, but does not like to be labeled: "If I should be expected to function as a corporate wife, they can damn well put me on the payroll."

Another articulate, lovely woman who emphasized the dilemma of expectations and preparation was Grace Wilson, whose husband, Thornton A. Wilson, heads the Boeing Company in Seattle. Mrs. Wilson has been growing into the job as chief executive's wife but admits to "feelings of inadequacy. I'm not as sure of myself as I'd like to be. I have gradually been learning a little more about how to live graciously, and acquiring a few of the things you need to entertain well." She noted that it is easier for women who were raised in wealthy families to play this role than it is for women who were raised "garden variety. It makes a lot of difference when you have to learn. I want people whom I entertain to have a good time, and good food, and not be bored spitless." One suspects, despite her modesty—or maybe because of it—that Mrs. Wilson is a joy to be around. She obviously knows who she is and where she is in life, but she proves that this is not an easy process.

Few of the women I interviewed were as candid and down-to-earth as Mrs. Wilson, but I suspect that her struggle is fairly typical. "T. always had a good job with Boeing, and the pay was good, but the rest wasn't easy. When the kids were little, he was never home. I've had arthritis since age twenty-four and wasn't well much of the time. I would get depressed and nasty, and was weeping a lot. One day my sister Jean straightened me out. She woke me up to the fact that I was just going to have to change things. I would just have to feed the kids and take care of things. Now I'm the best short-order cook in the world. The kids just had to depend on their mother more. I had to accept the fact that T. was getting ahead. That's what we both wanted. I had to accept the things that went with it. I still complained about a lot of things, but there were so many things to enjoy. The travel has been great, and we meet fantastic people."

Mrs. Wilson told of a recent trip to Jordan with King

Hussein, who had just purchased a Boeing airplane. They stopped in Washington on the way for dinner at the White House. "One of the most fun parts is learning that famous people are just people; so many other women never have the opportunity to realize this. We have gotten so many good friends in other countries just by visiting or having them in our home."

Many of the men who were interviewed also mentioned preparation and stressed the importance of trying to choose the right wife for the role. Stephen H. Fuller has been vice-president of personnel, administration, and development at General Motors for six years, and was for twenty-seven years before that a highly respected professor at Harvard Business School. This delightful, erudite man credits his wife for many of his values and says, "It would be wise as individuals to try to select our spouses with some perspective of the future. Even if it would be desirable, the executive cannot separate his business and personal life completely. I am one, not two people. I carry more home with me than just my briefcase. I carry my joy, my tiredness. And my wife carries her day home with her too. I rank my own ability to relate to my wife above my job. It is the stability around which everything else must orbit. It is the security system without which our sons would not be nearly so able to grow, to experiment, to gain self-confidence." Mr. Fuller's wife, Frances, is hardly the typical corporate wife, and he obviously relishes her accomplishments. "Thirty years ago, she was a lecturer at Harvard University when women faculty members could almost be counted on one's fingers. She has been an alumna trustee of Radcliffe College and the first and, until this year, the only woman member of the Board of Trustees at the University of Detroit. She continues her interest in management training for women by serving as chairperson of the Advisory Boards of the Simmons College Management Programs and by participating in seminars for newly appointed women managers." He added: "I question what it would be like for any couple to live with the uneven development that seems so

31

often to take place. It must create real problems within the home. But this would be true whether the man becomes a senator, president of a university, or chairman of a company. The impact of an executive's life on his wife is tremendous. In any organization, do the wives make a sacrifice! And this is not just in terms of entertaining or going to conferences. Their husbands are up early, home late, carry full briefcases, and are gone many weekends. I do not think the effect on Mrs. Fuller is quite so great as it is on many other wives—she is far more self-sufficient than most."

## IDENTITY

The answers for the corporate wife of today, and certainly the corporate wife of tomorrow, lie in the area of identity—the identity that has been almost totally denied her by the corporate world. No longer should that world be able to make tremendous demands on her and see her only as an extension of her husband. She is not an appendage; she must force them to take her seriously.

Among the few people in our survey who underscored the importance of identity were Kathleen May, Jane Dart, and Edward Donley, and their comments say it well.

Kathleen May, the attractive, gracious wife of the man who heads American Can Company, put it this way: "If you're not yourself, you're no good to anybody." Her personal philosophy is the antithesis of the corporate wife as dependent clinging vine. "I could not be faithful to a career or demanding volunteer job because of all the traveling we do. I have never worked, but Bill would be good about it if I wanted to. He would prefer to have things as they are now, with me at home, free to go on trips with him. But if I wanted it some other way, he would go along with me. I have lots of hobbies and interests that I do by myself that really absorb me. I find that corporate wives these days are very much personalities of their own, and you have to credit enlightened men

32

for a lot of this. Men are in touch with interesting women all the time. My feeling is that you have to hold people with a silken thread. You have to be able to let them go. When you let them go, then they want to be around. This applies to kids as well as husbands. It is like dogs who are always kept on a leash—if you let them loose, you probably never see them again. Of course, it helps to feel secure in the love of that key person."

Jane Dart is a warm, enthusiastic woman; her husband, Justin, heads Dart Industries in Los Angeles. She described a drastic change in women over the past few years. "This was part of a long shadow that finally came to a head in the sixties. Women had had these fragmented, kind of chopped-up little lives. I'm not part of the women's lib movement, but I guess it stemmed from that, and it is terribly exciting. I see it amazingly in the generation of our children. Two of our three children are married now, and the wives are very career oriented. Our daughter is involved in a fascinating job. Our daughter-in-law is raising two little children, but is also involved in the natural history museum and the ballet. All of their friends are doing something. The women are really blossoming. And it doesn't stop with the young ones. I have very few pals who aren't up to their eyelids in enthusiasms for museums, the Music Center, the Huntington Library, or whatever. But maybe it is different out here because of the creative vitality of the entertainment industry."

Edward Donley, who heads Air Products and Chemicals in Allentown, Pennsylvania, is one of the more liberated men I talked to, and says his business friends call him a liberal on sociological issues. He felt the identity characteristic was very important and said, "A person not concerned about her own identity could not perform the functions of a corporate wife very well. I think there is an age gradient here. It is a changing continuum. Most women in their fifties are not so concerned about these questions. But I see more young women in their twenties and thirties involved in careers of their own. The change is a continuum."

# SOME WOMEN ARE DOING BOTH

Finding corporation wives who are really independent and who are involved in their own career pursuits is a little like looking for the proverbial needle in a haystack. Most of the chief executive officers' wives I interviewed said they don't see this kind of woman very often, but they usually agreed that the trend toward careers was growing among younger wives. Following are the brief stories of two women who are trying to do both.

One example is Kashiyo Enokido, a thirty-six-year-old Japanese journalist, student, and mother of one child. Her American husband, Tom Crouse, is a vice-president of a large international bank. Both Kashiyo and her husband have a zest for new experiences, and they are into a routine in New York of entertaining or being entertained an average of twice a week. They feel this is a light schedule because during the time they were stationed with the bank in Asia, they were involved in business/social functions four or five nights each week. Kashiyo says, "Now I often have to juggle my graduate school classes, writing, and domestic chores with these bank activities, but my husband helps out a lot at home. We both love life in New York City, because there definitely is our private life. While we were overseas I felt we were both tied twenty-four hours a day, seven days a week to the bank. I believe that many women in overseas assignment frequently do their entertaining out of a sense of obligation, but without these activities they might feel alienated from other bank wives. After several years of life like that, many wives begin to feel that they are part of the company. When they travel, they expect to be treated the same way as their husbands by foreign staff. They are truly involved and, in many cases, they have no identity of their own. I see changes in myself after two years in New York. Now I can be myself, as an individual apart from the hundred percent (timewise) involvement of a bank life. Frequently we have visitors in New York from overseas who are still leading the kind of life we used to. Many of these wives talk about the bank with a strong sense of involvement and mission. At the same time, I see increasing personal and even professional independence among younger wives who have pursued premarital interests or developed new pursuits in an effort to create their own lives, and they seem to enjoy that. This appears to be very stimulating to the wife and, for that matter, the marriage itself."

Kashiyo is a strong, independent, very busy, and very interesting woman. Her husband has had to take a prominent role in household management and care of their small daughter, Alissa; but he is proud of Kay, and he also recognizes advantages for himself when he says: "My wife's education and her career are the best life insurance policy I could have."

Corky Miller is a thirty-one-year-old merchandising consultant who lives in Winnetka, Illinois. Until recently she was a highly paid buyer for B. Altman in New York, running a $4-million section of the company, traveling around the world three months out of every year, and carrying very heavy responsibility. When her husband, Paul, took a position in Connecticut, she decided to incorporate her business as a consultant; and when he moved again last year to Chicago as vice-president of marketing for the Cory division of Hershey, she moved her consulting business too.

The transition has been easy for her partly because of her contacts. "If you're good at what you do, people get to know you. We both needed to slow down a bit when we moved here, but I will always continue to work because that's the kind of life I choose. You have to be selfish enough to do what is right for you. Only you can make yourself happy; no one else really cares if you make a hundred thousand dollars a year or are president of a major corporation. You have to make the trade-offs. Cycles change and needs change. I enjoy being my own person and yet being married. I still travel to California and Europe, and often to New York."

Their son Andrew is now eighteen months old, and Corky has always depended greatly on live-in help, but she admits that their child takes more time and energy than she had imagined. Nevertheless, she would not want anything less than this combination of roles.

"Paul is incredibly flexible; I don't know that too many men could handle this kind of life so well. Some of our friends have blatantly said they would not tolerate it. Their attitudes seem to depend on their upbringing and on their own security. One key factor is the ability of the individuals to communicate and define priorities in the beginning. You have to come to some kind of agreement about whose job justifies making a transfer."

Do her two roles ever conflict?

"Yes, at times I am required to be the typical at-home wife, and I am terribly frustrated in a social situation when left to talk small talk to women when the truly interesting conversation is business with men. However, if I thought my presence would be of benefit to Paul, I'd be there. He has always been flexible about doing things for me too."

## CHANGES

It is an indisputable fact that women's roles are changing and that attitudes about women are being shaken up. One might expect that the current interest in businesswomen and the emergence of women into executive positions would be a bonus for corporate wives as well; but in practice, the effect is exactly the opposite. Until recently, women executives have not been much of a threat. They were few in number, and to use Asther Yogman's words, "Those who made it behaved just like the men. They were not the kind who had any feeling for the women's movement." Now the numbers and the types are changing; and honest corporate wives are beginning to feel the comparisons.

Introspective women are aware of some jealousy over the faddish interest in women executives, especially if they

36

have been discouraged from any such roles for themselves. Many opportunities are suddenly open for women in business. In moments of candor, most top executives admit that the primary reason for this change is the recent affirmative action legislation. No sudden attacks of conscience have occurred to enlighten male executives about equality for women. They have essentially been forced to help women and, in the process, themselves. Nevertheless, there appears to be an honest search under way for capable, knowledgeable women executives in all fields. There has been considerable litigation brought against major U.S. companies by women—with surprising success and substantial financial losses to the corporations. There is suddenly a frantic scurrying by executives to make sure they comply with the law.

However, there is no such legislation to protect the rights of corporate wives. And thus, although there are discernible changes here too, they are much slower and generally only in response to the demands of individual wives and their husbands.

As a complicating factor, women are just beginning to realize that work can be very sexy. As we work with people closely and get to know them well, we find things in common; that little French restaurant may be a favorite of both, or we may both be dying to see a certain movie. It is a few short steps from there to a drink after work Friday night, and only a few more steps from there to bed. Even women who have never held full-time jobs are conscious of attractions to men with whom they have worked on some project. One man on a church fellowship committee may have become much more appealing after a few weeks than he started out to be; a man on that school levy committee might suddenly become the subject of daydreams and fantasies after you've discovered that his opinions are so like yours or his reactions to people seem so like yours.

Working together on an exciting project can be the biggest aphrodisiac in the world, and that is one reason why people who work together often sleep together. The corporate wife has always been a bit more anxious when

37

her husband is on a business trip with a female co-worker or secretary. Now she has to face the fact that her husband is increasingly associated with women at work—not just secretaries, but other competent, intelligent, stimulating women at the executive level as well. As women are slowly infiltrating the ranks of sales positions, they can be found traveling with men, asking men to lunch, and staying in next-door hotel rooms—a phenomenon that salesmen's wives never had to consider until recently. What is the effect now of men being turned on by attractive, educated female associates, who also have power and money?

Will the woman whose main concern has been her husband and children be able to compete with these more worldly women? She may have heard sad stories of middle-aged women being dumped by successful husbands for younger replacements, but now there are even more ingredients than age. Her husband is becoming intrigued and fascinated and sexually aroused by a different type of woman. She always thought she had played her cards right. Now she is not so sure. She is beginning to read and hear about an alarming and fascinating new development in our society: The divorce rate among couples married twenty years or more is skyrocketing; and divorce in corporations is increasingly acceptable.

Just when it would seem that two people have shared enough intimacies to last a lifetime, just when they are finally secure financially and have raised a family together, one or both of them are opting out of a relationship that seems dead and worthless. Many experts are speculating on the cause for this, but one cause seems to be success. Often the man has fought and struggled hard to make it to the top, but when he gets there he says, "Is this all there is?" This reevaluation of his life includes his marriage, and increasingly these days he wants out rather than to accept the status quo. If the wife has lived her life primarily through him and has little separate identity, she is left confused and bewildered and hopeless. She is devastated and doesn't even know what went wrong. She was always loyal, self-sacrificing, adaptable, and "proper";

she took the road that was prescribed for the corporate wife. She probably doesn't even known what hit her.

In the old days, a woman who was the "victim" in a divorce action could at least look forward to the solace of a very substantial settlement. Alimony used to be seen almost as payment for the man's freedom. Now long-term alimony is gradually becoming a thing of the past. The courts are increasingly viewing alimony as a rehabilitative measure to aid dependent wives in making the transition to independence.

Even if a divorce or another woman is not part of the picture, there are other things around the corporate wife that are threatening to take away her security. Business executives are likely targets for early heart attacks and other stress-related illnesses. Her husband's death or disability can take away her comfort, her economic security, and her emotional stability in an instant. The concern for "displaced homemakers" is now receiving a great deal of serious attention, and federally funded centers are springing up all over the country.

Many corporate wives have distrusted what they call women's lib and have been sure it had nothing to do with them. They liked what they saw as their privileged position; but whether they like it or not, laws are now being passed that make them equal. They were happy being less equal but more privileged. The laws and the courts now seem to be taking that away from them. Affirmative action and antidiscrimination legislation are popping up in every level of government.

As a further development, the women's movement has made many men and women at least intellectually aware that a system in which one partner gives up almost total autonomy is not fair, and it often becomes boring as well. There is suddenly a buildup of pressure on women to reassess every area of their lives. There are some confusing and unnerving messages in the media that the choices open to women are boundless. Many couples are reacting with near panic to the increasing pressure in the message that being wife and mother are no longer enough.

Some women in the suburbs say that five years ago if

they were holding a job, they would have been asked at cocktail parties, "Why in the world do you work?" Two years ago they might have been asked with some skepticism if they were working because they wanted to or had to. Now there is more genuine interest by both men and women in any activity they have outside the home. One woman I know has been answering any man who thinks she is a housewife in this manner: "No, I'm not a housewife. Are you a househusband?" Five years from now—and in certain groups it is happening already—women who *don't* hold jobs will probably be asked, "Why in the world don't you work?" Gradually, in various segments of our society, the same questions about one's place in the working world are being put to both men and women.

At the same time, there are still tremendous constraints against this kind of equality. And one of the strongest bastions against these "new" roles for women is still the corporation. There is always a culture lag in getting attitudes into practice, but it seems that the business world is lagging far behind the rest of the world in this regard. Sensitive women are beginning to feel more and more caught and squeezed between two warring ideologies and factions. They see inequality all around them—in their own marriages as well as those of friends—and are aware that there is something wrong with this. It is becoming clear to them that unequal growth and experience, which happens so often to corporate couples, tends to damage and erode all areas of living. And yet, it is so hard to know what to do.

As A. A. Milne describes it in *Winnie the Pooh,*

Here is Edward Bear, coming downstairs now, bump, bump, bump on the back of his head. It is, as far as he knows, the only way of coming downstairs, but sometimes he feels that there really is another way, if only he could stop bumping for a moment and think of it. And then he feels that perhaps there isn't. Anyhow . . .

# PATTERN PERPETUATION

One of the early steps in liberation must be to understand the two-way process by which corporate wives have remained for years in the one-down position vis-à-vis the corporation. In no occupation except the corporate world is the wife's involvement so imperative, so prescribed, so regimented, and so demanded. It is too early to tell whether husbands of female executives will have the same kinds of demands placed on them, but limited experience indicates that this is a different ball game. The important factor in the attitude about corporation wives is that they are women.

But why should it be otherwise? Is it any surprise that corporations are reluctant to give up their hold on these heretofore corporate assets? The corporate world does not exist primarily to help people; it is in the business of making a profit. Business exists in the realm of economics, not psychology. There is much evidence that corporations are becoming more socially responsible; they seem increasingly aware of the human element, and are more and more forced to take people's feelings into consideration. But corporations are a long way from being social welfare agencies; their "bottom line" seldom includes feelings. The careless way in which wives and families have been treated seems to be the result not of malice, but of our total socioeconomic system.

First of all, it is a matter of money. Corporate wives provide untold hours and a good deal of uncompensated expense entertaining and being entertained for purely business reasons. What would it cost the company if these women all started charging at the rate, let's say, of $10 per hour for their preparation and entertaining time? If corporate wives suddenly went on strike, much of the work they usually do would simply not get done. But if their services *were* hired from professional caterers, maids, cleaners, restaurants, etc., it would cost a small fortune.

Second, there is a big ego kick for most men in having their wives available and presentable for company·functions, or having their wives totally flexible about a transfer. If you are not the head of a company, it's nice to know that at least you are head of a family, and it's comforting to prove to both cronies and superiors that you can manage your wife so well. Even Grant Simmons, who says he is—and truly seems to be—"sensitive to women's rights," expresses a fairly typical attitude about moving. Simmons Company recently moved its headquarters from New York to Atlanta, and Mr. Simmons was aware of no problems. "Normally when an individual moves it is because of a promotion. If he turns down a promotional opportunity more than once or twice, his career is ended. There are too many eager competitors. My own personal feeling is that a man should have the dominance over his wife just to say, 'We're moving.' If he doesn't have the dominance to handle his wife, he doesn't have the leadership ability we want." Are there any exceptions? "If the reason for refusing to move is someone's health, it may be okay. But if it is his wife's career, I am hard-boiled. I just wonder whose career is on top."

In addition, a wife who accepts her "proper" corporate role does, in reality, allow the executive much more time and energy to devote to climbing the corporate ladder. If you never have to cook your own dinner, take your own shirts to the laundry, arrange social engagements, hassle with the cleaning lady, worry about the details of a move, or stay home with a sick child, you can work harder and longer and more efficiently. And any man whose wife does all these things, plus boost his ego when he's insecure, coddle him like a baby when he's sick, accept all the responsibility when he's sexually impotent, and subjugate most of her needs to his, would be hard pressed to give up this way of life voluntarily. In fact, many a career woman has wistfully noted how much easier her life would be if only she had a "wife."

An added complication these days is the subtlety with which a husband's attitudes get played out. Up until recently it was quite acceptable for a man openly to oppose any independent activity on his wife's part. Lower-class men still get away with this machismo insistence on superiority, but middle- and upper-class husbands have been persuaded or bludgeoned into a situation wherein they cannot be openly antagonistic. In fact, the sophisticated man may consciously support equality, but he is often in great conflict between the social pressures he experiences and the deep-seated prejudices with which he was raised. In subtle ways, executive husbands tend to demand special preferences because of who they are. While they overtly talk about equal rights for their wives, they covertly put obstacles in the way.

Perhaps Martha and Phillip Smith of Pittsburgh are a case in point. Mr. Smith heads the Copperweld Corporation and is an articulate man with strong views on many subjects. His wife is a gracious charmer, who is also intelligent and wise. On the subject of the corporate wife, Mr. Smith says: "She is a very important person and has a right to live her own life. Some wives I see are sophisticated, some are bright, some are dumpy and dumb, but their husbands obviously love them and that's no business of mine. The important thing is the man; I don't ask to meet his wife. If I was looking for a job and as a part of the hiring process the prospective boss asked to meet my wife, I think I'd tell him to go to hell. That kind of thing usually means that some wife up the line is beginning to wear the pants, and the old man doesn't have the guts to tell her to back off." Sounds like a liberated man, right? Yet Mr. Smith also says about his own wife: "I work ten or twelve hours a day and don't like coming home to an empty house. I try to leave weekends free, and I don't want her away then either. If she wants to go out during the day when the kids are in school or when the housekeeper is there, that's okay. But I don't like her away when the children come home from school. In the evenings when the family is home, she should be there." Does he see many corporate wives who are involved in careers? "Very few. We tend to have dedicated and hard workers in the management group of this company. They need to have wives who are wives and mothers rather than career girls."

Martha Smith's modus operandi evidently complements her husband's views. "I do a lot of things—Girl Scouts, etc.—but I am not the least bit concerned about women's lib for myself. I am a person in my own right, but I am not concerned that my star isn't shining from day to day. There are rewards other than being identified. My work in volunteer organizations has helped me understand my husband's work better. When I've worked in a volunteer capacity in a responsible way, I've used my own talents and my management skills. The thing most gratifying to me in that my husband has had a chance to use his talents and his skills, that he has a leadership role where he can demonstrate the principles he believes in. He is very consistent and that filters on down through the organization. We sometimes get letters years later about how he has helped someone." Certainly Mrs. Smith seems to have made a happy adjustment; one should add that she also has six children. But one can only speculate on how the pressures from her husband have affected the use of her "management skills," and how her husband's ideas affected the choice she has made of being very concerned about her husband's identity while she seems so unconcerned about her own.

Finally, many corporate wives themselves struggle to maintain the stereotyped role. Accustomed to putting themselves last all these years, often untrained for any real position in the marketplace, they are timid about asserting themselves honestly and anxious to hang onto the position they have. As Lois Wyse found in her 1970 survey, "The wife apparently finds a sense of importance and meaning in life's scheme by providing the kind of support that makes it possible for her husband to meet the demands of his job . . . Apparently, they do whatever their husbands want—and whatever that turns out to be is called 'helping.'"[7] With this kind of investment in their husbands and so little investment in themselves, they are frightened by change and feel threatened by the women's movement. They often see younger or more independent wives as competitors and enemies. The fact that these women are usually very intelligent and well educated makes the situation even more poignant. The fact that they occupy a particularly affluent and privileged position is small comfort. Many feel bound by a situation in which they cannot do any real work or attain any real independence.

## RISKS AND REWARDS

It is common to hear corporate wives express the fear that any independent functioning on their part will mean disaster for the marriage. There is obviously some possibility of this, but most experts believe it is very slight. A woman has to be able to take some risks, and the ultimate risk, of course, is that the marriage will end. But there is no guarantee that it might not end for some other reason anyway. In direct rebuttal to those wives who hide behind the fear that their own independence would somehow damage their marriage, there is much evidence to the contrary. A wife who tries to combine some measure of freedom with her corporate role tends to bring life and excitement and stimulation into her marriage. This almost always results in better communication, and if the marriage has any solidity at all, the relationship will be enhanced.

Bill May of American Can paid tribute to this type of corporate wife when he said, "I sometimes find the wife stronger and smarter than her husband. Lots of times I have said, 'I wish I had her working for me rather than him.'" May's comment implies that corporate wives who are strong and smart *can* be highly valued by their husbands' bosses and can be seen as a real asset. The wife who is not afraid to show her strength and independence is, in almost every case, a positive force in the marriage. She opens up communication and shares in a more equal partnership.

Laverne Phillips, the wise, charming woman whose husband runs International Multifoods in Minnesota, talked about sharing and communication in a meaningful way: "I feel so strongly about sharing at home. It is really a fifty-fifty thing. She has to be interested and really want to hear; he has to want to tell her. She also has to be aware that she must keep her mouth shut. My husband has always felt free to confide in me because he knew it was not going to be told further."

A woman who cares about herself and her own identity need not be a detriment to her husband's career; she can be an asset. What may seem to be a very selfish stance can, in the long run, be a benefit to those around her. But, at this point in our history, she is still a maverick—sometimes labeled strange, or uppity, or even crazy.

We are all conditioned and controlled by the society in which we live, but equality is not an impossible dream. As more and more corporate wives become aware of the possibilities, many goals and actions will change, and the corporate powers that be will find that fewer couples accept the status quo. Once it is understood that women will not allow the corporation to get two employees for the price of one, the issue becomes one of justice rather than deviance. When this happens, psychologist Jane Torrey says, "The burden of proof is no longer on those who ask for change to show why it should be done. It shifts to those who resist to show why it shouldn't."[8]

The corporate wife, as well as wives of other upwardly mobile achievers, often feels quite alone in her struggle to deal with the complexities of her role assignment. Her husband doesn't understand her and seems too busy to be bothered with trivial and emotional complaints. Discussions with other women in her husband's corporation don't get into areas like this. Her role at social occasions is set; her loyalty is expected to be first to her husband and the nuclear family structure, which is a unit in the larger corporate structure. Corporate wives meet one another primarily within this already established social context. Even though their inner, secret lives may have much in common, wives within the corporation remain fragmented from each other.

Other women seem to be so accepting; each woman thinks she has no right to be upset. She enjoys an enviable position in the most privileged country in the world. She has a good mind, a healthy body, and adequate financial

46

resources. Both men and women put her down—she has no reason to bellyache!

But she is not alone, and there are growing numbers of women like her. As I've talked about this subject in seminars and workshops, I've been impressed with the poignant stories that come pouring out. It helps to be able to communicate feelings, to share them with people who are willing to listen, and to hear the same kinds of problems and struggles from other women. As Gail Sheehy says in her monumental study, *Passages,* the steps of inner growth are the most difficult, even when the apparent obstacles seem easily surmountable. The prizes in our society are given for outer, not inner, accomplishments. And yet, without some inner peace, without a sense of satisfaction with our most private being, all the accolades in the world are quite worthless.

We all are unique, and we often like to hang onto the feeling that we are special in our struggles. At the same time, we cannot escape the need for sharing and commonality. Sheehy says it well: "The older we grow, the more we become aware of the commonality of our lives, as well as our essential aloneness as navigators through the human journey."[9] As corporate wives become more assertive, there will be changes in the system, and the image or mold of the corporate wife will change. But, to a large extent, the dilemmas and the decisions will always be a matter of individual and independent choice.

The trick for the corporate wife who also wants independence is in sorting out the healthy parts of her corporate role from the sick ones. Can one woman play both roles and not end up schizophrenic? Can she be straight and honest about herself and her own needs without offending the often fragile egos of her husband and his superiors? Can she refuse to do something or to be available for some activity that would enhance her husband's career? What level of guilt should she feel for being unwilling to entertain or to move? Can she insist on equal sharing of household management or child care if she knows his company would never understand? Why is it that when emotional needs of corporate executives and corporate wives conflict severely, she often ends up in a psychiatric hospital but he rarely does? How can one enjoy the many benefits of corporate wifedom without becoming a nonperson?

The forces that keep the corporate wife in her place are powerful ones. Things are changing, but slowly. A corporation wife who also wants to be an independent human being has to struggle against a very tenacious hold on her, and she has to be able to take some risks. Hopefully in another generation or so this kind of struggle will no longer be necessary. But in the meantime she needs all the help she can get. It is important that she be aware of her own resources, and her own power, and her own very important part in the process.

It may not be easy to accomplish, but women *can* have enough personal flexibility, be shrewd enough analysts, and employ enough tricky mechanisms to put it all together.

# 2

# They Sometimes Call Me Looney

For the past sixteen years I have been trying, with varying degrees of success, to combine the role of corporate wife with some measure of personal liberation. My husband, Ray, has worked for three *Fortune* 500 companies during this time—Trans World Airlines, Indian Head, and Hewlett-Packard—and we have lived in four parts of the country. He started out as a cost accountant, and is now president of a manufacturing company that is part of a large conglomerate.

I have been fascinated by the pressures of corporate wifedom in various ways, at various levels of the career ladder, and in various geographical locations. One personal observation is that, during the ten years he spent in the "corporate jungle" of New York, the demands on me were minimal. In contrast to the usual feeling about New York's pressured living, I was less involved with his career there than when he was working in other parts of the country. Probably because most New York executives have families at some distance in the suburbs, most of the entertaining there did not include wives. On the other hand, when he was a junior executive with a California company, there were frequent company bashes, and the kowtowing by junior people to senior executives and their wives was almost nauseating. One was expected in that organization to look right, say the right thing, and entertain properly at small dinner parties; there was concern expressed by both executives and wives about any wife who did not fit the mold.

Ray now has one of those "senior" positions, and I had thought I might now relax a bit; but instead, there again are tremendous pressures to conform. The man whom he succeeded as president is a delight, and his wife is a warm, energetic woman whose life has revolved around her family and the company. The style she established seemed to fit her and obviously gave her many satisfactions, not the least of which is her feeling of contribution over many years toward the success of the company. She often entertained in her home, and was pretty constantly available for visiting bigwigs and their wives. Her hospitality probably sustained many customer relationships. Social relationships were intertwined with business ones. But her style is not mine, and the transition has not been easy.

Furthermore, it seems that there are more and more dinners, meetings, and trips that require my presence these days. They all seem to be legitimately important functions; and all the other wives seem to be going. How do I sort out these demands on my time and energies from other activities that I might prefer? What kinds of compromises can I make that will allow me the fun and stimulation of certain business-connected situations without depriving me of other activities that are purely my own?

## CONSCIOUSNESS RAISING

There were two indidents that particularly shocked my own consciousness about being an independent corporation wife. The first occurred at a week-long industry meeting that Ray and I attended a few years ago for the first time, but which is a twice yearly function for that group. It was held at the Greenbrier, one of the most elegant hotel resorts in the country, and when I first heard about the possibility of going, I thought it might be great fun. The attendees are mostly presidents or chairmen of their companies, with a smattering of vice-presidents, and I looked on such a group as a new challenge. However, when I was told that I *must* attend, I began to think about my limited, precious vacation time, and question whether I wanted to "invest" a week of it in my husband's career this way. I thought of all the workshops and conferences I could attend with that week to enhance my own career. I thought of all the mechanical problems with child care, coverage in my office, social plans to be rearranged, and so on and on. It seems clear in retrospect that my attitude was somehow connected to my ability to choose—the week looked like fun when it was voluntary, but like a noose around my neck when it seemed involuntary. In the final analysis, I realized that I did have a choice, and I went because I wanted to.

As is usual with such groups, there was a mixture of interesting and boring people, worthwhile and waste-of-time events. To the credit of groups such as these, they have recently begun inviting wives to attend some of the sessions where there are interesting speakers. The shocker came at the one "ladies' " luncheon which all wives were officially required to attend. There were about twenty women who had not been part of this group before, and the mistress of ceremonies, as a get-acquainted gimmick, asked each of us to tell something interesting about ourselves—"Tell us something about who you are and what you do." I was appalled at how many women stood up and said, "I just can't think of anything interesting about myself." The mistress of ceremonies must have had the same reaction I did, because after eight or ten women said essentially the same thing, she retorted, "That's really too bad. I hope by the time for this meeting next year, you will have found *something* interesting about

51

yourself." Most of the other women who spoke identified themselves by naming their children or saying something about "the great guy I'm married to." A couple of women said they were taking courses, but I was the only one who mentioned a career. During the rest of the week, several women came up to me to ask what it was again that I did and to say they had been impressed with what I said about myself. A few added some snotty comment like, "It must be hard on your family to have you away so much," but the more benevolent ones seemed genuinely amazed that I had time to work. They made comments like, "My life is so full being Sam's wife," or, "I'm just so busy with my husband and children, there's not much time for myself." It is worth noting that most of these women were in their late forties or fifties, and a couple of them were open enough to suggest that they might do it differently now.

The other event that wrenched my consciousness about corporate wifery was my recent move three thousand miles across the country to the West Coast. Although Ray and I had lived in three different locations during our marriage, the moves had always before been mutual, rather simple decisions, and had resulted in happy job changes for both of us. Various other transfers had been discussed from time to time, but as Ray repeatedly reminded me, I had never before been asked to move because of a company transfer, and this was extremely unusual in a sixteen-year marriage to a businessman. We had both arrived at similar positions of responsibility in our careers, and frequently were kidded by friends about how we would handle a transfer. We said proudly that either of us would move if the other had a significant promotional opportunity, but I knew somewhere in my gut that "either of us" really meant me, and "significant" would be defined primarily by my husband. We had also theorized about the place we lived being less and less important to us. He clearly preferred the West Coast, and I always felt more comfortable in the East; but we verbalized about our problems tending to follow us and our ability to find happiness and good friends anywhere.

Meanwhile, we had spent six years in a particularly lovely New York suburb, and without quite realizing it, the territory and I had become part of each other. We had looked a long time for, and finally found, an old French Normandy house, and I had spent a good part of my energy and time the last two years redecorating it. I hate to admit that I had become so attached to a "thing," but that is a fact. My position as director of social work in a private psychiatric hospital was a satisfying one, and I had developed an excellent staff. I had more referrals for my small private practice than I wanted. I was beginning to feel the need to move on to a new position and new challenges, and had made many professional contacts in the community whose help I could enlist in doing this.

But perhaps most important, I had made many good and close friendships, and had just come to realize, as I never did in my twenties, how cherished and significant these were to me. Some of these relationships were mutual with my husband and would be losses to him too, but others were totally separate and met all kinds of needs for me. Friends have always been an important part of my support system. For various reasons, most of which relate to our childhoods, Ray has always depended less on friends than I do. I don't mean that he has fewer friends, but that they are less important in his psychological support system than mine are. Why couldn't I keep these friendships even if I moved? Because distance changes things; frequent contact and shared experiences are needed to "feed" a relationship. Distance cannot end something meaningful, but work is required to keep it really alive. Why couldn't I make equally close friends in a new location? I can and I will, but not for many years. Only a very few of the strangers one meets will ever become friends, and that process at times seems very painful and lonely. Trust is never established overnight, and confidences cannot be shared without trust. It seems that the older people get, the more they cling to and protect their friendships of many years; there must be a common realization that some processes simply cannot be repeated and that certain times will never come again.

So the company is grooming my husband for bigger things, and a move to the West Coast is definitely in the game plan! He tells me this news with such pleasure! This is the kind of operational job he has always wanted, and it means a good increase in compensation besides. He knows I won't be happy about moving, but the company will make it easy—giving us plenty of time to plan and see the new location, taking over our house, and helping with other details.

How do I communicate what a spot I am in? How could I ever refuse to go without jeopardizing any future promotions and probably the marriage as well?

What about a compromise—a separate living arrangement for a while? We were not strangers to this possibility and had twice before survived periods of separation for career reasons quite easily. I had remained in California for three months after he moved to New York in order to get my professional certification. Recently he had taken an apartment in the South for eight months, flying home most weekends, because of an assignment that was known to be transitional. But even these separations caused some problems when they were extended for any length of time. Although our explanations both times were perfectly acceptable to us, they caused raised eyebrows among some business associates and friends. There were subtle questions about marital disharmony and subtle insinuations that my husband might not have "control" of his family.

But even from my point of view, this move was different. The distance between us would be too great for commuting; the transfer looked permanent; our son was growing and should have both parents if possible; and it would be very difficult for me to search for a job in absentia. Besides, the company would not put up with it; after all, I had duties to perform in the new location.

My "liberated" friends said they were surprised when I announced the move, and some even said they were disappointed in me. Some women in this kind of position would say they had no choice. The saving factor for me was that I felt I had many choices—none of them were ideal, but then few of life's choices ever are. My first choice was to maintain the marriage. Then I chose to avoid the responsibility of possibly hindering my husband's career. To be perfectly honest, I was more concerned about any loss of income and a way of life I had come to enjoy, than about the blame that might accrue to me from impeding his career and the guilt I might feel. I did not opt for a temporary separation partially because it was time for me to change jobs anyway, and I thought that perhaps company contacts could be used to locate the right position for me, too. The resentment at this dilemma did not disappear, and the loss of friends and security was no less painful. But the knowledge of power in the possibility of other choices made me a significant person in the process and a force to reckon with—not a victim.

Did the company help as much as it could? And did it try to ease the transition? Some companies have worked out elaborate procedures for dealing with transfers, and various writers on this subject have made interesting suggestions as to ways in which companies can help bridge the gap. From my point of view, however, it is important to stress that every family deserves privacy, and must protect itself at all costs from company encroachment into areas where the company just does not belong. Such things as psychological tests of wives and corporation-employed therapists get into dangerous territory, and any kind of psychotherapeutic help should really be a private arrangement. Similarly, wives of other executives have built-in hazards as guides for a new wife on the scene. They may offer to help, but they should be sensitive to "back-off" signals. In reality, I think the company can do little to help in the most important areas except financial compensation.

We lucked out with one hell of a terrible move—everything went wrong. Two anecdotes were the only humor in three months of horror!

For various reasons I had to work until the day of the move, while my husband had a week between assignments. He was left to supervise child, housekeeper, packers, movers, utility servicemen, Salvation Army pickup men, and other assorted people. The reversal of usual roles was good for both of us, and we laughed later about several frantic phone calls I got at work. "What drapes did you say we take?" "What food shall I throw away?" "How come I couldn't reach you earlier? Is your meeting *that* important?" "I've had a terrible day—I've got to get out of the house."

When we arrived at our destination the tables were turned, and I was left to deal with the multitude of claims, estimates, and repairs that resulted from damaged and missing items. The sportscar had been dented in three places; the mattresses had all been carried on the outside of the truck, and were ruined from the rain and freezing temperatures; the moving van had gone into a ditch in Montana to avoid a worse accident, and many things were broken. I once asked the claims representative, only half facetiously, if I could charge at my usual private practice rate of $25 per hour for the tremendous amount of phoning and coordination and paper work I put in. The answer of course was "no," and the job simply had to be done.

The crowning blow came a month after the move when the local police notified us that a bank in Connecticut had been robbed by two armed men wearing Ray's army fatigues. The robbers turned out to be our moving van driver and his helper, who had stolen not only army fatigues, but a favorite coat and ski hat, and the housekeeper's Afro wig as well. It was evidently a well-planned heist, which made us feel lucky that *most* of our belongings had arrived. More phone calls, notarized statements, and additional claims! Translation: more headaches, but also a few laughs!

Several company officials had been nice enough to express concern about my job possibilities. They held prominent positions in the community and offered to be of help when I arrived. In some ways I seemed lucky—I had degrees, credentials, and a proven track record of performance. I was not a teacher who was giving up tenure, a civil service worker who was giving up seniority, or a small businesswoman who was giving up clientele. But, as in every field beyond the middle management level, contacts are the means to significant jobs, and I was an unknown quantity three thousand miles away from the contacts I had made. When I tried to describe to certain executives and their wives the kind of position I wanted, I found they had no inkling of the kind of work I do, and some of the suggestions they made were off the wall. A couple of their referrals were helpful, but basically I learned I would have to do it on my own. It was a blow to hear from people in powerful positions that "we like to promote from within," and a shock to the ego to contemplate starting again several steps down the compensation and authority ladder.

The fact that my husband couldn't have been happier with his new position had its pros and cons. It was good to see him so contented and using his talents; he is obviously easier to live with when he is happy. But his sense of fulfillment was in such direct contrast to my professional frustration; I was so jealous of the easy transferability of his credentials; he was wanted and needed here; his support system was set. Nevertheless, the saving factors for me in this situation were that I do have credentials; I do have a strong sense of identity built up over many years in the marketplace; and I did have some realistic hope of recouping the sense of accomplishment I had had in Connecticut. Again, the important denominator was that I had choices—I could try to get into a new, very restricted Ph.D. program at the university; wait for the right job to come along; take a lesser position; pursue the contacts one needs for a private practice; or even go into a totally different field. I also had the choice of staying home, although that is not a realistic one for me (which comes under the heading of knowing oneself).

In increasing numbers corporate wives, like all women, are looking to careers for a sense of accomplishment and self-worth. Like their husbands, they need some achievement outside the home to feel fully alive. The more a woman's identity is connected with a professional or business situation of her own, the more reluctance she will have about any move related only to her husband's career. In some cases she may be able to transfer her credentials with minimal loss. But often the difficulties for her in moving will begin to outweigh the advantages, and her reluctance or resistance will become a major force in the marriage. Our world has changed, and corporations will have to reckon more creatively with a new type of corporation wife in their often haphazard plans for moving executives around the country and the world.

## SHARING

A few other personal concerns of this liberated corporation wife can be mentioned briefly. First is the matter of sharing household management and child care. I agree wholeheartedly with those who say that what a career woman needs most is a wife—someone not just to do housework or baby-sitting, but someone who can manage a household as most wives do. The management and organization part of a housewife's job is no small task. I have always contended that, in order to be really successful at the office *and* at home, a woman needs two basic qualities: (1) boundless energy and good physical health, and (2) the organizational ability of a superexecutive. One woman simply cannot do everything herself, but finding and managing other people can become another job again. Domestic help is no longer easy to find, and it is even more difficult to keep. Furthermore, it is the rare domestic worker who has any ability to organize. Therefore, the woman who employs any kind of household help usually finds herself making lists or giving lectures, and then dealing with inefficiency or simple laziness. Is there any reason why this task is almost invariably left to the wife? I have heard business executives act like helpless babies about household help. My own husband tends to be one of those who assume that the money they provide for maids and babysitters should solve every problem. There is usually some backhanded compliment like, "You've always managed the house so well by yourself;

58

I'm sure you can do it even better now that you have the housekeeper." Or there may be the casual insult, such as, "You have time to handle the maid; I have so many other [i.e., important] things to do." In any case, it seems to me that the insistence of men that their wives continue in this role is tantamount to saying, "You can have the frosting only if you eat all the cake."

In addition to dealing with help, any person who has run a household knows that there are many tasks that only he or she can do. While my husband has always shared some of these, I, like most other women, have assumed the greater share. How does this happen? Some of the reasons are as follows: There is pressure to perform all duties well; there is a little guilt about not keeping up with the Mary Joneses; there is often the feeling that it is easier to do it oneself than to have an argument. In a recent *Wall Street Journal* article about dual career couples, one woman described well what it feels like to try to do everything at home and at work—"I feel I even have to sleep fast."[1]

While many women smother their feelings of overwork, resentment builds up and tempers flare. My memory goes unhappily back to one summer evening shortly after we had purchased our "dream" house. I had come home from work tired, had made dinner, put the dishes in the dishwasher, bathed the baby, put him to bed, straightened up his toys, and then set about with hammer and screwdriver to fix several broken door hinges. On a trip past the family room, my eyes settled on a picture of my husband with beer bottle in hand, a smile on his face, obviously enjoying a baseball game on TV. I found myself standing about two feet away, with hammer and screwdriver poised at his head. There was murderous rage in my heart. He was saved by a moment of rational thinking. Was it his fault that he chose to watch the boob tube mindlessly instead of working compulsively like me? Couldn't some of this wait? Perhaps tomorrow I could work out a little more sharing with him. The tired martyr promptly collapsed into bed.

In line with our earlier understanding about roles, it should come as no surprise that the areas of housework and household management often become a struggle. No person, man or woman, who has enjoyed the benefits of someone else's household management would want to "get his hands dirty" voluntarily. Whether one does the housework oneself, or whether it is done by household help, these are rather thankless, repetitive, frustrating tasks which most of us would rather avoid. However, if a wife asserts herself and insists that these be shared, there may even be a few benefits for the busy husband. For example, his wife will be less tired and less resentful of having to carry this burden by herself, and he may even learn a few interesting things about how his household runs in the process.

But it is easier to talk about a household (an inanimate object) than to talk about the care of a child or children. Those little people, assuming they are under twelve or thirteen, should be equally dear to both parents, and are for the most part passive recipients of what those parents decide about their care. The matter is complicated by the fact that children are prime scapegoats for fighting out marital battles, especially those battles involving authority and responsibility. Traditionally, child care has been the province of mothers, and this is nowhere more true than in executives' families, where fathers are often absent more than they are home. For the same reasons as previously discussed, there is a tremendous pressure to keep it this way. Again, why would any man want to get involved in an often boring, repetitive, difficult job if he doesn't have to? The answer is simply that he may have to, and in the process he may even enjoy the benefits of getting to know his child better and having a bigger influence on his child's life.

And what of emergencies (which happen in most households on a pretty regular basis)? My own experience is that when I made my needs clear, my husband pitched in, but usually not without some struggling. We each have stayed home from work from time to time when there was no other person available, or when our son was too sick to entrust to anyone else's care. However, my husband was sure his company would never understand, and warned me that I should never breathe a word of this to his associates. In talking with other business executives, I am sure he assessed the business climate accurately, and he had to be much more secretive about any household responsibilities than I did. I suspect that if he were a teacher or lower-level office worker, it might have been a bit more possible to share the truth with co-workers; but any man fairly high up in the corporate structure, or any man hung up on the machismo ideal, will have a hard time divulging his part in child care. Equality in the child care area always seems to be one of the most difficult to achieve, and I cannot say I have yet arrived.

I have purposely not focused this book to any extent on the problems of corporate wives' children. There are innumerable scientific studies which show that, if any generality can be stated about children, it is that their emotional health tends to reflect that of their parents. Corporate wives perhaps worry more than any other group of mothers about the effect of moves, stress, paternal absence, and even affluence on their children. But at the risk of being overly simplistic, the message to these mothers has to be: Get it together for yourselves and your kids will be okay.

## MY NAME IS ME

One other example of the corporation's effect on our lives concerned my decision to return to the use of my maiden name. When we were married sixteen years ago, it was very rare for a woman to continue using her maiden name, and I frankly never even thought about it. But within a very short time after becoming Mrs. Looney, I began to realize what I had done. My husband admits that he got more than his share of teasing as a kid because he was a "Looney," and even had a few fist fights over it. But it became in his family almost a cause célèbre, and they have fierce pride in the name. Fortunately for them, none of his family is in the psychiatric field! As a psychotherapist, I have heard every joke and silly comment you can imagine about the name, and early on I was forced to learn the humor in it too.

One encounter came on a particular April 1, when I was trying to get some important information from a New York attorney. I told his secretary who I was, and she promised to have him call me back immediately. When I had not heard from him by the next day, I called again, and the secretary hooted! "Mrs. Looney! From Bellevue Psychiatric Hospital! I was sure it was April Fools'!"

Perhaps the sweetest incident over my name came after I had sent an appointment letter for a family session to the parents of a young patient at Mt. Sinai Hospital. The father, an official at the UN, obviously skilled in diplomacy, called to check if there really was a therapist named Mrs. Looney. He then asked me if I had been in this field before I married Mr. Looney or vice-versa. When I told him I had been a professional before I married, he said, "Well, all I can say then is that you must have loved him very much to marry him with a name like that."

Now that I am a Ph.D. candidate, the moniker Dr. Looney seems even more crazy and formidable. I think I can live very well without hearing all the nonsense that would come from colleagues, patients, and families about that!

Thus, my husband's name itself became part of my desire to change, but that was a relatively small part. The real me is still the identity or label I grew up with and spent two-thirds of my life with. My maiden name is a kind of personal possession; by giving it up, I gave up part of my identity. The decision to return to my original name has nothing to do with my husband as a person. It has to do with me. Maintaining my own name means that I keep part of my own heritage and family background in a more real way. Returning to that name perhaps also symbolizes the kind of marriage I would like: one that enhances individuality rather than implying possession of another human being. Clearly, I am the mate of my husband, but I won't be just another appendage or extension of him. I am an individual too.

State laws vary, and one state (Hawaii) has a law compelling a woman to take her husband's last name. But "the current trend in America supports the English common-law rule that a name is whatever the person chooses and that a wife's use of the spouse's last name is custom rather than law . . . Persons may give themselves or their children any name or as many first or last names as they wish, or even opt to have no last name at all, provided it is not done for fraudulent or dishonest purposes and is not considered obscene."[2] Feminist writings are full of explanations about the name dilemma, and all kinds of interesting, creative solutions are being tried by young marrieds these days. Some couples are even issuing wedding announcements with the discreet footnote: "The bride will retain her maiden name." In fact, it is now fairly common for a woman, regardless of professional status, to do this. But most parts of the business world seem never to have heard of it.

My husband, after some discussion, was really not threatened by the change. In fact, he told someone, "I'm keeping my own name, too." But he anticipated and had to field questions about why I did it and whether we were separated. Those business associates who have learned of the change for various reasons are often incredulous as to why his name was not sufficient for me. When he or I explain these days that my "old" name feels more comfortable and right, we tend to meet vague suspicion and a genuine lack of understanding. What is this business about identity? Who does she think she is? There is, of course, some acceptance too, and I hope it is growing.

(My husband says, with tongue only slightly in cheek, that I will aid his business career, when this book is published, by not carrying or identifying with his name.)

In the long run, any couple's total relationship and communication patterns are the important ingredients for working out problem areas; but in the short run, the nitty-gritty decisions can seem terribly important, and in fact, they become the battleground for working out larger issues. Each corporate couple must resolve differences in their own way, and no one can prescribe what a corporate wife should do in a given situation. Nevertheless, I can describe two recent incidents of decision making that give a flavor of my own success, as well as failure.

During a three-month period last fall, there were four out-of-town meetings that included wives. Ray brought home this news with some trepidation, knowing that it was that same period during which I had planned to cram for my oral comprehensive exams. My reactions went from panic, to anger, to defiance. I finally calmed down and said that I could afford to go to one; that he should pick the one where my attendance was most crucial, and I would work my schedule around that. Ray agreed readily to that strategy, and he went to three of them alone, deftly handling several questions about whether we were still together and whether my program was hard on him too. Happily for all of us, the meeting he chose for me to attend was in Anaheim, California, where we could also take our son to Disneyland and add a little vacation along with business.

The incident at Christmas was not so smoothly worked out. This was the first year he had been president, and we were pleased to receive several lovely gifts at home from other company presidents. When I asked if he would be writing thank-you notes to these people, he said "no," and insisted I do it—the gifts had been addressed to me too; I had met all of these people; and it would be "warmer" if a handwritten note came from me. I protested, but there was no precedent from last year, and I eventually relented. We took a vacation in Hawaii shortly after the holidays, and it is impossible to describe my emotions as I wrote those notes while Ray was lying prostrate in the sun. I did it under one condition: that he promise to show me any notes that arrived at his office in response to gifts he sent these people. A few days later Ray told me, with a sheepish grin, that all the thank-you notes from these people had been on company stationery, typed (and probably composed) by secretaries. I really felt terrific about that decision! I can imagine those men saying to their wives, "Maryanne wrote such a nice, personal note; you should do that too." And I can just hear those wives saying to me at the next corporate meeting, "Thanks a lot for being such a model corporate wife! And you are the one who wrote the book about how to be liberated and independent!?"

## THE GOODIES: AT WHAT PRICE?

Finally, on the other side of the coin, my consciousness has been raised by my increasing awareness of the pleasure the corporate world has afforded me. The monetary rewards have been more than adequate and have furnished me the financial security that makes all kinds of choices and activities possible. Furthermore, there has been travel; the seven years that my husband worked for an airline allowed me three trips to Asia, many visits to Europe, and countless learning experiences that only travel can provide. There have been interesting people; there has been a sense of vicarious excitement in watching my husband's career; there has been a wholly different atmosphere in my life than I would have experienced in my field alone.

Occasionally I envy my friends whose husbands are physicians or attorneys or whatever, and I especially envied them during my recent move. They can and usually do stay in one community forever; but then some of those wives long for a change and can never move because of their husbands' practices. Their incomes are substantial, but the maximums do not usually match the possibilities in business. They have seldom done much traveling because the costs must come totally out of their pockets;

most of their friends come from the same professions; and their horizons in many ways seem provincial and limited. By contrast, the wheeling and dealing of the business world can really be fascinating. It is something apart, something about which many volumes have been written. The political strategies and various kinds of people-power have been fascinating to watch from the sidelines. The stakes are high, the power is immense, and the exposure to it all can mean excitement, fun, and real learning for the corporation wife.

But how grateful should I be? How much allegiance do I owe my husband? How much allegiance do we both owe to the company? Where do *I* fit in—at the back of the line, front, or middle? My unqualified answer is: at the front. Unless I am my primary concern in all decisions and in all relationships, the rest is pretty shallow and can all very easily come apart. The opportunities are there, the obstacles are also there. The trick is to put all the disparate elements together as an independent corporation wife.

# 3

# What the Shrinks See

Psychiatric hospitals and therapists' offices are full of corporate wives. We know that about 70 percent of all psychiatric patients are women, and most therapists estimate that the corporate wife is a significant category in this group. If it were not for these patients, many (perhaps most) private practitioners of psychotherapy would go broke. If corporate wives did not break down so often, many of the fancier private psychiatric hospitals like Menninger's in Kansas, Austin Riggs in Massachusetts, and Silver Hill in Connecticut would have to close their doors.

In both institutional work and private practice, it is striking how many wives of corporate executives become patients, and how few of the executives ever come for psychiatric help. There are obviously many reasons for this, including the male reluctance to show feelings, the lack of acceptance among many employers of psychiatric problems, and the opportunities for most men to bury their problems in work. But also, it seems, there is a greater willingness on the part of these women to take the role of victim or scapegoat, and to act out the family traumas. The reasons for this are multidetermined. One reason probably is that they can afford it; another is the tremendous amount of leisure time that many corporate wives have; but another determinant surely is the unique and heavy pressure that corporate wives feel.

The corporation, as my survey showed, makes very real demands on their time and energies, and insists that they conform to a rather conservative mold. Furthermore, wives are very directly affected by the demands on today's executives; and the women very often act out the sickness in these relationships by breaking down. *Business Week,* October 6, 1975, did an article on "Young Top Management: The New Goals, Rewards, Lifestyles." It stated that there is "a new breed of Organization Man, exhibiting a commitment to the corporation that characterized the young executive in the 1950's, and at the same time a rebelliousness of spirit that grew out of the 1960's." What a grueling and exhausting combination! The article adds that these men are "wedded to their work, almost to the exclusion of outside interests, community activities, or even time for the spouse and the kids. For many overworked young executives, tension and fatigue are chronic . . . Besides the tension there is the need to conform —not as much as in the past perhaps, but few young executives stray far from the norm . . . When it comes to personal life, young executives are likely to demonstrate even less flair than in their corporate personalities . . . Most young executives are too busy working to do much else . . . One problem is that young executives seem no more adept than older managers at separating their business and social lives." Although this article relates specifically to young managers, it seems obvious that the older men too have to run hard to keep up and, in some cases, have to run even harder to stay ahead.

Women married to these rising stars, then, have tremendous demands and pressures placed on them—both physically and emotionally. They have little or no social life with their husbands that is unconnected with business, they have little or no help from their husbands with children or home, and they have little or no emotional rapport with a man who is so uptight and preoccupied with his work. Couple this with the discouragement and denigration all around them for any identity of their own; couple this also with the cultural "permission" women have been given to show feelings or to appear weak; and you have the recipe for instant collapse. In fact, in this light, it becomes amazing that any of these women are healthy at all! The fact that so many corporate wives break down emotionally—as an indicator of their own unmet needs as well as a barometer of their sick marriages—is more than understandable.

## THE NUMBERS

The statistics indicate that in nearly every category of mental health treatment, the women patients far outnumber the men. The only categories in which this is not true are admissions to Veterans Administration hospitals and admissions to state and county mental hospital inpatient units. The assumption here is that most of these patients are dependent, indigent men whose socioeconomic profiles would be quite different from those of corporate executives and their wives.

The latest national data available from the Department of Health, Education, and Welfare relate to 1975. The important totals are as follows:

Admissions to outpatient psychiatric services (excludes admissions to federally funded community mental health centers, VA psychiatric services, and private mental health practitioners)

| | |
|---|---|
| Both sexes | 1,406,065 |
| Male | 634,355 |
| Female | 771,710 |

Admissions to private mental hospital inpatient units

| | |
|---|---|
| Both sexes | 129,832 |
| Male | 55,706 |
| Female | 74,126 |

Discharges from public and nonpublic general
hospital psychiatric inpatient units[1]

| | |
|---|---|
| Both sexes | 376,185 |
| Male | 140,659 |
| Female | 235,526 |

Admissions to federally funded community mental health centers for outpatient treatment[2]

| | |
|---|---|
| Both sexes | 919,037 |
| Male | 439,381 |
| Female | 479,656 |

It is impossible to know what percentage of each of these groups is corporate wives, but perhaps we can assume that most psychiatrically hospitalized corporate wives would go to private mental hospitals; in these institutions, women comprise about 60 percent of the patient population.

There are also no national figures available for private outpatient psychiatric treatment, and this would be the treatment of choice for most corporate wives who do not need to be hospitalized. I have, however, done an informal survey of therapists in private practice, asking them what percentage of their patients are women. The estimates range from 60 to 95 percent, and the highest estimates come from those therapists who practice in the affluent suburbs of large cities. Women therapists appear to be treating larger percentages of women than their male colleagues, but both male and female therapists indicate that they treat many more women than men. It is difficult to guess what percentage of these are corporate wives, but all the therapists questioned said that corporate wives constitute a large portion of their practice. One person who practices in Fairfield County, Connecticut, said that about 75 percent of his total practice is corporate wives.

Statistics also indicate that the margin between male and female psychiatric patients is growing. In 1960, the number of men and women under treatment as psychiatric inpatients, outpatients, or in private counseling was roughly the same.[3] From 1964 to 1968, 125,351 more women than men were psychiatrically hospitalized;[4] and in 1971 alone, at least 100,000 more women than men sought psy-

70

chiatric help. The HEW figures for 1975 indicate that the trend is growing, and that many more women than men are being treated for mental illness.

There is much speculation about reasons for this. It is suggested that difficulties associated with the modern woman's role promote mental illness. It is also theorized that women more willingly express symptoms of mental illness.[5] Both of these theories appear to have merit, but the supporting data are sketchy.

More rigorous research has been done on the biases and prejudices of therapists themselves, and there is considerable evidence that sex-role perceptions are a source of trouble. One study, for example, assessed the sex-role stereotypes of seventy-nine clinicians (clinical psychologists, psychiatrists, and social workers). They were asked to describe a mature, healthy, socially competent adult (independent of sex), man, or woman, and an ideal standard of mental health was developed from questionnaire responses. Both male and female clinicians agreed on the behaviors and attributes characterizing a mentally healthy man, woman, and adult. However, the traits characterizing healthy, mature individuals paralleled closely the description of male behavior rather than female behavior. This negative assessment of women's behavior says they are submissive, more easily influenced, less aggressive, less competitive, more excitable in minor crises, more conceited about their appearance, and less objective. The adult and masculine concepts of health did not differ significantly, but a significant difference was found between the adult and feminine health concepts.[6] This and other studies of therapists' values suggest that therapists, as others, reflect the culture and values of our society, and are not much less bound by stereotypes than the rest of us.

Phyllis Chesler's book *Women and Madness* and her articles in professional journals[7] elaborate on the role of women as patients. It should be no surprise that both women and men prefer male therapists, since our culture connects most of the mature, strong, healthy characteristics with men. It should also be no surprise that, since

71

the majority of therapists are male, the image of the passive, weak, depressed female patient persists. Chesler suggests that the reason for the proponderance of women in psychotherapy is that women are oppressed and have no approved life recourse in this society other than marriage or psychotherapy, or both. They both maintain the status quo for women. There is a strong analogy between "slave" and "woman" as shown in the symptoms common to women patients; they can be best understood in terms of "slave psychology" and oppression.


## THE SYMPTOMS

There are different diagnostic patterns for men and women in the general population, and the following data give an overall picture of diagnoses in general (nonfederal) hospital psychiatric inpatient units, during the year 1975.[8]

| Diagnosis | Both sexes | Male | Female |
|---|---|---|---|
| All disorders, total | 515,537 | 211,569 | 303,968 |
| Alcohol disorders | 35,932 | 25,979 | 9,953 |
| Drug disorders | 17,849 | 7,621 | 10,228 |
| Organic brain syndromes | 18,981 | 8,074 | 10,907 |
| Depressive disorders | 194,399 | 60,831 | 133,568 |
| Schizophrenia | 124,458 | 57,754 | 66,704 |
| Other psychoses | 11,597 | 5,013 | 6,584 |
| Neuroses | 32,070 | 12,439 | 19,631 |
| Personality disorders | 30,100 | 15,013 | 15,087 |
| Childhood disorders | 4,625 | 2,142 | 2,483 |
| Transitional situational disturbance | 26,529 | 10,792 | 15,737 |
| Other | 18,997 | 5,911 | 13,086 |

This represents only the most serious diagnoses, only the situations that require hospitalization. Women far outnumber men in the categories of depression, neuroses, and transitional situational disturbance. Although the inpatient diagnosis of alcohol disorder shows a preponderance of men, it is quite possible that women alcoholics are often given the primary diagnosis of depression, neurosis, or "other."

Most of the corporate wives seen in outpatient psychotherapy present symptoms in one of two categories: 1) depression, often with accompanying anxiety, lack of interest in life, indecisiveness, guilt about being a drag on their family, feelings of worthlessness; or 2) alcoholism or abuse of other drugs; or both. The incidence of both depression and addiction seems to have skyrocketed in the last few years, but researchers are not sure whether they are actually occurring more frequently or whether increasing sophistication about mental illness and accessibility of treatment have led more people to seek help.

In any event, both depression and substance (alcohol or drug) abuse have their special complications for corporate wives. The professional literature has dramatically shown that both of these illnesses are more prevalent among housewives than among working women, and corporate wives, because of demands made on them or community image or whatever, tend to fall into the housewife category.

Several very specific and thorough projects on depression in women have been done by Yale researchers (at Connecticut Mental Health Center–Yale University School of Medicine and Boston State Hospital–Tufts Medical Center) during the past few years.[9] One part of the study compared workers and housewives in treatment and found that working offered depressed women real protection and distraction. The overall improvement was better for workers than for housewives. Working women felt more competent, were less frequently bored in their free time, and were more at ease in social situations. The study concludes that work may serve as a protection and diversion for depressed women regardless of social class. It further suggests that more efforts should be made to find satisfying alternatives for women—especially in the high-risk groups such as "empty-nesters," menopausal women, widows, etc.

Another part of the Yale study considered the effects

73

of moving on women. Patients treated in a research clinic for depressive episodes were evaluated, and it was clear that a pattern of depression occurred even when the moves were voluntary and related to presumably desirable circumstances such as improved housing and financial status. The study concludes that moving often places inordinate demands on the individual to adapt, and raises continued challenges to one's identity.[10] This finding is especially important for corporate wives, who often feel (and are told) that they have no right to be depressed when the move means so many good things for the whole family.

It is noteworthy also that women make suicide attempts four times more often than men, although more males actually commit suicide (by a ratio of three to one). It is assumed that men resort to more violent and more successful self-destruction because of their stronger aggressive drives, while women seem to use suicide attempts more often as appeals to the environment. Women seem more inclined to use suicide attempts as covert aggressive and defensive weapons, and for manipulation of relationships.[11] Corporate wives, who are denied more open and honest expressions of aggression, are often very skillful at using suicide attempts and suicide threats to give vent to their anger, rage, and frustration.

Alcohol and other drug abuse has many complications for women. Statistics are just beginning to surface about the increasing numbers of substance-abusing women. For various social and environmental reasons, women have been able to hide their addictions better than men. Our society often considers the hard-drinking man to be macho and acceptable, even for treatment, but the hard-drinking woman is seen as a slut and a disgrace. If she gets into treatment, the physician may "protect" her by giving her a different primary diagnosis and simply "drying her out." If she is a housewife and does not have to perform every day in the marketplace, she can probably hide and be hidden longer than most men.

For alcoholic and drug-addicted corporate wives, as for politicians' wives, physicians' wives, and wives of other prominent men, public acknowledgment and family image present added complications. Corporate wives are often shielded and protected by their families until the illness becomes impossible to hide anymore. The woman's excessive drinking at home may be ignored until a fire starts in the house or one of the children is badly hurt while she is in a drunken state. Or her usual tipsiness at parties may be tolerated until she gets falling down drunk or insults a superior in drunken irrationality. Although Alcoholics Anonymous and other treatment approaches for alcoholism stress open acceptance of oneself as an alcoholic, the executive will often collude with his wife to prevent disclosure at all costs. More often than not, this simply pushes the alcoholic wife further down the road of illness until treatment can no longer be avoided.

Similarly with women who become addicted to pills, all kinds of excuses are made: The doctor wouldn't give her prescriptions if she didn't need them; she just takes the barbiturates to get a few good nights' sleep; because her schedule is so heavy this month, she needs the amphetamines or pep pills to get through; the diet pills keep her looking slim and trim; she gets nervous at big gatherings —a few tranquilizers shouldn't hurt. Excesses and dependence on pills are denied or ignored until there is some kind of overdose or shocking event. The "protection" by executives in these cases may be motivated partly for the sake of their wives, but it is largely for the sake of their own reputations. Many of these corporate wives would get into treatment faster if their husbands weren't so "important."

Occasionally therapists also see the manic woman, the one who is too emotional and frequently out of control. This is the person who seems to have an excess of energy and emotions; she seems constantly to blow things out of proportion. Clinically we see the depressed woman much more frequently than the manic one, but in many ways they can be viewed on opposite ends of the same continuum.

Often one of the accompanying side effects of either

75

depression or anxiety is psychosomatic illness. In fact, many of these women are treated all their lives by general practitioners or internists for things like migraine headaches, backaches, insomnia, or hypertension, and they never recognize the psychosomatic origins of their physical ills. Medical science is just beginning to realize the tremendous effect of emotions on bodily functions, and some exciting new connections (such as biofeedback) are being made.

From time to time corporate wives also appear in therapists' offices with phobias, or unrealistic fears: They feel unable to fly in airplanes, or ride in elevators, or cross bridges. The most pathetic ones suffer from agoraphobia, an intense fear of any open places, and some of these women have not been out of their homes in years. In the last few years behavioral therapy has been able to offer relief for many phobic symptoms, even though their cause may not be clearly understood. But again, unfortunately, many phobic women lead isolated, frightened, timid lives, unaware that help is available, and often protected from exposure by their executive husbands.

When corporate wives do appear for treatment, any feelings of anger or rage are usually well buried. There tends to be little insight about causation of their illness; the request is often that the therapist "do something for me." The road back is a hard one. Very little of the work can be done for her, but the therapist *can* help her to help herself. And the therapist hopefully will involve her husband in a process that leads them both to recognize who they are as people, how the problems developed, and how they can learn new ways of problem solving.

Of course, every marriage is a delicate balance, and if the woman begins to change, the scales are tipped—the equilibrium is upset. This is one of the reasons that change is never easy. Although people think they want to change, they also resist. Old habits or life-styles, even though painful, are in a strange way comfortable; new ones seem frightening or may not appear adequate to replace the old ones. Furthermore, if change in one partner upsets the equilibrium, change is demanded in the other partner, and the executive's reaction may be too powerful or too negative for his wife to tolerate.

For every resistance that the therapist encounters, however, he or she also encounters a genuine longing by both patient and spouse to improve the situation. Unfortunately, therapists are often poorly equipped to deal with these couples because of the prevailing attitudes in our society about women. As our cultural ideas change, so do those of therapists, but there are still many professionals who see their main task as helping a corporate wife accept her traditional or expected role. Her mental health would be defined in terms of her acceptance of the usual feminine roles. The purely Freudian view of a woman places her, in almost every way, in a one-down position vis-à-vis men. Many therapists today have come to see Freud's theories as connected primarily to the social system and historical perspective of which he was a part; but his influence on psychiatry has been enormous. Furthermore, psychotherapeutic professionals tend to be as chauvinistic as any other group dominated (more than 80 percent) by men.[12] All too frequently for women, therapy has focused on their individual problems or seeming symptomatology, their inferior personalities or early childhood traumas, and neglected consideration of the social system in which they live.


## ONE WOMAN'S THERAPY

The following example of a corporate wife in treatment illustrates the complications of therapy, as well as the tremendous resistance we all have to change.

Amy was in her middle thirties, married to a very successful executive a few years older, and the mother of a small son. She was strikingly beautiful and had been one of the highest paid New York models during her late teens and early twenties. She was referred to the private psychiatric hospital in Connecticut where I worked by her

New York City psychoanalyst, a prominent and well-trained man who had seen her deteriorate steadily over the past two years.

Amy was the only child of a career army officer who rose to the rank of colonel, and a beautiful, though chronically depressed mother. She succinctly described her childhood: "We moved several times while I was growing up, but we always had plenty of money, and I always thought I had wonderful relationships with Mom and Daddy."

What she was not aware of at the time was that her relationships with both parents, as well as most of her relationships outside the family, were based primarily on her exceptional physical appearance. Many of the people around her related to her as a beautiful object—doting on her, worshiping her, even being a bit in awe of her. Her mother, recapturing her own fading beauty through comparisons with Amy, treated her as an alter ego, although there were also subtle signs of rivalry and competitive feelings. Her father was extremely proud of her, called her his "goddess," and very early began to compensate for his inadequate relationship with his wife by escorting Amy everywhere. Because Amy was also likable and fairly bright, she did well in school and was the center of much attention. Nevertheless, she remembered harboring a private loneliness and a feeling of emptiness from about the age of ten.

"When I was fourteen, my parents told me how unhappy their marriage had always been, and they got a divorce. I was upset at first, but soon I realized that they were both as involved with me as ever. They both used all kinds of contacts and energy to make a modeling career for me."

She was an instant success, and by the time she was nineteen, she had been on the covers of most of the leading fashion magazines. She had a brief, early marriage to a reporter, but her family helped her quickly dissolve that.

"At twenty-one I married Tom, who was then thirty and an already successful vice-president in a brokerage firm. I continued my modeling, but gradually I just lost interest in it. It was hard work, and it seemed like I had been working forever. I guess part of the truth is also that I began losing assignments to newer, younger models, and eventually I gave up my career. Instead I concentrated on being the perfect hostess and business wife, and I was often pointed out as an example to the wives of Tom's associates. We both enjoyed Tom's substantial income, our interesting friends, and our travels; but I found I was increasingly bored with life and at loose ends, so we decided to have a baby." Their son was born when Amy was twenty-eight, and six months after his birth, Amy was in a full-blown depression.

In the style of a successful and affluent executive, who also was extremely concerned about his wife, Tom made inquiries and arranged for her to see a well-known psychoanalyst. Amy entered analysis dutifully and saw him four times each week for two years. She seemed a bit better able to cope, but complained to Tom that it was a waste of time and money because she never got any advice from the analyst. Finally Tom gave Amy "permission" to quit, and she did fairly well for a few months.

"Then the old symptoms reappeared, and we went through the same process again. This time I stayed in therapy almost three years, but I gradually went down hill, and eventually I needed hospitalization. Whereas I had once been the perfect corporate wife, the envy of all Tom's associates, I had long since given up even trying to make the right appearance; I had become a drag at any parties we attended."

On admission to the hospital, she was disheveled and uncommunicative, resigned and quite hopeless about her future. She had considered suicide and had made one pseudo-attempt with an overdose of tranquilizers. Her attitude toward the professional staff was: "I doubt that you can do much for me." Her experiences with therapists had been similar to her relationships with other men—she had related like a dependent child and had been disappointed by them. They, in turn, had found her difficult to understand and had failed in helping her adjust to her life as it was. Our staff told her she was right—very little could be done for her. But the staff and other patients forced her into the knowledge that she could do something different with her own life. They reminded her in countless ways that she had choices in every aspect of her life, and as this began to sink in, Amy began to come alive.

One important aspect of Amy's therapy was her understanding that she had never been encouraged to develop many inner, emotional resources because people around her had tended to relate so much to her as a beautiful object—almost a nonperson. Although Tom was well-meaning, he too had fallen into this pattern to some extent, and had unconsciously used her in his business life to enhance his own image. Amy and Tom had collaborated in a system where he made all the important decisions for them both; Amy had grown up believing this was the only way to function, and Tom had some hidden fears that Amy was not really capable of much independent thinking.

The other important aspect of therapy was joint sessions, which helped both Tom and Amy get to know each other in a new way, get more honest and explicit about their expectations of each other, and become aware of the delicate balance in their marriage. At one point Amy started to tell Tom why she had married him—insight she had gained from her individual and group therapy—and he tried to shut her up twice with comments that changed the subject. When the therapists pointed this out, he admitted, "I think I know why Amy married me, but it's too painful to hear her say it. I think she needed someone to take care of her; her parents really couldn't do that anymore, and they had gotten rid of her first husband. I think I was convenient; I was making good money, and she knew I would not purposely hurt her. I was in awe of her beauty and her fame and success, but I also knew that, under all that, she was kind of a little girl. In a way, I guess I was flattered that she wanted me to take care of her; but I've always been a little hurt that she didn't love me."

Amy seemed shocked to hear this from Tom, but she did not deny it. "I was going to tell you that I was a little girl emotionally when I married you. You said it better than I could have, but I had no idea you felt so hurt about it. I did love you, Tom, in my own way; but I didn't even know who I was at that point. And I never thought you loved me very much either. I know you liked to show me off; I know you liked having your friends say what a terrific wife you had; but you sure were never interested in talking things over with me. I never thought you respected me; I figured you thought I was pretty dumb. All you cared about was whether I looked good for all those other people—those clients and the guys you worked with. You never much cared if I was hurting inside. You liked having a little boy who would look like me and like you too, but you were never around to spend time with him, and you never would listen when I complained about how hard it was to take care of him."

Now it was Tom's turn to look surprised. He too had known these things on some level, but had preferred to keep them hidden. Unfortunately, the issues surfaced in other ways—primarily in Amy's depression, which was used to some extent to act out problems that they both had. Now that they were out in the open, they somehow began to seem less catastrophic. In fact, both Amy and Tom developed a sense of humor about how superficial their relationship had been; they began to talk of themselves in the past as "old Tom" and "old Amy."

I saw Amy and Tom in family therapy with a male co-therapist for two years after hospitalization. Amy began slowly to assert herself and to talk about some of her resentments toward Tom. He had really prized her as a showpiece and had unconsciously sabotaged any efforts at self-assertion. The alliances are always shifting between patients and therapists in a foursome such as this, but probably the strongest alliance was in the identification process between female patient and female therapist. Amy had never seen women operate that way before, especially in relation to men, and she was a quick learner. She eventually went back to college, and although they frequently hit snags when her schedule conflicts with Tom's business needs, they have learned how to talk things out and make compromises.

Most of the time a woman is just plain lucky if she gets a therapist capable of helping her in her struggle for identity. Often such a woman is in therapy for years without much success, or she jumps from therapist to therapist with seeming inability to relate to any of them. This may not be just a "bad patient," as some professionals would like to label her, but rather a person whose resources for finding the right therapist are limited. It is terribly important that this kind of woman find a therapist who considers her in the context of her environment, who assesses what rewards and punishments she gets from the people around her for various kinds of behavior. Most corporate wives find that there are many rewards in their environment for passive-dependent behavior and very few supports for the opposite.

The tasks of therapy should ideally be: (1) to see how the problems developed, (2) to help the woman become aware that she has choices (including the choice to remain as is rather than to change), (3) to help the woman accomplish change if she wishes to, (4) to help her integrate those changes into all areas of her life, and (5) to help her evaluate those changes over time.

On the clinical level, one sees a range of corporate wives, a range of symptomatology, and a range of measures that can help. The most common problem, if it can be so labeled, is confusion about the right to make choices and the possibility of independent decision making. Corporate wives, despite their middle-class, educated, affluent life-styles, tend to be a passive, accepting, dependent group. Probably more than any other group of American women, they have allowed themselves to be victims, not only of their husbands, but of very powerful, male-dominated organizations as well. Those who are trying to change or liberate themselves need various kinds of help: The most severely disturbed woman obviously needs professional services. The woman whose symptoms are labeled neurotic may choose psychotherapy with a professional, consciousness raising among friends, some kind of growth experience such as assertiveness training, or a combination of these. And probably any woman struggling to resolve for herself the inconsistencies between liberation and corporation could benefit from the self-help suggestions in the chapters to follow.

# PART TWO

# The View from the Top—
# <u>Fortune</u> 500 Survey

# 4

# Attitudes at the Top

In order to get a reasonably accurate picture of how the corporate world sees the role of corporate wife, a questionnaire was sent to the heads of the 500 largest industrial companies listed in *Fortune* magazine, May 1975. A similar questionnaire and explanatory letter was included for their wives. Of the 500 questionnaires sent to chief executive officers, 126 were completed; 112 of the wives' were returned. This is a rate of approximately 25 percent—a relatively high response when one considers all the other demands on this group of people. An additional 32 letters or notes were received indicating business or personal reasons why the questionnaire would not be returned; usually this involved a company policy of not responding to any unsolicited material because of time limitations.

The chief executive officers of the *Fortune* 500 companies and their wives were chosen as a target group for several reasons. First, this is a homogeneous group and a recognized entity; these companies have been grouped together and evaluated for two decades by *Fortune* magazine. Also, these men and their wives tend to make the most important decisions and set the tone for all that happens in their organizations. In an indirect way, their attitudes about wives affect the wife of every executive in that corporation. Furthermore, although the *Fortune* 500 list does not include businesses like banks and transportation, and although it does not reflect the practices of small companies, it does include a wide range of industries and a considerable differential from the largest of the 500 to the smallest. It should be recognized that these men and women tend to be older, more affluent, and more successful than the "average" corporate executive and his wife; this means that they would not necessarily be representative in their attitudes of younger, less affluent middle-management people. Nevertheless, it is precisely because of these qualities and the leadership positions these people hold that their attitudes and opinions are so important. They have tremendous power over wives within their own companies, as well as wives of bankers, attorneys, suppliers, clients, and others who deal with the *Fortune* 500.

The picture that emerges of today's corporate wife is quite clear and quite conservative:

• Her most desirable qualities are sense of humor, graciousness, intelligence, adaptability, and friendliness. Her least desirable qualities are gregariousness, independence, creative thinking, punctuality, and the ability to be a skilled conversationalist.

• She is expected to communicate well with her husband and others, and be devoted to her husband and children. She should not be concerned about her own identity. The abilities to entertain well and manage her household smoothly are seen in the moderate range of importance.

• She should not be alcoholic or have extramarital affairs. She should not be part of an open marriage. It is acceptable for her to seek psychiatric treatment or to use a surname other than her husband's. It is acceptable if she is occasionally unavailable for entertaining because of career conflicts, but not if she is often unavailable. And it

88

is fairly acceptable if her husband occasionally takes time off to care for a sick child while she works.

• She is expected to make many moves in connection with her husband's career—approximately one every five years.

• Her responsibilities for entertaining and being entertained vary according to many factors, but her estimates of these responsibilities are consistently higher than her husband's.

• In our era of changing consciousness about women and their roles, very few men at the top of the *Fortune* 500 and their wives have changed their opinion of the corporate wife's position.

## MECHANICS OF THE SURVEY AND INTERVIEWS

The schedule of questions was purposely brief and concise (two pages); it was addressed personally to the chief executive officer as he or she was listed in the *Poor's Directory*. If the chief executive officer was not listed as such, the questionnaire was sent to the chairman; if no chairman was listed, it was sent to the president. To my knowledge, the only female chief executive among this group is Katherine Graham of the Washington Post Company. Unfortunately, her response was that "her schedule does not permit her the time to participate in your project."

The questionnaire was designed for anonymity if the respondent desired it, but more than half—about 55 percent—chose to include their identity. There was a section, which could be torn off and returned separately, which asked whether they would like to receive a copy of the results and whether they would be willing to be interviewed. For the many people who left this section attached, one can guess that they are used to taking credit for their ideas. These are people who are frequently giving speeches and being quoted; anonymity is not particularly appealing to them.

The content of questions for chief executive officers

and their wives was similar, though different in certain areas such as attitudes toward moving. The similarities in the questionnaires were designed to compare the responses of husbands and wives, to see whether they tended to put emphases in the same places.

The difference between the number of executive respondents (126) and wife respondents (112) may be explained by a variety of possibilities: executives never gave wives the questionnaire; wives resented being asked to do another task that came through their husband's job; wives did not consider this survey important; or several other possible reasons. There were indications from a few women that they were completing the questionnaire even though their husbands were not (usually because of time demands)—i.e., some husbands did pass the questionnaire on to their wives, allowing them to make the decision of whether or not to respond, even though the husband chose to not complete his. However, it seems likely that most of the executives who did not complete the questionnaire themselves also did not give the opportunity to their wives. In other words, they made this decision, as they do many others, for their wives. It also is apparent from talking with chief executive officers that their secretaries sort out much of their mail; one can assume that many of the people who did not respond never even saw the request.

Of the 126 chief executive officer respondents, 23 said they would be willing to meet with me personally to discuss their attitudes and experiences. Most of these men were interviewed either in person or by telephone. Thirty-one of the women said they would be willing to talk in more depth, and most of them were also subsequently interviewed. All of these people were interesting, and they were usually very gracious. Their reasons for offering to help the survey in this way ranged from personal curiosity about the subject, to seeing this as part of their job, to: "If you're doing the work, I'm willing to help."

# SURVEY FINDINGS

The eleven areas covered in the survey can be categorized as follows:

*Qualities most valuable in the "ideal" wife of a corporate executive*

The respondents were asked to indicate which of these qualities, listed in alphabetical order, they would consider most valuable:

| | | |
|---|---|---|
| Ability to entertain well | Flexibility | Sense of humor |
| | Friendliness | Skilled conversationalist |
| Accomplishments of her own | Good health | |
| | Good manners | Unselfishness |
| Adaptability | Graciousness | Versatility |
| Attractiveness | Gregariousness | |
| Cooperativeness | Independence | Other _____ |
| Creative thinking | Intelligence | _____ |
| Efficiency | Punctuality | |
| Enthusiasm | Resourcefulness | |

Most of the people circled several of the above qualities, and a few circled them all. However, there was a clear preference for certain qualities and a clear omission of others.

To the chief executive officers, the most desirable qualities are sense of humor, intelligence, friendliness, and adaptability. The least desirable qualities are gregariousness, independence, punctuality, and skilled conversationalist.

The most desirable qualities, as listed by the wives, are graciousness, intelligence, adaptability, and sense of humor, in that order. The least desirable ones are gregariousness, independence, and creative thinking. (See Table I.)

The most preferred attribute of a corporation wife, as these men see it, is an interesting one—sense of humor. Out of 126 men responding, 88 (or 70 percent) list-

TABLE I—QUALITIES MOST VALUABLE IN THE "IDEAL" CORPORATE WIFE

| | CEOs who consider this valuable (Total N = 126) | | Wives who consider this valuable (Total N = 112) | |
|---|---|---|---|---|
| | Number | Percent | Number | Percent |
| Ability to entertain well | 54 | 43% | 52 | 46% |
| Accomplishments of her own | 34 | 27% | 35 | 31% |
| Adaptability | 86 | 68% | 91 | 81% |
| Attractiveness | 44 | 35% | 48 | 43% |
| Cooperativeness | 49 | 39% | 69 | 62% |
| Creative thinking | 28 | 22% | 20 | 18% |
| Efficiency | 28 | 22% | 41 | 37% |
| Enthusiasm | 59 | 47% | 56 | 50% |
| Flexibility | 71 | 56% | 69 | 62% |
| Friendliness | 86 | 68% | 66 | 59% |
| Good health | 59 | 47% | 66 | 59% |
| Good manners | 63 | 50% | 48 | 43% |

| | | | | |
|---|---|---|---|---|
| Graciousness | 73 | 58% | 87 | 78% |
| Gregariousness | 5 | 4% | 7 | 6% |
| Independence | 15 | 12% | 20 | 18% |
| Intelligence | 86 | 68% | 87 | 78% |
| Punctuality | 20 | 16% | 45 | 40% |
| Resourcefulness | 34 | 27% | 48 | 43% |
| Sense of humor | 88 | 70% | 73 | 65% |
| Skilled conversationalist | 20 | 16% | 38 | 34% |
| Unselfishness | 63 | 50% | 48 | 43% |
| Versatility | 32 | 25% | 28 | 25% |

ed this quality. A charitable interpretation of this would be that any situation in life requires a good sense of humor, and any corporate wife who can combine humor with other characteristics is likely to have a pretty good perspective about her role. Since a high percentage of chief executive officers' wives (65 percent) also listed this quality, we can assume that these couples are in some agreement on its importance. A much less charitable interpretation of this fact would be that, because the traditional role of corporate wife is such a ridiculous, demeaning one for any woman, she can get through it best if she can see its comical quality, if she can appreciate what is funny or amusing about it all. The more reasonable interpretation is probably somewhere in the middle and could not really be verified without questioning each of the respondents further.

The other highly rated qualities—adaptability, friendliness, intelligence, graciousness—are relatively easy to understand: An adaptable woman would be able to handle all kinds of situations, would be able to entertain with little notice, would be willing and able to adjust to a new location if her husband's job demanded it. A friendly and gracious woman would be able to meet all types of people easily and would enjoy the myriad of opportunities she has for seeing new faces and places. An intelligent woman would make good assessments of people and situations and would be able to talk and conduct herself appropriately.

A woman who has these five qualities, then, can be easily pictured as an "ideal" corporation wife. The very low priority given to independence is a bit less understandable, especially since corporate wives find their husbands quite unavailable for most things that involve home or child care. The best explanation is probably the one given verbally by several men: "Independence would tend to make her less available."

There is general agreement between the chief executive officers and their wives on the order of preference for qualities of a corporate wife, but there are a few significant differences in emphasis. The wives placed more im-

94

portance on adaptability (wives, 81 percent; executives, 68 percent), cooperativeness (wives, 62 percent; executives, 39 percent), efficiency (wives, 37 percent; executives, 22 percent), graciousness (wives, 78 percent; executives, 58 percent), punctuality (wives, 40 percent; executives, 16 percent), resourcefulness (wives, 43 percent; executives, 27 percent), and skilled conversationalist (wives, 34 percent; executives, 16 percent) than their husbands did. By contrast, the executives put more emphasis on friendliness, good manners, and unselfishness than their wives did, although these percentage differences are not as great.

The "other" qualities that individual chief executive officers chose to list as important to them were: ability to keep her mouth shut, sincerity, dependability, good mother and/or wife to the husband and family, and "a decent Christian woman." Some wives added other qualities they would value. Mrs. Justin Dart, whose husband heads Dart Industries in Los Angeles, included three very articulate words in her list: "sensitivity, compassion, awareness." Another woman added "dependable, trustworthy." Someone else suggested: "The ability to listen and not act as a corporate wife who thinks she is very important." One other wife noted the importance of "discretion—not taking sides in interpersonal relations within the company."

*Qualities that would be detrimental to the functioning of a corporate wife.* The respondents were asked to cross out any of the above qualities they would consider detrimental to the functioning of a corporate wife. The numbers here are statistically small, but the choices are significant. The three qualities selected were gregariousness (by 10 percent of the men and 9 percent of the women), independence (by 8 percent of the men and 9 percent of the women), and accomplishments of her own (by 2 percent of the men and 3 percent of the women). The ages of the respondents who listed these qualities as detrimental were found not to be relevant or statistically significant. On further questioning in interview situations, it became apparent that the definition of the word "gregarious" may be a factor in the way it is valued or devalued. Although Webster defines it as "fond of the company of others; sociable," it appears that many people think of gregarious as pushy or assertive in a rather nasty way.

*Five characteristics ranked in order of importance.* The survey group was asked to rank from one to five, in order of importance, the following characteristics of a good corporate wife:

Able to communicate well with husband
and others
Able to entertain well
Able to manage household smoothly
Concerned about her own identity
Devoted to husband and children

Clearly, the most devalued characteristic of a corporate wife is concern about her own identity. Almost all of the respondents listed it third, fourth, or fifth; only two men and three women listed it first. Forty-nine percent of the men and an amazing 72 percent of the women listed the identity characteristic last.

The ability to communicate well was important to everyone; all 126 of the men and all 112 of the women rated this first, second, or third. A significantly high 48 percent of the men and 44 percent of the women rated it number one. The other important characteristic to both men and women was devotion to husband and children. Forty-three percent of the men rated it number one, and an even higher 50 percent of the wives rated it first. The ability to manage a household smoothly is seen by most of these people as moderately important. The ability to entertain well was also valued in the middle range in this ranking. (See Tables II and III.)

*Attitudes about emotionally charged situations.* The questionnaire listed seventeen situations involving attitudes both about executives and about corporate wives. The situations were very briefly described and obviously ambiguous, allowing the respondent to interpret them in subjective ways. It is not clear from the questionnaire results how the attitudes would get played out in practice, but it is clear that there are some strongly negative attitudes among chief executive officers and their wives about various kinds of behavior. There is also neutrality in some areas, which would indicate that the average executive and his wife have flexibility in certain situations. (See Table IV.)

It is interesting to note some surprising spots of conservatism within a particular individual's generally liberal responses, or vice versa. For example, one man was neutral about almost everything, but negative regarding a wife who uses a surname other than her husband's. These seeming inconsistencies probably imply no more than personal idiosyncrasies, but they do suggest that the wise corporate wife should assess whom and what part of that person she is dealing with.

The respondents were predominantly negative about alcoholism in either the executive or his wife, although the chief executive officers were slightly more tolerant if the alcoholic is the wife. One cannot be sure why a few people listed their attitude as positive, but they probably were making the same interpretation as did William F. May, chairman of American Can Company, who said that his reaction to alcoholism is "constructive, not condoning."

In the area of extramarital affairs, both men and women were predominantly negative in regard to other executives and wives, and overwhelmingly negative in regard to themselves and their spouses. Seventy-two percent of chief executive officers were negative about their executives having extramarital affairs, and 76 percent of them were negative about affairs for wives. An overwhelming 84 percent of the wives were negative for both. The old sexual double standard is somewhat apparent in this survey: Among the respondents, the chief executive officers tended to be slightly more liberal in sexual attitudes than their wives. Also, the chief executive officers expressed a little more neutrality toward men's having extramarital affairs than toward women's having them.

These findings are interesting in light of the image of many businessmen as swingers, men who enjoy an extramarital sexual fling almost as a reward for their hard work. It is also increasingly acceptable in the corporate world for an executive to be divorced and still be promotable if he is otherwise capable. And as most sophisticated people know, divorces are often preceded by some extramarital activity. How then can these findings be explained? First, it seems that this is a very conservative group of people, primarily in their fifties and sixties, who are probably by nature very conscious of responsibility, and who are certainly burdened by the obligations of their positions. Second, sex is probably the most taboo subject in our culture, and as most researchers know, responses to sexual questions are notoriously unreliable. It is complicated in this situation by the fact that many of these men and women chose to identify themselves, and therefore limited further the reliability of their response to these questions. Third, my choice of the words "extramarital affair" and "extramarital sexual relationship" implies something long-term, and some emotional commitment. As one chief executive officer said so succinctly in an interview, "A ballsy fling in San Diego is okay; an affair seems much more intimate and long-term and threatening." As it applies to themselves, one can imagine how exposed these people must feel and how their standards in extramarital matters might be affected by fears of exposure as well as moral beliefs.

One other recent survey, published under the title *Executive Life Styles,* indicates that infidelity is not as prevalent among executives as most people think; but this picture is less conservative than my survey indicates. Nearly six thousand men examined at Manhattan's Life Extension Institute filled out questionnaires about their sex lives. "The most notable finding in the entire survey is that in these permissive times nearly 80 percent of the married men are faithful to their wives." Of the 20.6 percent who engaged in extramarital affairs, there was little variation from one age group to another. There *was* a difference, on the other hand, between city husbands (25.4 percent) and suburban husbands (19.9 percent) who had extramarital relations. There was also a "strong

## TABLE II—CHARACTERISTICS OF A GOOD CORPORATE WIFE AS RANKED BY CHIEF EXECUTIVE OFFICERS

N = 123*

|  | #1 | #2 | #3 | #4 | #5 |
|---|---|---|---|---|---|
| Able to communicate well | 48% | 29% | 23% |  |  |
| Able to entertain well | 3% | 7% | 12% | 42% | 36% |
| Able to manage household smoothly | 4% | 25% | 23% | 34% | 14% |
| Concerned about own identity | 2% | 9% | 20% | 20% | 49% |
| Devoted to husband and children | 43% | 30% | 22% | 4% | 1% |

## TABLE III—CHARACTERISTICS OF A GOOD CORPORATE WIFE AS RANKED BY CHIEF EXECUTIVE OFFICERS' WIVES

N = 110*

|  | #1 | #2 | #3 | #4 | #5 |
|---|---|---|---|---|---|
| Able to communicate well | 44% | 44% | 12% |  |  |
| Able to entertain well | 3% | 3% | 19% | 53% | 22% |
| Able to manage household smoothly |  | 22% | 47% | 25% | 6% |
| Concerned about own identity | 3% | 9% | 6% | 10% | 72% |
| Devoted to husband and children | 50% | 22% | 16% | 12% |  |

*Three of the men and two of the women did not respond appropriately.

TABLE IV—ATTITUDES OF CHIEF EXECUTIVE OFFICERS AND WIVES REGARDING VARIOUS KINDS OF BEHAVIOR

| | CEOs* | | | Wives | | |
|---|---|---|---|---|---|---|
| | Positive | Neutral | Negative | Positive | Neutral | Negative |
| Male executive who is alcoholic | 8% | 4% | 88% | 3% | 19% | 78% |
| Corporate wife who is alcoholic | 4% | 16% | 80% | 3% | 19% | 78% |
| Male executive who has extra-marital affairs | 2% | 26% | 72% | | 16% | 84% |
| Corporate wife who has extra-marital affairs | 2% | 22% | 76% | | 16% | 84% |
| Male executive who is homosexual or bisexual | 4% | 18% | 78% | | 34% | 66% |
| Corporate wife who is lesbian or bisexual | 4% | 20% | 76% | | 31% | 69% |
| Male executive who seeks psychiatric treatment | 38% | 49% | 13% | 41% | 53% | 6% |

100

| | | | | | | |
|---|---|---|---|---|---|---|
| Corporate wife who seeks psychiatric treatment | 32% | 60% | 8% | 41% | 56% | 3% |
| Corporate wife using a surname other than husband's | 2% | 78% | 20% | 9% | 66% | 25% |
| Male executive living with woman but choosing not to marry | 2% | 47% | 51% | 3% | 41% | 56% |
| Male executive occasionally taking time off to care for sick child (wife works) | 30% | 49% | 21% | 50% | 31% | 19% |
| Male executive planning vacation to coincide with working wife's | 67% | 29% | 4% | 75% | 22% | 3% |
| Corporate wife occasionally unavailable for entertaining—career conflict | 28% | 61% | 11% | 41% | 56% | 3% |

TABLE IV—(continued)

| | CEOs | | | Wives | | |
|---|---|---|---|---|---|---|
| | Positive | Neutral | Negative | Positive | Neutral | Negative |
| Corporate wife often unavailable because of career conflict | 6% | 56% | 38% | 6% | 44% | 50% |
| Executive & wife who follow principles of "open marriage"* | 2% | 31% | 61% | 6% | 41% | 50% |
| Yourself having an extramarital sexual relationship | | 11% | 89% | | 3% | 97% |
| Your spouse having an extramarital sexual relationship | | 9% | 91% | | | 100% |

*CEO = chief executive officer
*6% of CEOs and 3% of wives did not answer this question

102

correlation between income and infidelity, with nearly one-third of the over-$50,000 group engaging in extramarital sex. This affinity is all the more striking because the men earning the higher incomes would tend, of course, to be older."[1] Since our chief executive officers are all in the over-$50,000 salary range, their attitudes can be seen as more conservative and restrictive than the norm.

| Annual income | Percent engaging in extramarital sex |
|---|---|
| Less than $20,000 | 13.5 |
| $20,000 to $35,000 | 20.2 |
| $35,000 to $50,000 | 28.7 |
| More than $50,000 | 32.0 |

Table based on *Executive Life Styles* (New York: Thomas Y. Crowell, 1974).

Another survey, done by *Town and Country* magazine, which looked just at chairmen and presidents of the 100 largest manufacturing companies—179 men in all —found that 95 percent of them are still married to their first wife. Considering the death of some wives, the divorce rate at the top is lower than 5 percent, and one might assume that infidelity is also low. "The plump paychecks and fringes smooth out some of the rough spots in married life, and social pressures to stick together also help marital stability."[2]

The picture of sexual practices for our society at large is mixed and sometimes confusing. A recent book by Anthony Pietropinto and Jacqueline Simenauer, *Beyond the Male Myth,* reports that approximately half of the 4,000 men surveyed have cheated on their wives or steady girlfriends. This confirms the findings of Dr. Kinsey's pioneering sex research back in 1948.[3]

Other accounts are more conservative. *Time* magazine, in the November 21, 1977 issue, reported a survey on "The new morality; an exclusive poll on what Americans really think about sex," and one of the questions was about extramarital relationships. Is it morally wrong

103

for a married man to be unfaithful to his wife? A solid 76 percent said yes. Is it morally wrong for a married woman to be unfaithful to her husband? Seventy-nine percent said yes. *Time* notes that women are more conservative than men on these issues; they are also just as quick to apply the double standard—that is, like men, women condemned female adultery more than male adultery. Several "experts" were quoted as saying that the sexual revolution of the sixties appears to be over. The nuclear family has survived intact, and "we're not as swinging a people as we think we are."

My survey indicates some neutrality (31 percent of men; 41 percent of wives) about the concept of open marriage. Three of the respondents indicated they did not know the term, but the others obviously interpreted it in various ways; openness to many of these people evidently does not include sexuality.

Homosexuality or bisexuality is frowned on for both executives and wives. A little more than three-fourths of the chief executive officers would feel negative about such a situation; about two-thirds of the wives would take negative positions. This is fairly consistent with attitude surveys of the general public about homosexuality.

The attitude about an executive who lives with a woman but chooses not to marry her is a slightly more liberal one; about half of the chief executive officers and wives would take a dim view of it, while the other half would be neutral. As in other situations, one must assume that the particular circumstances would help to determine the attitude, along with the chief executive officer's or wife's idiosyncratic beliefs. Nevertheless, these situations are occurring and are having to be dealt with.

The chief executive of one very large and well-respected company told about one of his vice-presidents who is a current example. The chief executive officer and his wife had known and liked the vice-president's wife and were surprised when they divorced ten years ago. They were subsequently surprised and delighted to meet his new companion, who proved to be bright, witty, interesting, and extremely good for him. They were amazed to find that she would live with him but refused to marry him. Over time, the situation seems to have been totally accepted within the company and the man has had two significant promotions, but there have been a few sticky problems. Many people have had to be corrected after introducing her as his wife, and one convention planner who felt that her presence would· be awkward can no longer expect his attendance either. There is only one major dilemma: The next promotion would be to a position that involves essentially representing the company to the world, and there has been some real questioning about whether his marital, or rather nonmarital, status would be acceptable at that level. This vignette illustrates that all kinds of marital variations and alternatives are happening. Whether they will be increasingly accepted and at what levels in the hierarchy is an open question.

One area where there is significant acceptance among this group is psychiatric treatment. It would be interesting to be able to compare this with findings ten years ago; I suspect that general attitudes about psychotherapy have been greatly liberalized in the past few years. Although people in this survey are a bit more understanding if it is the wife rather than the executive who seeks treatment, their attitudes in this matter should be encouraging to both men and women. Approximately 35 percent of the men and 41 percent of the wives are positive about people who seek psychiatric treatment; approximately 55 percent of the men and 54 percent of the women are neutral.

They are also primarily neutral about a wife using a surname other than her husband's. However, one-fifth of these chief executive officers and one-fourth of their wives would be negative about this. Women who want to use maiden names for professional or other purposes should beware; they should try to assess whether they are dealing with one of the 20 or 25 percent.

The group was significantly positive (67 percent of men; 75 percent of women) about an executive planning his vacation time to coincide with that of his wife. Although this could obviously present some problems to the corporation, it is probably seen as just another factor to throw into vacation preferences. In addition, most top executives seem to recognize the importance of vacations and good vacation planning to the productivity of any worker.

There is an interesting mix in attitudes about an executive occasionally taking time off to care for a sick child while his wife works. Thirty percent of the chief executive officers would be positive; 49 percent would be neutral; 21 percent would be negative. Fifty percent of the women would be positive; 31 percent neutral; 19 percent negative. This would seem to be a fairly liberal position. It also indicates, as might be expected, that the women see more need for shared child care than men. In reality, attitudes would probably differ with the individual circumstances and might not be as understanding as the above would imply. However, it should be encouraging for those couples who want more equality in child care. And it should also be discouraging for those husbands who have hidden behind the idea that their bosses would never understand that kind of thing.

The last item in this list concerns demands on the corporate wife for entertaining, and indicates an interesting neutrality if she is occasionally unavailable because of career conflicts. In fact, 28 percent of the men and 41 percent of the women would be positive if a wife were unavailable occasionally, probably indicating some respect for a woman who pursues a career. However, 38 percent of the men and 50 percent of the women would be negative if she were *often* unavailable, indicating that her first priority should still be her husband's career, or possibly indicating that she should be able to arrange her life to include both.

With the men and women who were interviewed, some effort was made to determine how their negative attitudes in all these areas would get played out. On the whole, the chief executive officers would draw the line at any behavior that interfered with company functioning.

They would be more tolerant if the individual exercised discretion.

J. B. Lanterman (AMSTED Industries) said, "I would watch the productivity of the individual to see if there was any impairment. It would be one of those brown marks—not a black mark—against a person. It would send up a flag." If the offender was the wife? "Discussion would be through the husband mostly. We have an industrial psychologist who visits with all of us about once every three months. I might mention the situation to him, and he might discuss it with the man in the patient-doctor relationship. He would go to the wife only at the insistence of the husband."

Henry C. Goodrich, president and chief executive officer of Inland Container Corporation in Indianapolis, had a case in point: "One of my men was having an extramarital affair. I called the individual in and told him what he was doing was his own business. But if his behavior resulted in any scandal, he would have to get another job. He subsequently divorced his wife and married the other girl. In a community like we live in, we are somewhat in a fishbowl. I am not so concerned about the individual's morals as I am about how it looks for the company."

Are wives of executives ever enlisted to straighten out other wives? Goodrich said, "I have personally seen situations which have backfired. Sometimes a chief executive officer has tried to use his wife to influence a tough situation that he didn't have guts enough to handle. My wife and I do assist people and of course we talk about things privately. The company makes pastoral counseling and industrial psychological counseling available. You see all kinds in a company, and we've gone through some nasty divorces. But most people are relatively normal. You can't be a moralizer. I'm convinced that corporate people are no different from those in other fields, and their level of integrity is higher than most of the publicity indicates."

Most of the wives said they would not get involved directly in these situations even though they might feel strongly about them. However, a few said that they might be asked by their husbands to tactfully talk with a wife. One woman, who asked not to be identified here, said, "I'm well liked, so I can jokingly make suggestions that might be picked up. But generally it would be handled within the company, and my husband also makes counseling very available. We had a situation where a man was divorced and was having an affair for quite a long time. He brought the gal to conferences, and everyone liked them both. Most people were nice to her, but there was disapproval of them traveling together. The men talked to him; they told him they didn't think it was good that they were traveling together on business. Then my husband and I just happened to have one lovely evening with them following a business meeting. Well, the next morning they told us they had decided to get married. They said they figured if we could be happily married for thirty-one years, they would try it too." The influence of this CEO's wife was certainly positive, and she is the kind of warm, sincere person who could carry it off.

*The number of moves an executive and his family might make.* The respondents were asked to estimate how many moves an executive might be expected to make if he worked for that company from age thirty to age fifty and rose to the rank of executive vice-president. This is admittedly a very vague situation, and it is difficult to think in terms of an average. As several people noted, the marketing executive would tend to move many more times than would the man who comes up through finance, for example. Nevertheless, a picture emerges of a significant amount of moving within the corporate world. The mean number of moves that a man in this situation should expect to make is four. The overwhelming majority of executive families would be expected to make three to five moves during the twenty-year period, working for the same *Fortune* 500 company and rising to the rank of executive vice-president.

These figures reflect only intracompany moves; they do not include the moves those executives might have made before coming to that company at age thirty, nor do they reflect any moves after fifty that would presumably include retirement. The data should be considered in contrast to most other occupations and professions where moving is not part of the picture and is in fact made quite impossible by the financial cost and loss of contacts. (See Table V.)

The wives were asked their own attitudes about the moves they had made, and also what they think the attitudes of other wives are about moving. Forty-one percent said their own attitude was enthusiastic, but only 6 percent thought other wives were enthusiastic. Other women are more often (76 percent of the time) rated "accepting." This difference between our respondents' attitudes and those they ascribed to other women could be explained by the fact that chief executive officers' wives tend to make big jumps in status and salary on their way to the top. Or it could also be explained by the "leader of the pack" phenomenon: The fact that these women are in exposed leadership positions requires them to appear more enthusiastic, more "well adjusted" than other women. Only a very small percentage termed themselves or others resentful about moving (two women substituted the word "reluctant"), and this too has many possible interpretations.

For most executives, as for many corporation wives, moving has its pros and cons. For the man who is moving up in the organization as well as moving geographically, the balance is usually weighted on the positive side. Several chief executive officers who were interviewed did say that the lateral moves in the corporate world are much less frequent than they used to be, simply because of the tremendous cost of moving a family these days. If an executive quit or died or got fired in Cleveland, for example, the company used to just fill the position the most expedient way. Now a lot more thought goes into that decision: Is there already a man in Cleveland who could fill the bill? The man in New York would be right for the job, but is this what he wants? What would then be his next step in the company?

TABLE V—THE NUMBER OF MOVES A MAN WOULD BE EXPECTED TO MAKE IF HE WORKED FOR COMPANY FROM AGE 30 TO AGE 50 AND ROSE TO RANK OF EXECUTIVE VICE-PRESIDENT

|  | 1 | 2 | 3 | 4 | 5 | 6 | 7 | No response |
|---|---|---|---|---|---|---|---|---|
| Chief executive officer | 2% | 6% | 25% | 27% | 27% | 8% |  | 5% |
| Chief executive officers' wives | 13% | 13% | 30% | 23% | 13% | 9% | 3% | 9% |

TABLE VI—ATTITUDES OF WOMEN ABOUT MOVING

|  | En-thusiastic | Ac-cepting | Re-sentful | Other Answers |
|---|---|---|---|---|
| Chief executive officers' wives' attitudes about moving | 41% | 47% | 3% | 9% |
| Attitudes attributed to most other corporate wives about moving | 6% | 76% | 6% | 12% |

Another advantage of moving for the executive, and also perhaps for his wife, was expressed by Henry C. Goodrich (Inland Container Corporation). Mr. Goodrich went to that company about ten years ago, after many years in sales and marketing. The move to Indianapolis, he said, "was good because we got out of a lot of things we had been pushed into; it is a relief now not to have to get into certain things. In the previous environment, we did much more outside of business hours. Now I'm in the paper business, and we've made our friends primarily at the association level. There is not/as much entertaining of customers now; we have a large department to do this." Several other executives and wives also said or implied that they enjoyed the months right after a move when they were less involved in community activities and had more time to spend with their families.

*Number of business-social functions corporate wives host or attend.* The chief executive officers were asked specifically how many functions their wives and the average corporate wife in their company would be expected to be involved in.

For their own wives, there was a considerable range in entertaining expectations. Forty-four percent would be expected to host zero to five business-social functions in one year. However, 12 percent would host more than thirty. Thirty-eight percent said that their own wives would be expected to attend six to ten functions in one year. But 15 percent said their wives would attend more than thirty.

The expectations for the average corporate wife are relatively modest and are somewhat less than the demands on the chief executive officer's wife. Several men indicated here too that the expectations for the wife would vary according to the executive's position in the organization (e.g., they would be high in marketing). (See Table VII.)

The wives were asked specifically how many business-social functions they and the average corporate wife would host, and how many they would attend in one year. Their answers show a range similar to their husbands',

TABLE VII—CHIEF EXECUTIVE OFFICERS' ESTIMATES OF BUSINESS-SOCIAL ENTERTAINING EXPECTATIONS FOR CORPORATE WIVES PER YEAR

| | 0–5 | 6–10 | 11–15 | 16–20 | 21–25 | 26–30 | More than 30 | No response |
|---|---|---|---|---|---|---|---|---|
| Your wife hosts | 44% | 20% | 18% | 6% | | | 12% | |
| Your wife attends | 27% | 38% | 6% | 10% | 2% | 2% | 15% | |
| Average corporate wife hosts | 69% | 21% | 6% | | | | | 4% |
| Average corporate wife attends | 41% | 37% | 14% | 2% | 2% | | | 4% |

112

but they consistently estimated more entertaining responsibilities than their husbands gave them credit for. It is possible that the women inflate their own importance by estimating higher than actual responsibility for entertaining. It seems more likely, however, that men are not aware of, or do not focus on, the heavy responsibilities that are handed to their wives for the entertaining part of their business careers. As several women pointed out, these responsibilities do not include just the little dinners at home or at the club, but they also involve charity functions, receptions, and many out-of-town trips for dedications of branch offices, retirement parties, plant open houses, conventions, etc. (See Table VIII.)

Jane Dart (Dart Industries), who does an enormous amount of entertaining, said, "I could get along awfully well with half as much having to go here and there. I often think I would just as soon sit on the rocks at Carmel and have some islands of calmness in my life. Every day there is a deadline of some sort. People are coming through Los Angeles constantly, and there are a lot of impromptu things. We have to be on the march." How did she manage this when her children were small? "There was a terrible conflict. But I was extremely lucky that my parents lived out here. My mother told me when I got married at twenty-one that I should be ready to pack a bag and go whenever my husband needed me, and she really helped out a lot."

Several chief executive officers who were interviewed also admitted that their own attitudes about entertaining largely affected the expectations for their wives. A common feeling among these very busy, pressured men was that they like to keep as much privacy as possible for themselves. Three men said they really do not like large gatherings. Mr. and Mrs. Edward Donley (Air Products and Chemicals) agreed that he is "not much of a party giver or goer." He has been president since 1966; he acknowledged that "perhaps the amount of entertaining in the company has been unconsciously shaped by my own life-style." One woman, Martha Smith (Copperweld), said that she would prefer to do more entertain-

113

TABLE VIII—CHIEF EXECUTIVE OFFICERS' WIVES' ESTIMATES OF BUSINESS-SOCIAL ENTERTAINING BY CORPORATE WIVES PER YEAR

| | 0–5 | 6–10 | 11–15 | 16–20 | 21–25 | 26–30 | More than 30 | No response |
|---|---|---|---|---|---|---|---|---|
| You host | 37% | 25% | 16% | 6% | | 3% | 13% | |
| You attend | 22% | 28% | 9% | | 13% | 3% | 25% | |
| Average corporate wife hosts | 22% | 33% | 21% | 9% | 3% | 3% | | 9% |
| Average corporate wife attends | 16% | 27% | 13% | 13% | 13% | 6% | | 12% |

ing than her husband will tolerate. "He prefers to relax on the weekends. We do about as much as he is interested in doing." Both Mr. and Mrs. Smith said they do very little socializing within the company. Phillip Smith, who has been chief executive officer of the company since 1968, added: "I discourage intramanagement entertaining within the company. Martha and I do it two or three times a year on a corporate basis, but more than that, I think, is an imposition on the wife and children. I also think that kind of thing can lead to a lot of political jockeying." Another CEO described a lot of customer entertaining as "a crock; it just leads to a lot of in-breeding."

On the other end of the continuum, Marjorie Lanterman does a great deal of entertaining. Her husband has been chief executive officer of AMSTED Industries more than eighteen years, and they have developed a wide circle of people who are both business and social friends. She said, "We like to entertain and we do it mostly at home—small dinner parties of six, eight, or ten. We both love our home and like to have fun. Through the business, either directly or indirectly, we have met wonderful people. Through our travels, we have made wonderful friends." The Lantermans have no children and this pace of life clearly suits them both.

Some companies have policies that limit wives' involvement in entertaining. Grant Simmons, who is chairman of the Simmons Company, expressed the view that entertaining should be done on a purely business—usually stag—basis. He said that Simmons very rarely pays any expenses that include wives, and they usually entertain in hotels or clubs. Any wife who wanted to go on a Simmons business trip "would probably find herself a fifth wheel—out in left field—and would go at her own expense."

One other company that seems rather exceptional in its entertaining policies is General Motors. Stephen H. Fuller, GM's vice-president of personnel and development, said, "Our company entertains very little, and typically, we do not allow entertaining on expense accounts if it is done at home." Business entertaining and business

115

trips are usually quite separate from wives, and Mr. Fuller suggests there are several good reasons for this. He adds that "GM is rather extreme in some ways—for example, no officer of the company enjoys a paid club membership —but we feel we offer the best salary and benefit package —period." His statements imply that while entertaining on the company payroll may be a chore to some, it is also a benefit.

It is clear that the chief executive sets the pattern for entertaining standards, as well as other standards, in his company. Men who had been in those positions for many years expressed a lot of security about doing things their way; men who had been chief executive officers a short time were a bit less secure.

*Promotability of a man who is married vs. single or divorced.* The chief executive officers were asked whether it would help a male executive in their company to gain a promotion if he were married rather than single or divorced. Twenty-three percent said yes, it would help; 77 percent said no, it would not. Most of these men are presumably saying that they would evaluate the executive's ability alone in promoting him. However, it is also possible that, because of the equal rights and antidiscrimination laws that everyone is so conscious of right now, this question would not always be truthfully answered.

Those who said it would help a man were asked why. Edward Donley (Air Products and Chemicals) said a married man is "likely to be more stable." Henry Goodrich said the "wife is a great asset." P. Goff Beach, who heads Oscar Mayer & Company in Madison, Wisconsin, said that his company "considers the wife or husband of an executive to be a helpful and valuable part of the management team." Another explanation was, "Married men tend to be more balanced, stable, emotionally mature." Another: "Marriage gives a man the ability to give and take, live and let live; it gives emotional stability."

Two chief executive officers suggested in their responses that there is a big difference between a man who

116

is single and one who is divorced. One man said, "I'm pretty cool towards divorced people. However, the fact that a person is single doesn't affect the decision." Generally, however, there is indication that divorce is a much more acceptable reality in the corporate world than it used to be.

*Attitudes about husbands of female executives.* Both chief executive officers and wives were asked whether their attitudes would be approximately the same for the husband of a female executive as for a corporate wife. A somewhat surprising 92 percent of the men said their attitudes would be the same. However, this statistic must again be considered in light of the antidiscrimination emphasis in today's corporations. It should also be remembered that there are still today very few female executives in the *Fortune* 500 companies, and there has been little opportunity to test out theories regarding this question.

Of the few men who said their attitude toward the husband of a female executive would be different, the reasoning of one is typical: "The female executive's husband would probably (and properly perhaps) be too tied up in his own career to be as helpful as a male executive's wife would be."

The wives' answers to this question indicated considerably more recognition of differences. Forty-eight said their attitudes about corporate husbands would be the same, while 52 percent said they would be different. Kathleen May (American Can) said, "Their 'maleness' gives them license to do what they wish, regardless of their wives' obligations." Marjorie Lanterman (AMSTED Industries) said, "I feel men are much more independent." Mrs. William Norris, whose husband heads Control Data, added to her questionnaire, "I think it would be the unusual case where the responsibility for home management, care of children, and entertaining would be expected to the same degree of the husband of a female executive."

Laverne Phillips (International Multifoods) put it this way: "Men would be treated more as their own per-

117

son. Men would be excused more readily if they could not attend functions with their executive wives due to their own commitments." Bettye Lee, whose husband, Frank, runs Foster Wheeler Corporation, said, "Husbands of female executives would generally be employed themselves and would be less free to participate socially with their wives. I doubt as many corporate wives are employed." Mrs. Robert C. Cosgrove, whose husband heads the Green Giant Company in Minnesota, added this interesting observation: "Very often the female executive has more drive than her husband does."

Other comments on this issue were: "Husbands would not be expected to share in company functions and activities as much." "He wouldn't be expected to entertain at home." "I'm sure that the husband of a female executive would want to be known for his own accomplishments and not so much by those of his wife." "If husbands of female executives are not recognized for their own accomplishments, they are usually having difficulties in this role. Wives of chief executive officers and other executives can bask in the husband's accomplishments."

*Changing attitudes about corporate wives.* The respondents were asked whether, in the past few years, their attitudes about corporate wives had changed and, if they had, whether drastically or slightly, and in what ways. Fifteen percent of the men and 30 percent of the women said their attitudes had changed; 85 percent of the men and 70 percent of the women said they had not. Most of the changes were said to be slight rather than drastic. In light of the women's movement and the changing consciousness of most of the world, this finding is really quite shocking.

There are several possible interpretations, and age is certainly a factor here. As many sociological studies have shown, our ability to change and be flexible decreases as we grow older. Our basic ideational structure is formed by the time we are twenty. Most of the chief executive officers and wives surveyed were raised in depression or postdepression years, and it might be expected that they

118

would be resistant to change. However, these are also the leaders of large organizations that employ many women and which are part of the very real world in which the women's movement has had a quite profound effect. The fact that the heads of the *Fortune* 500 companies and their wives seem so unaffected by these changes is a sad commentary indeed on the business world. It is also an indicator of the formidable odds faced by the independent corporate wife.

Nevertheless, there were some very poignant statements made by men and women whose attitudes have changed. It is obvious that some of the chief executive officers surveyed have been very much affected by their own wives as well as the world around them. Perhaps the strongest statement came from J. I. Miller, who heads the Cummins Engine Company: "Women should pursue their own lives insofar as they are able. Husbands should give the same consideration to wives which they expect from them. Corporations must respect this relationship." Grant Simmons said he has become "more sensitive to women's 'rights.'" Bill May of American Can said he is "more tolerant of the new social values and norms." Another man said he has become "somewhat more accepting of wife's independence and identity." Still another chief executive officer said he is "more open—expecting wives to realize their own selves." These kinds of statements come from a statistically small sample of the chief executive officers who responded, but one might hope that it is the beginning of a trend.

Several women expressed the same kind of sentiments. Kathleen May has become aware "that we are entitled to separate identities, i.e., not rubber stamps or reflections necessarily of our husbands." Jane Dart thinks corporate wives are becoming "much more interesting. More wish to be involved in arts, hospitals, education, politics, personal intellectual pursuits, sports. Less 'ladies bridge luncheons.'" Mrs. Robert Cosgrove put it this way: "She takes her role as a helpmate, and is far more graceful about it than the wife did twenty years ago. She is well traveled and better educated." Another woman ex-

119

pressed "admiration of a good corporate wife—not sublimated to her husband but a true partner." One other wife said, "They should have more freedom to be themselves—not have to fit a mold." Bettye Lee said, "I don't think corporations expect as much of wives now as they once did. In any case, a good wife in the first place can cope with being a corporation wife. If a man is happy at home, that's her best contribution toward his and his company's success."

*Age.* As might be expected, the chief executive officers of America's largest industrial companies are men over fifty. Fifty-eight percent of the chief executive officer respondents were age fifty to fifty-nine; 26 percent were age sixty and over; 15 percent were forty to forty-nine; and just one man was in his thirties. Their wives are only slightly younger: 63 percent are fifty to fifty-nine; 28 percent are forty to forty-nine; 6 percent are sixty and over; and 3 percent are thirty to thirty-nine.

*Marital Status.* An overwhelming 92 percent of the chief executive officers and 91 percent of wives in this group are in their first marriage. The remaining 8 percent of men and 9 percent of women are in their second marriage. Not one person who answered was in any of the following categories: single, never married; living with someone, not legally married; married, third or later marriage; divorced; widowed. It is possible that the chiefs of the *Fortune* 500 companies are very conservative men who marry once and forever. Their age could also be a factor in the very low divorce rate. It is also possible, however, that the nature of our survey colored the response in this area: Since the questions were about corporate wives, it would tend to be married men who replied.

Some effort was made to determine whether the small group of people who were married for the second time were any more liberal in their attitudes than their colleagues who were in their first marriage, but this was not

120

the case. Among the second marrieds were ultraconservatives, semiliberals, and in-betweens.

There were a few people who objected to the idea of categorizing corporate wives. J. I. Miller (Cummins Engine Company) said, "I do not like the idea of evaluating corporate wives—or the expression. Wives are *not* hired by the corporation." Mrs. Fletcher Byrom, whose husband runs Koppers Company in Pittsburgh, put it this way: "I know many chief executive officers' wives. Each one is different. Some good, some bad, some great, some indifferent! You can't lump them together and say 'this is what a corporate wife is like.' Every company is different." J. W. Van Gorkom, president of Trans Union Corporation, would not complete the questionnaire but wrote a very articulate letter: "Our company does not really involve the wife of any of our top executives. We almost never have business-social affairs at high levels, and our wives are not called upon to entertain or otherwise contribute to the corporate picture. We respect the privacy of the lives of our executives, and a man's promotion does not depend in any way upon the conduct or capabilities of his wife."

The survey indicates that this kind of attitude about corporation wives is the exception rather than the rule. But these comments give us a clearer picture of the range in the corporate wife role. It will be interesting in years ahead to see which way the pendulum swings.

# PART THREE

## How to Put It All Together

# 5

# Know Yourself

Probably the hardest work anyone can do in life is to be honest with oneself. It is also the most rewarding. In these days of psychological awareness, most intelligent people like to think they are straight with themselves and fairly introspective, but massive denial still exists in most of us. We learn it almost from the moment of birth. A tired or hungry baby is told, "Don't cry"—that is, deny your feelings. He or she is raised by parents who set a pattern of denial in their own lives. If an angry little girl tells her mother she hates her, the response is usually, "Don't say that. Apologize for even thinking that." If a teen-age girl aspires to one of the "male" professions, she is often told she doesn't really want all those years of school if she is going to get married and have kids anyway.

Traditionally girls have been encouraged more than boys to show certain kinds of feelings. Girls have been allowed to cry, act silly, and exhibit various kinds of hysterical behavior. Probably this has provided a healthy outlet for women, and possibly it has contributed to women's longer life span. But these emotional outlets have their price; they have also been used against women and have been labeled as weak characteristics. One can only speculate about how many management jobs have been withheld from women because male superiors saw women as poor decision makers or prone to crying. At the same time, girls have traditionally been forced to deny, or at least sublimate, the more "masculine" or aggressive emotions such as anger, competitiveness, and toughness. Although little girls growing up today have a somewhat better chance of avoiding these pressures, most of us had to conform in order to be accepted by families, teachers, and peers. Thus, denial of feelings, dishonesty with ourselves is an ingrained, easy path for most of us. The opposite—facing ourselves honestly and courageously, even in unpleasant situations—is the harder, more frightening way of operating.

This personal dilemma can be expanded, of course, to the societal, national, and international levels. The recent Watergate and so-called Koreagate scandals are examples of dishonesty and deception at the highest levels. Questions about the functioning of the FBI and the CIA are rampant. Sexual scandals linking congressmen with Fanne Fox and Elizabeth Ray indicate deceptive tactics, questionable morals, and misuse of public funds.

We are also suddenly aware of large-scale dishonesty within corporations. The media have focused lately on corporate bribery that runs into millions of dollars, illegal political contributions from corporations which are assumed to buy influence, and a number of high-level executives who've been caught with their hands in the till. The Bert Lance affair was a recent scandal that besmirched the images of both businessmen and politicians.

These are only examples of the attitudes and atmosphere all around us. They make it blatantly clear that deception and dishonesty are often the rule rather than the exception. The crime almost seems to be not in the doing, but in the getting caught.

Applied again to the personal level, there is precious little encouragement, particularly for women, to be gutsy and honest with themselves and about themselves. Corporate wives especially are discouraged from looking at their situations honestly because the corporation might lose its control over valuable assets if these wives began to think more independently.

## EGO SYNTONIC OR EGO ALIEN?

Why should one strive for this goal of honesty with oneself? And how does a woman go about it? The primary reason for putting value here is that good decisions about anything in life are always based on valid and accurate information. It is common knowledge that a computer is only as good as its input, and in many ways this analogy can be used. Garbage in: garbage out. We all make millions of decisions in a lifetime, large and small. In fact, the course of one day might be described as a long series of decisions, many of which are made unconsciously or semiconsciously. But in order for these decisions or actions to be the best ones, they must be based on accurate information, particularly about ourselves. This does not refer to "right" decisions in absolute or moral terms; there are really few if any absolutes about living. Rather, you must discover what is right for yourself. You must be able to make choices that are based on an honest assessment of what fits your needs and aspirations.

The psychological concepts of ego syntonic and ego alien are applicable here. If an action or decision or relationship or experience is ego syntonic—that is, if it basically fits or can be made to fit with your inner needs and desires and picture of yourself—it will work. It will make your life more full or happy or complete. If it is ego alien, contrary to your character structure, destructive to something in your being, or, to use the vernacular, "goes against your grain," it eventually will not work. Something ego alien may have been chosen because it seemed the right thing to do, because someone else wanted it that way, or because you wanted it to fit, but it still will not work. It may seem to fit for a while, but problems will crop up in other areas—often vague somatic areas

127

that are difficult to understand or cure. The tendency in such a situation will probably be to blame something else or someone else. It is often too painful to look inward to see why the choice was wrong.

The important decisions in a woman's life that require self-knowledge are multitudinous. Among them certainly are the choice of a mate, the choice of a career (or lack of one), the choice of whether to have children and how many, the decisions about how to raise those children, the choice of whether to stay in a marriage or get out, choices about other relationships with men and women, choices about interests to pursue, choices about retirement and how to spend old age, and so on and on. All of these must be based primarily on information about ourselves, but few of us are really prepared or armed with accurate, honest guidelines.

If a woman has *not* been gutsy or motivated or energetic or knowledgeable enough to do some pretty rigorous self-examination, she will probably take one of three courses: (1) Much of her life will just not work out right and she will develop a vague sense of dissatisfaction, probably blaming her unhappiness on her husband or children. (2) Her denial mechanisms will continue stronger than ever, and she will present an intact facade to the world, but her emotional life will be quite empty and her relationships will be shallow. (3) She will avoid making decisions and choices herself and will appear content to let other people, usually her husband, take responsibility for her life.

## LISTENING AND ASKING

With the knowledge then that introspection is not a natural, easy process, but that it is necessary for a fuller kind of existence, what should you do? How can you approach your own background, needs, desires, character structure in a more open way? How can you begin to shake off the "excess baggage" that was put on you by others without your ever being aware of it?

First, you should really make a conscious effort to listen; you must listen to what you say about yourself and to what others say or imply about you. As patterns of communication grow old, they often grow stale also, and tests have proved that we all hear only what we want to hear. We tune out much of what is going on around us—and within us. We almost have to shake ourselves psychologically to hear in a new way. Therapists for years have used the phrase "listening with a third ear"; we can all train ourselves to do this. Not only should we try to hear more of the words that are said, but we should also try to understand the words better. It is something like reading between the lines; it is a process of hearing what is implied or meant as well as what is said. It is an effort to comprehend the nuances of the complicated thing we call communication. And it must usually be prefaced by some kind of motivation to open up in order to hear in a new way.

Second, you must convince yourself that you are a big girl now and can tolerate some psychological pain. There will be pleasant surprises in introspection too, but if you do not feel some pain, you are surely not going deep enough. The most common pattern for pseudo-introspective people is to see all the bright, witty, successful traits in themselves, then block emotionally when something unpleasant rears its ugly head.

But what allows a woman the strength to tolerate unpleasantness or pain? It is partly motivation to change, but it is more a conscious lecturing of herself in this manner: "After all, no one is perfect. I'm no longer a naive, frightened little girl. I've had a lot of successes in life. I have friends. I have———. I have ———. I'm not going to fall apart if not everyone likes me, or if I'm not the prettiest woman in the world, or even if my marriage is in trouble. I have lots of strengths."

At the first sign of pain, you may have to lecture yourself again, but gradually the process becomes more automatic. As you learn to live with more honesty and maybe a little more emotional pain, the gratifications begin to build up also, and the pain somehow seems worthwhile.

## SELF-ASSESSMENT QUESTIONS

| Question | 1st answer | 2d answer | 3d answer |
|---|---|---|---|
| 1. How do I really feel about my mother? | | | |
| 2. How do I really feel about my father? | | | |
| 3. What would I like to have changed about my childhood? | | | |
| 4. Why did I marry my husband? | | | |
| 5. What are my real relationships with my children? | | | |
| 6. What things give me the most pleasure? | | | |
| 7. What things make me sad? | | | |
| 8. What things make me angry? | | | |

## Self-Assessment Questions (continued)

| Question | 1st answer | 2d answer | 3d answer |
|---|---|---|---|
| 9. How do I express anger? | | | |
| 10. How do I express love? | | | |
| 11. What am I afraid of? | | | |
| 12. Whom do I really trust? | | | |
| 13. What things would I like to change in my life now? | | | |
| 14. Do I want a career or not? Why? | | | |
| 15. What do I hope to be doing five years from now? | | | |
| 16. What do I want my life to be like ten years from now? | | | |

This process will also add to a feeling of being more alive, more in touch with everything, and more of a complete person.

Third, you should try to develop a sense of curiosity about yourself. Unfortunately, many women have been taught by insinuation and innuendo that women are not very interesting. If you are even remotely aware of the tendency in yourself to see women as dull and uninteresting, you should try vigorously to shake it. You can and should be the most fascinating phenomenon in the world to yourself. You should stop to consider what a miracle it is that the little girl of your earliest memories developed into the woman—with both the good qualities and hangups—that you are now. You must be at least a little curious about how that happened. How come you took this route instead of another one? Do you have any real idea what makes you tick, what turns you on, what keeps you going? Curiosity about yourself is an escalating process. Once established, it can be exaggerated and become almost an obsession. But hopefully, put in proper perspective, it simply serves to open up new areas, new ideas, to develop a new sense of respect—and even awe —about yourself.

Fourth, you should ask yourself lots of important, difficult, basic questions. It really might help to approach this simplistically by writing down several questions first, then writing the answers, and letting a little time pass. Later you might read the answers again, evaluate them critically as though looking over your own shoulder, revise the answers where they were not really honest or not very deep, and then repeat this process again three or four times. The passage of a few days between the evaluations can allow the subconscious or unconscious some time to work; it can allow the conscious mind time to think things through; and it can allow current life experiences time to shed new light on the questions. You might even have dreams whose interpretations could add new insights.

The kinds of questions you might ask are: How do I really feel about my mother? How do I really feel about my father? What would I like to have changed about my childhood? Why did I marry my husband? What kinds of relationships do I really have with my children? What things give me the most pleasure? What things in my life make me sad? What things make me angry? How do I express anger? How do I express love? Do I want a career or not? What am I afraid of? Whom do I really trust? What things would I like to change within myself? What things would I like to change in my life now? What do I hope to be doing five years from now? Ten years from now? All of these questions of course can be answered on several different levels, and you should try to do just that. There are no right or correct answers to any of these questions, but you have to be very critical of yourself in order not to give evasive or partial responses.

Another fascinating, seemingly simple question is, "Who am I?" You might quickly list ten answers, and then sit back and ponder why you gave those priorities, made those choices, or made certain omissions. It sounds like an easy question until you try it. Women are often surprised by their own responses. If you can't list several answers without repeatedly referring to yourself as the possession of husband or children—Tom's wife or Mary's mother—you are probably in trouble. Our identity, the way we see ourselves, is crucial, and this question gives a quick way of indicating identity.

Besides the basic questions, you really should learn a process of examining actions constantly. Why did I make that decision? Why didn't I tell my husband the truth about that? And gradually you begin to sort out what the honest answers are from what the dishonest ones are. The honest answers begin to "feel" better. You get a fuller, richer picture of yourself, and consequently your life—and you—become much more interesting.

Fifth, you should begin to ask difficult, forthright questions of those whose opinions matter to you. This list of people might include husband, children, parents, siblings, close friends, or a trusted employer. The questions could be things like: What do you see as my strengths? What do you see as my weaknesses? What things about me have worried or concerned you? What kinds of

133

work do you think I'm best suited for? Do you think I am honest with myself?

At first, the people who are asked will probably be shocked by such direct questions, and the tendency might be to give evasive answers. This is certainly not the light, cocktail-party kind of social interchange that most of us are used to. But if you have picked people who care, and if you can communicate the seriousness in the question, some worthwhile answers will probably be forthcoming. There may be some testing at first to see if you can take or really want the truth, but you can usually pass this test be continuing to ask another question on the same subject. The importance of listening to the answers cannot be stressed too strongly, because there is so much implied communication and double-talk. The woman who wants information and feedback about herself can use further questions to clarify and make sure she really understands.

It should be emphasized that you never accept the answers or the other person's opinion at face value. You must realize that the person who is answering has an emotional stake in it too. Even those closest to us can never be really objective; they see us more clearly in some ways than we see ourselves, but it is always through their eyes. Nevertheless, it is fascinating how differently we often appear to others than to ourselves. By hearing the reactions of a few other people, you can get a bit more objectivity. You will undoubtedly hear some things this way that are hard to hear, but there will probably be some unexpected compliments too, and all of this is the stuff of which relationships are made.

If comments are made that do not ring true to you, the source should be evaluated. What did that person have to win or lose by saying that? But in addition, you might try to curb your defensiveness, wonder a while if there might be some truth to it, and check it out with a couple other people. Someone else's opinion should never be accepted automatically, nor should it be rejected automatically. Rather, a woman on the way to knowing herself should be able to really hear it, understand what is meant, evaluate it critically, reject the invalid parts, and

# WHO AM I?

| Answer | Assessment of answer |
|---|---|

1.

2.

3.

4.

5.

6.

7.

8.

9.

10.

accept the valid parts. At the very least, asking some of these questions of loved ones should be provocative to the relationship and should provide some food for thought.

This may all seem to be little more than common sense to any person who has a strong feeling of identity. Unfortunately, many corporate wives have really lost their sense of self and have existed a long time by someone else's rules. They have done what was expected of them, but have somehow abdicated the primary controls to husband, children, or corporation. As Ninki Hart Burger so eloquently puts it: "To devote her energies to living according to the book, authored by an expert, is to exist spiritless in someone else's house."[1]


## GROWING UP FEMALE

In addition to the personal focus in self-knowledge, it is important to recognize that women *are* different from men, and that your identity as an adult woman is conditioned by both how you grew up female and how all girls grow up female. Biological differences between men and women are the most obvious, but it is, at this point in our history, impossible to sort out all the biological differences from the cultural ones. Our psychology as women cannot be understood apart from the social context; the image of women in our society has conditioned us individually and as a group. From babyhood, girls tend to be trained for one kind of life, while boys are trained for another.

The little boy is expected to be aggressive, and he is rewarded for it by parents, other authority figures, and peers. He is expected to be independent, to initiate activities, and to run himself ragged at games. He is given confirmation for channeling aggression into useful paths, and the constructive use of aggression is supported in itself and for itself. The pressures of socialization for a boy make two routes clear: first, the externalization of aggression; and second, denial. In the process, he may mourn the loss of his ability to express hurt, inadequacy, or fear; but he is well compensated. Society tells him

136

that those "feminine" things are not worthwhile anyway; they are "soft"; instead, as a man he is inherently superior to more than half the human race.

The little girl starts life with most of the same feelings and struggles as a little boy, but she is part of a world that says boys are more desirable. If she is very lucky, she may have a father and/or mother who encourage her to show independence and aggression, but she runs the risk of being labeled unladylike—a tomboy. Even if she persists in following her parents' wishes for her, she gets many opposite signals from outside the family and must make some extremely difficult choices. If she chooses to be independent and aggressive, she may have trouble with both male and female peers. If she is the average little girl, she will probably just give up. Repression is developed as the primary coping mechanism.

While boys develop the ability to say it isn't so, it isn't my fault—an ability that helps immeasurably to preserve their self-esteem—girls turn inward and repress their last efforts at "masculinity." Research shows that boys score much higher than girls on "lie" and "defensiveness" scales, which are designed to assess the avoidance of self-evaluation and the tendency to present oneself in a favorable light. Boys do not reveal thoughts and feelings to others as readily as girls do, and they defend their egos by "turning against a real or presumed external frustrating object whereas girls engage in more self-blame."[2] Research also shows that boys boast more; more often than girls they perform acts simply to become the focus of attention. And they believe much more in their ability to control their own fates. Jacklin and Mischel found, in a 1973 study of elementary school textbooks, that "when good things happened to a male character in a story they were presented as resulting from his own actions. Good things happening to a female character (of which there were considerably fewer) were at the initiative of others, or simply grew out of the situation in which the girl character found herself."[3] Boys see themselves as stronger, more capable, and more dominant than girls, and as they grow older, the ability to see the positive side of life expands. "Even with respect to social sensibility—a presumably feminine trait—young men seem not to 'hear' comments to the effect that they are insensitive, and their self-ratings of sensitivity are scarcely affected by negative feedback."[4]

While boys, then, expect to succeed, girls develop the fear, or perhaps the certainty, of loss and disappointment. As Hennig and Jardim put it in *The Managerial Woman:*

> If loss or failure is seen as the outcome of one's actions it is so much simpler not to want to achieve, not to have to decide, to keep one's options endlessly open so that one never closes anything off. And this in itself has a double edge: nothing is closed off so nothing is lost; because nothing is closed off no action can be taken which might lead to loss.[5]

This means that girls do not set goals for themselves and tend not to think in terms of long-range planning. They also learn to fear success because it will bring with it so many other losses and disappointments.

In childhood and adolescence, in groups and teams, boys work together and support each other. Even while they compete fiercely, they work together in a team relationship, and they learn to work together toward a task. Being liked and liking everyone they work with is not so important; the task becomes predominant. Team sports allow both real and vicarious achievement, while failure as a team can be accepted in smaller and more tolerable pieces than failure as an individual.

At the same time, girls are learning that, if they are going to be successful in this world, they will have to do it through a man. Very few girls ever are socialized to think of supporting themselves or working all their adult lives. Rather, their mission in life is to "hook" the right man. Other girls become competitors in this contest; "feminine wiles" get reinforced and rewarded. The potentially assertive, bright girl has tremendous fears of loss of feminine identity. Psychologist Jane Torrey says, "To divest oneself of the feminine image is to risk being thought 'abnormal.' What's sauce for the gander may be something else again for the goose. A woman has to tread a thin line between too little assertion to get what she wants and more assertion than can be tolerated in a woman."[6]

This process is the source for the frequent saying that "women are their own worst enemies." Their own psychological reactions often reinforce rather than overcome the obstacles that exist. While most women want more equality with men, they thoroughly "buy into" the system that says that men are still better. A recent Gallup poll[7] revealed that, by six to one, women would rather have a man than a woman as their boss, and most women would rather deal with male doctors, lawyers, and bankers.

Growing up female means many things in our society, and every woman is affected by it to some extent. In Hennig and Jardim's study of twenty-five successful businesswomen, they found that all had unusual family backgrounds: All twenty-five were either first-born children or had experiences that were similar to first-borns. All had extremely close relationships with their father and had been involved in an unusually wide range of typically masculine activities in the company of their father, beginning when they were very young. "They believed that they had been given unusually strong support by their families in following their own interests regardless of the sex-role attributes of those interests."[8] These women went on to achieve high positions in the "man's world" of business, but they did not do it without cost. The women who married did so quite late in life, and none of them bore children.

In order to understand who we are as adults, each of us should examine what our own experience was in growing up female. How did our immediate families treat us as girls? And how did the world at large socialize us into the feminine role? The answers to these questions can help us sort out what our real needs and desires are versus the ones that have been laid on us by others. We

139

cannot be truly introspective and honest in our assessments of ourselves unless it is done against the background of our environment. Girls who are growing up now may have somewhat different experiences than we did, but unless parents are aware of the culture and the societal norms, they may try to repeat their own experiences with their daughters. And this, in turn, will be out of step with peer pressures, possibly causing confusion and concern for our daughters. The process by which all of us grew up male or female accounts for a large part of our identity, and serves as a basic model for all our relationships with others.

## HOLDING ON

Most of us started out as spontaneous children. We were anxious to try new things, loved play and pleasure of any kind, and lacked inhibitions. But all too soon, critics of every kind started ripping away at our confidence—all for our own good, of course. Even our peers learned to echo the criticisms of grownups, and by the time we were old enough to know what was happening, we were listening to a cadre of authoritative voices. "You can certainly do that better." "Your brother got all A's at your age." "Just make sure your parents will be proud of you." "You'd better practice hard so you can keep up with Sally."

The young woman who marries a budding corporate executive may not realize it, but she has bought herself much more of the same. She will find little time and no encouragement for independent pursuits or activities. Her life has taken on a new, very complicated set of prescriptions. She must realize that she and her husband are not married just to each other; they are both married to his job. And that complex fact explains the difference between a wife and a corporate wife.

Lacking security within themselves, corporate wives frequently overcompensate by acting terribly important. I know the wife of a bank vice-president who really feels

140

she is part of the company When she travels, she must always stay in the best hotels because she thinks anything less would be a slur on the bank. One CEO's wife I interviewed said she knows many corporate wives in Chicago whose "behavior is almost laughable. They really think they are running their husbands' companies. Actually, there is not a wife I know who had much to do with her husband's success. I always felt it was my duty to speak out in private if I thought my husband was doing something wrong, but I never had any idea I was running things. We all know women like this. It is funny and sad that they feel this way Most of them just talk too much when they should be listening. They think they are overly important. They forget that everyone usually starts at the bottom." The kinds of women described here are certainly out of touch with themselves and who they are. They are unable even to sense or hear the ridicule and pity of those around them.

Martha Smith (Copperweld Corporation) says, "Most corporate wives have good marriages and a good understanding of their husbands' business. It seems like they are much more realistic in the past ten years. Some middle management wives think they're more important than their husbands, more important than they have a right to feel. They end up making their husbands very uncomfortable. But most of those people who took themselves too seriously are out of the picture. It used to be very important to go play bridge at the country club, with your silk suit and your gold pin on the lapel. But upper middle management wives have changed a lot. Now it is probably more important to go to a tennis clinic or take a postgraduate course. Many wives are doing volunteer work that requires a great deal of training. In Pittsburgh the socially conscious woman is taking a three-month training course to answer the telephone for contact phone calls, a three-month training course to conduct guided tours through the art museum, etc. It is a marvelous, mind-stretching dedication to others in the community that gains recognition in the eyes of their peers. As one of my friends expressed it, after she had helped me tremendously with a Girl Scout National opportunity, 'Thank you for bringing me back to the real world.' As a result of this kind of involvement, most wives are not too caught up in flattery or misconceptions about their roles in the corporation."

Nevertheless, it is extremely difficult for any woman to hold onto a strong sense of herself when she must cheerfully and graciously entertain anyone her husband brings home; when she must move without complaint wherever and whenever her husband is transferred; when she must accept his long hours and travel like a trouper; when she must even change her personality and attitudes and habits as he moves up. If she tries to do her own things, she is a maverick and is censured. The easiest route is to accept her role as an extension of her husband and gradually give up parts of her own being, her own uniqueness. As Seidenberg says, "The self sometimes slips away; only the fortunate get a warning signal. Atrophy from disuse, whether of one's limb or of one's liberty, is a particularly painful deprivation since it is a largely self-inflicted condition. It is bad enough that fate, biology, and the ravages of time diminish one, but to allow parts of the self to slip away passively is particularly distressing."[9]

This loss of self-interest and self-knowledge will eventually go hand in hand with a crushing sense of loneliness. Ours is the era of alienation generally, and many corporate wives are alienated not only from others but, more important, from themselves. They speak of loneliness because their husbands are away so much, but they seem to have little concept of what they are really saying. To use Seidenberg's words again, "It is when the self is lost or communication with the self is severed that 'the other' becomes so desperately important. Being alone then becomes a particularly fearful experience because there is literally no one at home. The *house* is empty because the *person* is."[10]

When a corporate wife speaks of loneliness, she may mean many different things. She may have been obsessed with the care of her children, but they are increasingly independent or have left home. She may be finding that none of the friendships she has made over the years are very deep or meaningful. She may realize on some level that her husband has grown from experiences that she has not had, and that they have gone in separate directions. She may find that her volunteer work is just a time killer, and she is not really very interested in it. Her shopping expeditions or TV watching may seem increasingly boring. Without the ability to find good household help, she may have devoted large amounts of time to the care of her big, status house. Much of her time may be spent on things rather than people. She may find herself tagging along on business trips because there is nothing else to do, and then spending many lonely hours in a hotel. She may have lost or let go any skills she once had as a musician, dancer, artist, teacher, or whatever, and may not have replaced them with anything very tangible or meaningful.

But, let's consider the argument of those who do not agree. It is often men who do not understand this kind of thinking. They wonder what all this nonsense is about a woman wanting to fulfill herself or feeling lonely. They envy the leisure that most women have. After the children are sent off to school for six or eight hours, a woman may go back to bed, or she could paint or write or be creative in a thousand ways. They wonder why women don't consider themselves lucky and use their freedom better. Many people have questioned why there isn't more artistic, philosophical, intellectual production coming from women. What are they doing with all their free time? The answer, one would like to shout, is not in leisure time or available activities. It is the purpose, the motivation for, the goal of the activity that gives it pleasure and makes it worthwhile. Furthermore, the world at large adds to the pleasure if it places value on the activity. The usual "woman's work" is not very often valued by the world at large and is not taken very seriously.

Many of us are not really alive, and that is a hard thing to face in ourselves. It is painful; it is not easily cured. There is no magic key to unlock the door to pleasure and happiness. It might seem easier *not* to know that parts of oneself have been allowed to die or have been killed. But the important fact is that a woman can stop this psychological dying-off process and can, in fact, reverse it. Perhaps the first step is to try to throw off everything the experts—sociologists, psychotherapists, physicians, historians—tell us we should be like and should do as "normal females." The influence of all the experts is enormous, and their authoritarianism is really amazing, considering what opposite conclusions many of them come to. Nevertheless, most insecure and frightened women would rather find an expert whose dogma they can follow rather than look carefully into their own souls. For the corporate wife, this approach is only substituting one set of rules for another. She can become a disciple of some expert instead of accepting the corporate definition of the perfect wife. However, the best answers can be found only within herself.

## WORK, COMMUNICATION, AND SEX

Some of the most common trouble spots are in the questions about work, communication, sex, and other relationship areas.

Should I work or not? Part-time or full-time? This is one of the hardest problems to sort out because of all the input over the years from parents, teachers, husband, friends, and the media. It really takes some digging to find out exactly what is right for you. You may not have been educationally prepared, and working at something satisfying might mean a return to school. When women are exploring new possibilities for themselves, they often say they don't want to go out into the working world; they like the roles of homemaker, wife, mother, and volunteer. The important question for these women to ask themselves is whether they avoid entering the work world outside the home because of fear, or because they really like what they're doing.

Most of the women who have found it easy to enter

the career world have had a combination of circumstances that made this possible—a father who stressed competition, a mother who set an example by working, or even parental values that the person rebelled against aggressively. More and more women, however, are accepting the belief that every whole person has a need for the sense of achievement and recognition that can come through a career or other meaningful work, but which is often lacking in the lives of women who confine themselves to the nurturing wife and mother roles. The importance of independent income also should not be underestimated. Even women whose husbands make very good salaries feel strongly about earning money. Their own salary may give them the psychological freedom to save or spend in a totally different way.

For better or worse, there is something in our society that says an activity is more valuable when it has monetary worth, when it is compensated for. And being part of the marketplace where goods and services are bought and sold is pretty important for feeling really alive. Even those women who are getting a great deal of publicity these days for advocating traditional roles for women are part of the marketplace. While Marabel Morgan and Phyllis Schlafly are preaching the values of motherhood and homemaking and subservience for women, they are lecturing and writing books and appearing on television—earning handsome livings[11] and selling their services.

Thus, every woman should ask *herself* primarily whether she should be working, why she might be avoiding work outside the home, what she might get out of it, how it would affect her life. I am not advocating that a corporate wife do this in a vacuum. Your husband should be an important part of this process, since his life will certainly be affected either way. Ideally this should be a joint decision; a couple might even decide that he would stay home (househusband is a legitimate new term) while she works! But in the final analysis, you must really do the emotional work to know what is best for you.

Many women with young children or young husbands are choosing part-time work as a compromise. In some situations the part-time job will graduate into a full-time one as her household obligations lessen—that is, as her children become more independent or her husband resists less. There are a few interesting part-time jobs around, and certain occupations lend themselves to part-time work more than others. A few employers are trying to accommodate women by splitting a full-time job between two people or making other concessions to child care arrangements. The woman who works part-time will surely gain some of the advantages of both worlds, and she will probably feel less guilt or pressure that way. But a part-time job will probably be more of a *job,* while the full-time job has a better chance of being a career. The salary and responsibility of part-time work will most likely be on the low end of the scale, and it is quite possible that the woman who starts out to achieve recognition and status will not be able to do it through part-time work and will feel disappointed and cheated. The assertive woman who looks for many gratifications from her work will very likely have to make a full-time commitment—plus extra hours and energy. But she of course will have to struggle with how to accomplish everything and will be spreading herself pretty thin at times.

If a woman has specialized training or special talents, her chances of achieving status and recognition through work will be pretty good. She will be in demand, will get a good salary, and will be promoted. However, the woman who lacks this skill or training, and chooses not to get it, may have to be satisfied with other gratifications, such as peer contact, receiving a salary all her own, and gaining experience that can be applied later. Work, for either men or women, is never an all-or-nothing situation. No one can ever achieve all the things he or she wants, but the experience is never useless. Rather, certain needs can be met in certain ways. For example, the woman who decides on a career after twenty years' absence from the marketplace will not be in the same position as the woman who never stopped working. But she may have other advantages and will have had other life experiences. Each woman has to assess honestly what work does or could mean in her life, and then make decisions without the excess baggage of other people's expectations, fears, insecurities, and guilts.

Another important area of self-knowledge is communication. Whole books have been written about the importance of good communication in a marriage. It takes guts to assess honestly what the patterns of communication are in your own delicately balanced relationships. After years of marriage many couples have learned to tune each other out in significant areas, and it is easier to deny or avoid this than to find out why. Most couples have secrets from each other, but certain kinds of deceptions spell trouble. There are communication patterns of omission as well as commission. There are subtle insults or putdowns that couples learn to tolerate and seldom face. How do you show anger toward each other? How do you show love, concern, or affection? Are you satisfied with the level of communication with your husband? What can you do to change it?

In terms of communication, the corporate wife has been stereotyped as the listener. The husband is encouraged to get his problems off his chest; the woman who bores her husband with details about the household is the butt of cartoons and jokes. There is little encouragement in the corporate world for true two-way communication. Burger's advice is:

Every intelligent woman realizes that if her husband represses his anxieties and tensions, it can lead to anything from ulcers to ultimatums. It is *her* job to encourage some release from *his* job. Through the months and years, she creates a warm environment that welcomes his thoughts and words. If he simply wants 'to get it off his chest,' she is his listening post. If he elicits her opinion, she is his sounding board. She feels her way according to his mood and personality . . . Her role is neither that of a verbose critic nor a professional expert.[12]

147

No description of communication could be more offensive to a strong, equal partner in a marriage than the one above. Few liberated corporation wives would be satisfied with this definition. It makes no provision for the woman's needs and demands in terms of communication. It might only possibly be acceptable if the pronouns could be easily reversed as the situation warranted.

One test of communication is its openness and honesty. Another test is its sharing quality or its two-way direction. Yet another specific test is how decisions get made. Unfortunately, decision making is so threatening to our basic security that couples often cling to traditional notions of what is "woman's work" or "for men only" in order to avoid conflict. But democracy in decision making is truly a worthwhile goal within a marriage as well as a government, because if decisions are not basically agreed upon and worked through, they will be sabotaged in subtle ways. Equality in decision making requires mutual respect and faith, but this must be built on respect for oneself and faith in one's own ability. As with any good business decision, the first steps are usually open discussion and an atmosphere of trust. Then there must be the assumption that each individual is competent and is ready and able to make a contribution.

Unfortunately again, so many corporate couples have solitary or autocratic decision making either because the husband does not trust the wife's opinions or value her judgments, or because the wife is unsure of herself and would rather let him take the responsibility. In other situations, decision making becomes an arena for winning or losing. Both partners try to prove something to each other or bolster their own self-confidence by oneupmanship tactics.

Decision making and communication patterns in general are hard for the people involved to examine without bias or prejudice, but they are the core of a relationship. Even if these patterns cannot or will not be changed, it is better to see them for what they are than to continue deceiving yourself and building on that deception.

Another area, actually part of communication, which deserves honest examination is the sexual relationship. Women traditionally have been taught to be submissive sexually, and most have been loath to deviate from the norm. If they refuse sex, they are labeled cold and frigid; if they seek sex aggressively, they are called nymphomaniacs. Most corporate wives feel it is their duty to engage in sex when their husband wants it. Few of them can say no directly, although they use excuses like headaches, menstruation, or menopause. Another group of women use sex as a weapon to wield over their husband, but this is a tricky maneuver. A woman's negativism may punish her husband temporarily or make him feel guilty for something, but it may also be counterproductive. He may not ask again, or he may seek sexual gratification elsewhere. Sexual abstinence may be what she wants, but if she wishes to replace her husband with other partners, she may have more trouble finding them than her husband does. Sexual distance between husband and wife often erodes other areas of living, and it should be looked at from emotional viewpoints as well as physical ones.

Very few couples really achieve open communication in sex, but it makes pure common sense that those who can talk about and ask for what they need have a better chance of getting their needs met. How much more flattering it is for either a husband or wife to know that your partner is engaging in sex because he or she really wants to. What a compliment it is to know that someone is choosing you as a sexual partner; this would surely more than compensate for the damage to your ego when your spouse says no. Seidenberg's general hope for the future can be applied to sexual communication: "The future breed of spouse will be neither submissive nor obstructive. Individual human beings will maintain attitudes and behavior consonant with their own personal growth and fulfillment."[13]

Although this kind of egalitarianism is being increasingly accepted, it is difficult to achieve, especially when the husband and wife have grossly unequal positions in the outside world. For some couples the idea of an "open marriage" with total freedom to develop independently would seem shocking and offensive. For many couples it is a matter of degree; there may be a series of steps toward more equality in the future. But it is imperative that the corporate wife look honestly at what she has and what she wants. Who she is as a person—not what anyone tells her she should be—should be the primary determinant of the marital relationship and other aspects of her life.

# 6

# Therapy in Many Forms

The previous chapter assumes that you have at least a beginning sense of identity and want to try to know yourself without professional help. A second route is the semi-professional path, such as consciousness-raising groups, assertiveness training, church groups on communication, and other so-called self-help experiences. A third alternative is psychotherapy with a professional; this offers, among other things, the factor of objectivity. We can never be completely objective about ourselves; nor can relatives and friends be completely objective about us. The therapist, of course, sees things from his or her own perspective also, but he or she has been trained to have no particular stake in the relationship or the eventual outcome. The process of change is a complicated, difficult one, and a woman might seek the support, as well as the objectivity and skill, of a therapist in her efforts to know herself better.

Although choices about therapy and therapists may seem overwhelming to a novice in the psychotherapy area, most women—even a woman who is in some emotional distress—can make these choices if they have a glimmering of insight about their own rights, and a beginning sense of power over their own life. If you have an average IQ and a reasonable ability to "hear," you can tell pretty quickly whether the therapist respects you as a person and is primarily concerned with your identity. If the therapist does not fit this profile, you may as well quit wasting your time and money and energy.

## GROWTH EXPERIENCES

Several kinds of growth experiences are available to corporate wives who do not wish to label themselves as patients. Many of these evolve into something very close to therapy, but their lack of that label makes them more acceptable to people who view psychotherapy in a negative way. Many mental health clinics are offering groups on parenting, divorce, communication, self-worth, etc.; often they are available in the evening, and sometimes they are run by professionals. They are usually considered more educational than therapeutic, but what happens in those groups is a function of group membership and leadership. Churches and synagogues too are doing a great deal of pastoral counseling, and many groups around a variety of topics are ongoing. Some of these remain on a fairly superficial or intellectual level, while others get into very gutsy, sometimes dangerous areas. Again, the quality of the process and outcome depends largely on membership and leadership.

As a corporate couple, you may avail yourself of an exciting, stimulating opportunity by attending a residential seminar for executive couples. The Menninger Foundation in Topeka, Kansas, last year developed its first "Couples and Companies" seminar in response to the frequent lament of its executive alumni from other types of seminars: "I wish my wife could share this experience with me." The focus of these groups is to explore potential conflicts between the couples' home and corporate lives. The Menninger bulletin, February, 1977, says,

152

The business community has come to see the ultimate profit in preserving a balance between the executive's professional and personal lives. Conflict arises when, for example, the family and the company view one another as competitors for the time and devotion of the executive . . . When greater integration is achieved between family and professional roles, everyone profits. Satisfaction in one sphere does not come at the expense of satisfaction in the other.

If your husband is a student at Harvard Business School, you both may take part in a course run by psychiatrist Barry Grief; it includes about thirty couples and focuses on corporate-family conflicts. In addition, the Center for Family Studies at the Dudley House in Duluth, Minnesota, has an active program for executives and their spouses. And there are probably others across the country. These are excellent opportunities to work with your husband on problems of communication, sharing, pressures, and other things that busy couples seldom take time to discuss.

However, I would strongly caution you, as a woman and a corporate wife, to assess the nature and purpose of the group. If the focus is primarily on your executive husband, and he remains the center of interest, you should protest strongly or leave. No session is worth your valuable time if you are not seen as an equal partner. Furthermore, these groups are much more useful if a woman, as well as a man, is included in a leadership role. As an identity model for corporate wives, and as an indication that the sponsoring organization sees the importance of women, a co-leader, male-female arrangement is really essential.

If you find yourself in a couples group situation where there is *not* a woman in a leadership position, or where the designated woman leader is very weak, it is your responsibility as a woman to confront the situation directly. There are several ways to do this, but the ultimate purpose is to make clear to the group and leadership the ways in which this fact stereotypes women and handicaps the entire group. You might choose to make this point as an individual woman, and encourage group discussion of everyone's reactions to this. Alternatively, you might informally, outside of the group, gather support from other women, and form a sort of coalition that can then confront the issue together. You might even find a few men who are conscious of the effects of this type of sexism in leadership, and who would join you in an even more effective presentation to the group. Often those in leadership positions are quite unaware of their own sexist actions and attitudes, and professionals are no exception to this rule. Furthermore, for economic reasons, a sponsoring organization will often engage only one leader, and if the group includes many executives, you can bet that the leader engaged will be a man. This sets the tone for the within-group leadership to come from men, and in a couples group where the men are already executive leaders, this could be disastrous. The women easily get relegated to secondary, supportive positions. The assertive woman is ridiculed or made to look out of place. For those women who prefer to see themselves as equal, effective partners, this kind of group can be a frustrating, difficult experience. The strong, independent women in the group suffer, but more important, the whole group is hurt because the stereotype of the traditional corporate wife is perpetuated, and very little learning or growth takes place.

Two other kinds of group experiences are worth mentioning for corporate wives—both usually run and led by women. These are connected with clinical practice, but are not officially in that realm; they give many women the opportunity to discuss problems and feelings with others in similar positions, and they may be very therapeutic, but they are not therapy.

The first kind of experience, something quite familiar to most of us, is called the consciousness-raising group. Sometimes guided by professionals, these groups more often develop spontaneously and do not have formal leaders. Certain organizations such as the National Organization for Women may sponsor them or provide guidelines. The usual format is a weekly session of two to three hours, and the meeting usually takes place in the home of one of the members. Most women who join are amazed at how quickly a sense of honesty and openness occurs. A topic, such as loneliness, relationships with children, sexual hangups, etc., is usually chosen for each session, by consensus. The group members may take turns talking for a few minutes each about how they relate to the subject, and then share reactions and feedback afterward. Or the group may decide to discuss the subject more informally.

Most women who have participated in consciousness-raising groups feel they have accomplished just that —that is, their consciousness has been raised to a surprising extent about why they do certain things, how they allow themselves to be dominated by men, what the ramifications might be if they made other choices, and how they can take more control over their own life.

One other enormous benefit to most women in these groups is that they learn to enjoy and appreciate and trust other women—a phenomenon that is generally discouraged in our male-dominated society. It is painfully true that the roles women carry are almost universally devalued. The roles of wife and mother are generally taken for granted and are not very well compensated. Occupations that are primarily female, such as teaching, nursing, and social work, are less prestigious and less well paid than other "male" occupations requiring far less education. Many studies have demonstrated that the media continue to portray women in degrading, demeaning ways. Thus, women have been taught essentially to devalue themselves and each other as females, and a consciousness-raising experience can go a long way toward changing this.

One study of a consciousness-raising group demonstrated a massive resocialization process for women. Twenty-five sessions were observed, and eleven regular participants were interviewed during one year of operation. All of these women said that the sessions provided an experience and a language through which they were able to make shifts in identity, self-understanding, and world view. They became more aware of their individual potentialities and vulnerabilities, and by the end of that year, they all made impressive shifts in active pursuit of goals and skills.[1]

Another kind of group experience that has developed recently, and is spreading like wildfire, is something called assertiveness training. The theory behind this technique is that women have great difficulty making themselves heard or known—asserting themselves—and have been taught from childhood to be reticent. There is a huge payoff in the environment for women to be passive and subservient, and up until recently a woman who really asserted herself would have tended to meet considerable resistance. The leaders of these groups differentiate strongly between assertiveness and aggressiveness. In either men or women, aggressiveness has negative connotations and often involves hostile or obnoxious behavior. An example of three kinds of responses might be in a woman's reaction to criticism: The usual female, nonassertive response to criticism is an immediate acceptance—"Of course you're right. I did that badly. Thanks for pointing it out. I needed that." The aggressive response is a counterattack—"Who are you to criticize? Last week you did something worse . . ." The assertive woman would be able to question the criticizer, figure out exactly what is meant, assess the source of the criticism, mull it over in her own mind, accept the valid parts and reject the invalid parts. How many women are really able to be assertive and effective with husbands, teen-age children, employers, surly repairmen, and all the other people one encounters day after day? And even if a woman is able to be fairly assertive and effective, is she able to do without undue anxiety?

There have been studies of group situations where both men and women are interacting, such as work conferences, cocktail parties, or town meetings; and by any conceivable guideline of assertiveness, the men always come out ahead. The men do more talking in quantity of time filled, they tend to talk in paragraphs rather than sentences or half-sentences, they are more adept at handling interruptions, and they tend to state stronger opin-

156

ions and be more controversial. By contrast, women usually ask more questions (thereby reinforcing the male speaker), they do a lot of nodding and agreeing, they are seldom controversial, and they allow themselves to be easily interrupted. These studies, interestingly enough, are in contradiction to the image of women as chatterboxes. It seems that in sex-mixed situations, and especially in goal-directed activities, women take a back seat. The four situations that are found to be most anxiety provoking for women are no surprise, considering the socialization of girls to be agreeable and to "make nice." The most frightening areas are (1) being able to disagree, (2) handling criticism, (3) saying no, and (4) giving negative feedback (being in the role of criticizer).

People who do assertiveness training find that women need positive reinforcement, from both outside and inside themselves, of their ability to say something worthwhile in order to succeed; and there is indication of tremendous success so far from this method. The common suspicion of women that this kind of training could result in a lot of chaos with their husband has not been borne out. The usual procedure is for women to role-play in the groups (sometimes with trained men brought in for this purpose), to give each other feedback, and then to try out some kind of assignment at home. To their surprise, for the most part, they get positive responses from husband, children, and almost everyone else. They find that when they are more clear and direct and assertive, they are more respected and better liked. And they certainly come to feel better about themselves.[2]

One interesting finding has been that women who score highest in assertiveness also score highest in sexual satisfaction. But this only makes common sense, since a woman who is able to communicate her needs and desires sexually has a better chance of getting them fulfilled than her more passive, less assertive sister. One woman described her progression to sexual satisfaction as follows: "I was raised in a very strict, religious family, and I was a virgin when I married Mike. I assumed, since he had been away at college and in the service, that he had a lot more sexual experience than I did; but I know differently now. His friends convinced him to go to prostitutes a couple of times, but he knew nothing about making love.

"Mike was always considerate in bed, but we were pretty square—sex with the lights out, in the old missionary position. He never complained, and I never complained through six years of marriage and the birth of two kids. But in my heart I knew something was wrong, and I began to feel I was cheated out of something. I'd never had an orgasm, but I was always an avid reader, and I knew I wanted that experience if possible. I read something once about masturbation being a normal and healthy thing, so I started to experiment by myself. All the while, I felt guilty, but I continued telling myself that what I'd been taught wasn't necessarily true, and eventually I was able to masturbate to orgasm. I was also helped by a neighbor of mine, who leveled with me about some of her own sexual problems. A few years back I would never have discussed sex with a friend, but this neighbor was in a consciousness-raising group, and she invited me to join too. I didn't go to her group, but I took an assertiveness class at the community college, and I decided to tell Mike my concerns.

"I first bought a couple of books on sex and left them around the house. Mike seemed shocked when he saw them, but he smiled and started to tease me in a nice way. I tried very hard not to accuse him, but at first he got defensive anyway. He said I was never very exciting in bed, and I said that's right, but that I had trouble knowing how to make it better. That seemed to disarm him, and he acknowledged that he really hadn't had much experience. We both read some books after that, and I got the idea from the Masters and Johnson stuff to take it in stages. So we arranged a little vacation away from the kids, and we kind of did our own sex therapy course. I found that Mike liked it when I told him to do this, or not to do that. We were like a couple of kids in a way, and when I got excited it really turned him on more. Sometimes now I'm the aggressor in our sexual relationship, and sometimes he is. I also feel I can say no when I don't feel like it. I don't always have orgasms, but when I do, it's pretty terrific."

## COUNSELING OR THERAPY
## WITH A PROFESSIONAL

There are so many different kinds of therapy that it would be useless to try to describe them all here. But a few basic facts can be stated.

Therapy can range from a few weeks to many years in duration. The first session or few sessions with a therapist are usually termed consultation. This is a process in which both people decide whether they can or want to work together; it is also a time during which the therapist makes some tentative diagnostic formulations, and both talk about some tentative goals of therapy. One or two sessions per week is the usual therapeutic regimen; psychoanalysis may mean as many as five sessions per week. The cost can range anywhere from $100 or more per hour for a few big-city therapists to zero for a subsidized clinic. Basically, psychotherapy is done in two kinds of situations: private practice, where the fee is pretty much standard, and clinic practice, where there is usually a sliding scale of fees according to ability to pay. An in between step is certain kinds of group practice, where therapists have gotten together to share overhead, etc., and offer a limited sliding scale.

Psychotherapy has its fads and fashions as well as any other field and one can usually choose from several catchy, often gimmicky labels for approaches to the human psyche. Some of them are truly new, worthwhile types of intervention and will remain in good therapists' repertoires; others are simply new jargon for old words; still others are quite unscientifically founded and are potentially quite dangerous. The three basic methods for psychotherapy are still individual, group, and family (or couples). Some therapists use only one method; others use two or three as the situation warrants. The patient who wants group or family therapy may have to search a little longer for a therapist, but the practice of both these modalities is increasing. (A recent *Business Week* article provides an excellent overview of "Marriage Counseling."[3]) Family therapy especially is an exciting development within the past few years and is catching on rapidly. Very briefly, it assumes that no one person in a family should be labeled "the patient," and it concentrates especially on patterns of communication and methods of problem solving. Family therapists, as well as group therapists, often work as a team (conjoint therapy), but many work alone.

My own personal preference for working with corporate wives is a combination of individual and couples therapy, but each situation is so different that it is impossible to generalize. The decision to involve your husband, and to what extent, in the therapy is dependent on the awareness, ability to be open, and motivation to work together of both partners.

The researchers at Yale, dealing with depressed women, concluded that involvement of the husband depends on the degree of pathology in the marriage before onset of the wife's illness. A patient with an adaptive healthy marriage benefited when communication with her husband was reestablished and both were reassured about the wife's treatment and progress; this kind of treatment involves the husband in a peripheral role. However, when a marriage was termed maladaptive, a long-term course of couples therapy was indicated, wherein the marital conflict became the major focus for discussion.[4] Most of these depressed women were hospitalized with fairly severe symptomatology. I would add that the typical corporate wife, who is seen in outpatient therapy, may have many reasons to want family therapy in addition to the ones suggested above. Most of her questions and problems may concern role and relationship areas, and one cannot make changes in a vacuum. Whether the marriage is called adaptive or maladaptive, changes in the wife will require some changes in her husband, and there are many advantages to having him as a full partner in that process.

The inclusion of children in family therapy is increasingly common, and women who are involved in the complicated equilibrium of corporate husband—corporate wife should at least consider it. The Yale group found direct connections between depressed mothers and deviant behavior in children. Children of all ages may become part of the treatment process as needed.

Therapy groups also have merit, especially for a woman who is at the very beginning stages of an identity struggle. It is always enlightening for a person to know that her problems are not unique; I have seen women react as if light bulbs were turning on in their heads when another woman in a group describes a problem similar to theirs. Other group members can give the kind of support, as well as hard-hitting confrontation, that one lone therapist could never provide.

Psychotherapists come primarily from three disciplines: psychiatry (MDs), clinical psychology (Ph.D.s), and psychiatric social work (MSWs); other therapists might be nurse-clinicians, clergy, school counselors, or marriage counselors. There is no central licensing agency for psychotherapists, but there is specific licensing and/or certification within most of the professions themselves. The differences in training and background between psychiatrists, psychologists, and psychiatric social workers are not easy to describe. It is also possible for various people within the same profession to have had very different training.

I would venture the wrath of other professionals to state these differences: Psychiatrists are trained in medicine and all that that implies, and they are the only therapists able to prescribe medication. Psychologists tend to have had more emphasis on testing and research in their backgrounds than the other professionals. Psychiatric social work training tends to emphasize family dynamics and sociocultural factors more than the other disciplines do. But these differences are very rough, and most good therapists have had additional training beyond the formal degree. More years have been spent in academic and clinical training by the psychiatrist than the psychologist, and more by the psychologist than the psychiatric social worker. The fees tend to be correspondingly less for the therapists with the shorter training period. However, the work actually done by the three disciplines is quite similar. There are several professional organizations that combine them, and there are movements within the mental health field to give one degree in psychotherapy. A few such academic programs have begun, including the best and most appropriate elements of the three disciplines in the training process.

In addition to those who do psychotherapy, there are also those who do psychoanalysis. Analysts are usually people who have attended a psychoanalytic institute beyond gaining the MD degree and completing a residency in psychiatry; they learn under supervision to do psychoanalysis, which is a quite different procedure from therapy, and they must be analyzed themselves. (Although many, perhaps most, therapists have had psychotherapy themselves, there is no requirement for this.) There are also lay psychoanalysts who do not have the MD degree but have had analytic training; they usually come from backgrounds of psychology or psychiatric social work, and their work is usually identical to that of the MD analysts.

Many of these terms are quite confusing to the public. For example, the term psychoanalyst is often incorrectly used to include all therapists. Some people refer to all therapists as psychologists. There has traditionally been a mystique about psychotherapy which is just now being debunked and brought down to common-sense levels. But the hardest aspect of the process still is to find the right therapist for the individual. The person who has little contact with the "world" of therapy is often at a disadvantage in finding the appropriate professional, but there are a few tricks that every woman should know about. Hints like these can be like a road map through the maze. They do not eliminate the problems; trial-and-error experiences may still be necessary. But they make the territory a bit more familiar and the traveler a bit more comfortable.

The first tricky part is whom to ask for a referral.

The most frequent advice is that the patient ask her family physician, a clergyman, the county medical society or local psychiatric group, or trusted friends. Any of these can be helpful, but none is fool-proof, and they all have built-in hazards. The training of physicians and clergy in psychiatric problems is changing, but up until recently it was almost nil. People who run courses in psychiatry for general practitioners or clergy are often shocked at their lack of knowledge in emotional matters. Their ignorance may be especially appalling in sexual areas. One must emphasize that this is not always the case, but many physicians and clergy, in ignorance, have simply found a convenient resource to refer people for therapy; or they may, at times ineptly, try to do it themselves. They may mean well by a particular referral, but there may be little assessment of the needs of the patient and the style of the therapist. The physician or clergyman may find it most convenient to refer to a therapist he or she knows from the golf course or congregation or whatever.

The local medical society or psychiatric group will usually give three or four names of psychiatrists to anyone who calls. But one should realize a couple of basic facts: First, these groups represent only psychiatrists; second, they are obliged not to rank any of their members in terms of competence or appropriateness. If they consistently gave certain names and not others, they would be open to libel suits, and they usually try to refer to all members equally.

Similarly, asking friends can be a shot-in-the-dark procedure, since everyone chooses according to his or her own biases. Often a friend of a friend has been the actual source, and the opinions about the therapist are quite diluted. Friends can be most helpful in referrals if they will go into some detail about why the therapist worked for them or why that therapist did not; the kinds of problems they were dealing with; and what they wanted out of therapy. The questioner can then make some assessment as to whether her friend's situation bears any similarity to hers.

One must realize, then, that no person is going to be

able to make the selection of another person's therapist. The most fruitful approach is to talk to as many trusted professionals and friends as possible, get their ideas, and try to sift through what they say.

The second point, which is too often forgotten, is that the patient is the consumer who is buying the service. Insecure people that most of us are, we are often so concerned about whether the therapist will like us or will find us interesting enough, that we easily assume the child-like role while the therapist becomes the parent. Any secure and competent therapist should not resent questions about his or her background or orientation, and any patient or potential patient should not hesitate to ask questions. There are other sources also for validating credentials, such as lists that are kept by each professional organization. Certainly the patient has a perfect right, if she wishes, to know something about the person she is dealing with. This does not include personal questions that have no relevance to the person as therapist; the justified retort to a very personal question will probably be, "Why do you want to know?" But any question relevant to the therapy deserves a thoughtful answer. The kinds of things that the patient would probably want to agree on fairly early in the game would include fees, probable length of treatment, and family involvement.

Many people in distress are anxious to settle on a therapist immediately, but the most practical approach is to shop for a therapist just as you would for any other service. You can make appointments with three or four therapists with the expressed purpose of consultation, and be ready to make a decision only at the end of that process. This involves some expense and some time, but it is really well worth it since therapy in general is a very expensive and very time-consuming procedure. Besides the information that you will gather in the course of this shopping, you should not underestimate the importance of feelings. For lack of more precise terminology, we might say that good chemistry is an important ingredient in any relationship. And the chemistry in a therapist-patient relationship is enormously important. There must be some feeling of mutual respect, some quality in the therapist that allows you to want to open up, some feeling of interest—hopefully even excitement—in working together toward the goals. If that chemistry is lacking, all the credentials in the world will not compensate. You may remain in treatment, but the outcome will be disappointing for both you and the therapist. So, although it may sound callous and hard, shopping for the appropriate therapist is a very crucial step.

Taking the referral of someone else—especially a trusted professional—may seem like the right way to find help. Who am I to choose? What do I know about therapy? Don't they all act alike? But this is really a cop-out. As with every other decision in life, it is very important for a woman to take the responsibility of choosing her own therapist. This takes just a glimmering of insight about your own resources, and just a beginning sense of power in yourself. If the relationship or the therapy doesn't work out, it is of course easier to blame the failure on the person who referred you than on yourself. But it is much more productive to try to analyze what went wrong, why the choice may have been the wrong one. That way, if you decide to try another therapist, you can benefit and learn from past errors or mistakes in judgment.

What about the controversial matter of a male or female therapist for the corporate wife? Many women will find themselves leaning toward the male therapist for a variety of reasons: They may subconsciously have bought the belief that men are really better than women; they may imagine the therapeutic relationship as a replacement for the father-daughter dependency situation; or they may fantasize engaging the therapist as a lover, or seducing him into rescuing them sexually. Another group of corporate wives might see themselves as ardent or budding feminists, and might feel that the only person who could understand or really help them must be a woman. In my opinion, choice is appropriate, but closed-mindedness may be counterproductive and dangerous. The sex of a therapist is only one of her or his characteristics, and the patient who is adamant in either direction should really try to evaluate her reasoning.

There are, however, some very real dangers for women in therapy, and the personal attitudes of the therapist toward women should not be minimized. There is general agreement among professionals that the double standard still exists in the mental health field. Traits considered healthy in men tend to be seen as unhealthy in women. Many more women than men are seeking psychotherapy, but many of these women are getting little help from tradition-bound therapists. These traditional therapists include women as well as men, but since 80 percent of the psychotherapeutic profession is male, most of the feminists' anger is directed at the men. These traditionalists do not even try to shake the sexist stereotyped roles of male assertiveness and female nurturing. Consequently, they "deprive women of their anger, competitiveness and directness and encourage them to have an over-abundance of seductiveness, cheerfulness and helplessness."[5]

Women who want both careers and family relationships often seek therapy because they are in conflict and feel some guilt. They frequently are told that they can't have both. Men would seldom, if ever, get this advice; the stereotypes that apply to men are different. Men may be expected to be extremely strong and virile. Tradition-bound therapists have little idea of some men's need to be weak or of what it means for a woman to break free of sexist stereotypes. They are incapable of helping a woman who would like to compete on an equal basis with men; and they can actually do some psychological damage.

Few therapists today are totally Freudian in their attitudes, but Freud's influence on psychiatry is still enormous. The classical Freudian, psychoanalytic view of femininity might be described as follows:

• Anatomy is destiny: Woman's nature is determined solely by her anatomy, specifically by the fact that she does not have a penis. Thus, reproduction is the ultimate purpose in life; and

166

the psychologically normal woman is chiefly concerned with the roles of wife and mother.
- Penis envy: Because she does not have a penis, the female child considers herself defective and is envious of the male.
- Faulty development of the superego: Because the girl has more difficulty than the boy resolving the Oedipal conflict (attachment with father against mother), she has a lesser capacity for sublimation.
- Masochism and passivity: As a result of the woman's general feelings of inferiority and inadequacy, aggressiveness is forced inward, which in turn results in a masochistic personality. Furthermore, because of her sexual role as receptor, the woman naturally develops passive tendencies in all social roles.[6]

Thus, Freudian theory emphasizes the male as the model of normalcy. Even the neo-Freudians minimize the importance of the female and correlate feminine identity with biological function. Therefore those therapists whose personal biases tend to be anti-women have a significant theoretical base to cling to.

By contrast, the newer theories suggest that all behavior is learned. There is considerable evidence for the view that "the girl is taught not only how to think about her reproductive role, but how to think about herself in intellectual terms. Little girls are taught at an early age to have certain aspirations and standards of achievement. Data even suggest that independent, bright, and creative girls receive less affection from their teachers than do boys."[7] It seems that, just as other roles for women are prescribed, women are encouraged to seek therapy for their emotional problems or weaknesses. Once in therapy, the woman is judged by primarily male standards of what is "normal."

The therapist's attitudes about women will be communicated in subtle and uncontrollable ways—by tone of voice, facial expressions, posture, and areas focused on. If

167

the therapist has contempt for you as a woman, he or she may actually reinforce your own poor self-image. Consciousness-raising as it pertains to sex-role identity should be part of every therapist's training, but it has not always been so. As Wilma Scott Heide says, "Frustrated human potential in the search for 'femininity' and 'masculinity' may be a significant component in the etiology of mental illness. Mental health researchers, practitioners, and educators are urged to relate to clients in terms of ideal personhood, which transcends gender."[8]

One final caution about therapy is the occasional incidence of sexual acting out among therapists. The CBS program *60 Minutes* did a segment on February 19, 1978 about several disgraceful episodes of therapists taking advantage of vulnerable women patients. At least one of these women was a corporate wife, and it was clear that all of these male therapists convinced their patients that sex was part of the treatment. The final effect of this arrangement was extremely painful for the patient, and under no circumstances can it be therapeutic. What may start out seeming like a romantic interlude or sexual excitement usually ends up feeling like rejection and loss and pain. Even sex therapy, which deals directly with sexuality in other ways, does not include any sexual acting out between therapist and patient. There is no excuse for this kind of behavior, and all of the professional associations forbid it. Unfortunately, it is difficult to confront or sue in these situations because the accused parties always try to place the blame on the patient. The best defense against this travesty of therapy is a good offense: Do not let it happen to you.

A relatively new aid for women seeking a nonsexist therapist is the feminist referral service, which screens both male and female therapists and tries to match patients with the appropriate professionals. Many women are reluctant to think of themselves as feminists, partly because the media have pictured this group as aggressive, hysterical, angry, bra-burning, frustrated women. The spokespersons picked up by the media have often been the extremists of the movement, and many women have said that if these are feminists, they don't want to be. Therefore, they may be reluctant to use a feminist-oriented therapy referral service. However, the definition of feminist seems to be changing as many more women of all kinds identify themselves by that label, and a women's therapy referral service is a very good resource. Their list can help you find a therapist, male or female, whose ideas are in harmony with the women's movement. You will still have to shop and be a discriminating consumer, but the service will assist you; and if you cannot pay the full therapeutic fee, women's therapy referral services usually can suggest low-cost resources also. Although these referral services do not exist in many parts of the country, they are available in most large urban areas. Groups of women therapists have also banded together in some cities to form women's institutes or counseling services.

Beyond these aids, the individual woman must assess for herself whether her therapist is truly concerned about her identity, or is more caught up with traditional roles and how others in her family will be affected. It takes awareness, but any woman with a modest ability to "hear" can tell pretty quickly whether the therapist respects her and is really tuned in to her as a whole person. She should listen for the therapist to focus on these areas: Who are you? What do you feel? What do you want? What are you doing to get what you want? She should be able to assess whether there is some reciprocity in the patient-therapist relationship, and whether there is good two-way communication. If these components of the therapeutic relationship are not present, the woman will end up knowing how she should feel and think and act. But she will have little chance of really coming to know herself. On the other hand, if the therapist is tuned in to her, respectful of her, and fairly open in attitudes about women, the female patient can learn to know herself as she never could just on her own, and she can get valuable help in reshaping various areas of her life.

As Lisa Kelly put it, following two years of therapy with a renowned woman psychologist, "She introduced me to an entirely new person—part of myself that I never

# POTENTIAL THERAPIST RATINGS

| Issue | Therapist #1 | Therapist #2 | Therapist #3 |
|---|---|---|---|
| 1. Source of referral | | | |
| 2. My compatibility with referral source | | | |
| 3. Professional credentials of therapist | | | |
| 4. Therapist's willingness to answer questions | | | |
| 5. My comfort with fee arrangements | | | |
| 6. Negotiations about problem areas | | | |
| 7. Negotiations about time expected in therapy | | | |
| 8. My comfort with modality of therapy (individual, group, couple, family) | | | |
| 9. Indications of therapist's concern about my identity | | | |
| 10. Therapist's attitudes about women | | | |
| 11. My assessment of the "chemistry" between us | | | |

knew existed, or perhaps I wouldn't admit existed. Very long ago I had given up the dreams of adolescence that I would be a somebody; I did all the things I was supposed to do as a wife and mother, and I thought it was maturity that came in the place of my dreams and aspirations. Instead, it was a kind of emotional death. I was dying a little inside every day until I started seeing her." With a little, embarrassed laugh, she said, "I hate to admit now how much time I had wasted with my previous shrink. He was very good looking, and I kept hoping he would fall in love with me. Somehow, if that happened, I would be really alive again, and my life would be exciting. But it never happened, and I began to feel like even more of a failure. I'm not blaming him. If I had stayed with him and worked it out, he might have been able to help me. But I never understood the games I was·playing until I started seeing her. I feel very lucky that a friend of mine suggested her; she was just what I needed. I'm not saying that I didn't try to play games with her too, but seduction was not one of them. She helped give me the courage to look at my life as it really is, and she had confidence in me when I didn't have much in myself. When people ask me just what problem my therapy solved, it's hard to answer, 'cause it wasn't that specific. The process just helped me look at my life so differently; it really helped me to know who I am, and I'll never let go of that way of thinking again."

Thus, whether the corporate wife decides to go it alone or get professional help, she can begin to be really liberated as a person only if she knows herself pretty well. She must try very hard to-be honest with herself, even when it is painful. She must try to separate what has been prescribed for her by parents, husband, or experts from what she really wants. She must try to stop herself when she is denying or avoiding the difficult things. She must develop some real excitement in self-discovery. And she must have some faith that her future decisions in every area of life will be better, more effective ones if she is really in touch with who she is.

# 7

# Be Selfish;
# Put Yourself First

Unselfishness in women, from biblical times onward, has been lauded and rewarded; but this concept has often been used to mask something else. Is there really any such thing as unselfishness? I certainly hope not, because that would imply that there is no self, and it is clearly more than a cliché that one must love himself or herself before one can really love anyone else. Surely we can find a more honest way of looking at behavior. Certainly we can be strong enough to take responsibility for our own actions and to admit that all behavior is motivated. The time is long overdue for women to come "up front" with what they want instead of couching it all in terms of subservience and obeisance. It is an injustice to women to live through another person or persons and to forgo the excitement and the responsibility of taking their life in their own hands. But perhaps even more dramatic, it is an injustice to men who must take responsibility for these dependent, half-alive women who have somewhere learned to believe that they can accomplish the life they want by being "un-selfish," devoted semi-servants.

## NEW DEFINITIONS

It is no coincidence that the virtue of "unselfishness" is primarily associated with women—both throughout literature and in every aspect of daily life. And it is no surprise that the business world, which has used the corporate wife to get two employees for the price of one, has tenaciously emphasized the need for wives to be unselfish and flexible. The strong, iron-willed, determined businessman is valued and given all kinds of positive reinforcement, but his wife is expected to complement him by being just the opposite. The world has now changed enough to value also the tough, hard-driving business*woman.* The next step is to stop all the double-talk about unselfishness and flexibility in corporate wives and to recognize honestly that this too is selfish, motivated behavior—designed precisely to accomplish various goals. And wouldn't it be wonderful if the world had really changed enough so that corporations could recognize the value in a corporate wife who was every bit as strong and selfish as her husband!

So, perhaps we can now redefine our terms. Everyone is selfish. Everyone determines his or her own behavior and life to a very large extent. It takes honesty and guts to admit selfishness because it makes one more visible. It puts the individual squarely in control of his or her own life and makes that person primarily responsible for the outcome. We can therefore state, in a sweeping generalization, that the more selfish you are, the more in control of your life you are. And the more in control of your life you are, the more influence and control you can have over the world around you.

In the cause of human liberation, the time has come for more equal sharing of all things in life by men and women. This new definition of selfishness or self-centeredness lacks the negative connotations that have historically

174

been associated with these words. And basically it is a more honest and therefore more productive approach to life.

This is not meant to suggest that women should stop trying to help their husband's careers; after all, a married woman's life is very much affected by her husband's position on the career ladder. I am stating emphatically, however, that she should consider her own needs and desires and motivations first and foremost, and that she is defeating herself if she couches her efforts in some kind of selfless devotion.

The message is: Be selfish—whatever benefits you will benefit the people around you. This is in many ways a difficult concept for both men and women to comprehend—it is so much in opposition to the usual advice that we consider the consequences on those we love before taking any action. In therapy, this concept is especially hard for the insecure and frightened person to grasp. If that person is the usual corporation wife, she fears much of the world and has been constantly used to hiding behind her life of selfless giving. But it is exactly this concept that can most likely help her—allowing her to establish her own identity, her own self-worth, and her own growth as a person.

## UNSELFISHNESS, CORPORATE WIFE STYLE

People have been writing and giving advice about marriage for hundreds of years, and the most common piece of advice, especially directed toward women, is to be unselfish. I have often heard women refer to the biblical epithet "It is better to give than to receive," but I can scarcely remember hearing any man say this. Although women in general are supposed to accept this kind of life, nowhere is there more emphasis on self-sacrifice and unselfishness than in the role that is prescribed for the corporate wife.

She is told how to act, how to dress, how to entertain, even how to think, in both open dictates and subtle hints. And these directions come from a whole range of people—her husband, his superiors and associates, and their wives. Many corporate executives anonymously admit frustration that they cannot control the corporate wife quite as much as they can her husband. Wives must be assets to the company, and must above all be aware that their husbands belong to the corporation. Most of this, of course, is the handiwork of men and is perfectly understandable, as noted previously, in terms of the benefits that have accrued to men through this social system. How can all these new ideas about a seemingly selfish, "me-centered" person ever be reconciled with the traditional picture of the selfless, helping corporation wife?

My contention is that this in reality will not mean very much change in the way men and women operate. Instead, this seems to be a way of restating what has always been true. The difference is that, for various reasons, women can now be more open about what they want for themselves; hopefully, these new ideas will help them to be less devious and less manipulative in their relationships with men.

The important difference between selfishness and unselfishness may be in the definition. How does an unselfish wife operate? And is there really such a thing as unselfishness in any human being?

Let us look at the stereotype of the unselfish, husband-oriented corporation wife. She takes care of his needs ahead of her own; she organizes the household and children around his schedule and desires; she is willing to do whatever would be helpful to his career. Whatever time or energy is squeezed out just for herself takes last priority. She would seem to be doing all these things for *him*—but this is nonsense! She has made choices, and every bit of her behavior is motivated by forces inside her, even though this motivation is often unconscious. She has chosen a life-style of "unselfishness" to accomplish what she wants for herself. This is the image she wants to project. This is the image that is most successful in getting the things she wants out of life. This is the image that gives her the most psychological comfort.

If she is the typical American woman, she has learned from life, and especially from her mother, that her own future and the destinies of her children depend almost totally on her husband's upward mobility. The world has made her a clinging vine, and she clings tenaciously. But this is not unselfish behavior. It is for herself primarily and what she thinks she wants that she uses all her intelligence and charm and resources to promote her husband up the ladder. To do otherwise would be rebellious to the social system in which she was raised, and it would be especially rebellious vis-á-vis the corporate world in which she and her husband operate.

No one can deny that the world in which we live has given women many rewards for appearing passive and unselfish. For many corporate wives the rewards are tremendous: They fit comfortably into the system and are compatible with other corporate wives; their husbands brag about how efficient they are and how accepting they are— "Not like George's wife, who gives him so much shit every time they move." Their compensation for staying in their place may include jewelry, mink coats, and suitable homes in the suburbs. Do they perform all these unselfish chores for their husbands? Certainly not. They do it to get exactly what they want out of life, or rather, what they have been taught to want. They do it to perpetuate a certain life-style for *themselves* primarily.

In its healthier version, the goal of this "unselfish" behavior is to project the "proper" image of the corporate wife, and concomitantly to collect whatever rewards come from that. In its more sick or neurotic version, however, seeming unselfishness or selflessness allows the woman to look like a victim and to acquire the sympathy and compassion of those around her. This kind of "doormat unselfishness" is the extreme, but it is not uncommon among corporate wives who thrive on the pity of their friends and families. Of course, this kind of motivation is often below the level of consciousness, and would be denied by women who have been taught to regard unselfishness as a virtue and selfishness as a sin.

177

So many women cling to "unselfish" behavior because it allows them to avoid responsibility. If they do everything for "dear old John" and what looks like very little for themselves, "dear old John" has to take credit or blame for most of what happens in both of their lives, and the little woman can simply be dependent on him. This is certainly a safer, more protected position for a woman who has been taught to stay in the background. Therefore, the idea that "unselfish" behavior is very selfishly motivated will not be a popular one with many women—especially those who are insecure and frightened of facing life on their own. Nevertheless, we as women must all face this squarely and stop accepting the nonsense handed down mostly by men that unselfishness—that is, for women—is a virtue. If a woman chooses what looks like an unselfish way of life, she must recognize that this is a choice—as selfish as all other choices—and take some responsibility for that choice.

Most men who are secure and not easily threatened find it a drag to have a dependent, clinging wife. It is not uncommon for a man to have married young when he was not very sure of himself, and to have been attracted at that stage in his life by a child-woman who seemed to boost his ego by her dependence and devotion. However, as his self-esteem and position in the business world grow, he finds himself attracted to a very different type of woman. If his wife has not grown also, their marriage is either unhappy or dead or over.

The CEO who described the difference between his two marriages as "the difference between companionship and slavery" was implying that his needs were quite different at those two times in his life. On further questioning, he said that his first wife was a campus beauty queen, who was quite happy to leave college after her sophomore year; she was much impressed by his family business and wealth, and she always seemed to be insecure about how to act or dress properly. "She did everything I suggested or asked her to do, but she never had many ideas of her own. It got so that I involved her less and less in my life. But she didn't even have the initiative to want a divorce. When I told her it was over, she was pretty shaken, but she eventually accepted that like everything else." Why did he marry her in the first place? "She was very pretty and seemed to worship me. I was flattered by that; I liked the idea that I had control over such a gorgeous creature. It never occurred to me then that companionship would turn out to be so important."

If women take responsibility for their own lives, they can be partners in the fullest sense of the word. Two selfish people can then come together in a relationship that both want, but neither needs for survival. The implications of this are much more satisfying and more adult than in any situation in which growth and responsibility are unequal.

Two psychotherapists, one a man and the other a woman, have written about this kind of responsible, selfish relationship. Frederick S. (Fritz) Perls:

> I do my thing, and you do your thing.
> I am not in this world to live up to your
>     expectations,
> And you are not in this world to live up to mine.
> You are you and I am I,
> And if by chance we find each other,
> It's beautiful.

Virginia Satir:

> I want to love you without clutching,
> appreciate you without judging,
> join you without invading,
> invite you without demanding,
> leave you without guilt,
> criticize you without blaming,
> and help you without insulting.
>
> If I can have the same from you,
> then we can truly meet and enrich each other.

# CHILDREN

Women who flaunt their unselfish devotion often refer to their children as well as their husbands. This is not a simple situation, for good parenting in general takes tremendous resources from both mothers and fathers. However, again it is a matter of choices. A mother who decides to spend most of her time and energy raising children does it because *she* enjoys that way of life and wants to influence all aspects of their growth; or she would feel guilty if she did it any other way, or any combination of these reasons. On the other hand, a woman may choose to spend a great deal of time away from her children because she enjoys other parts of her life and feels her children will benefit if she is happier. Many parents, in fact, believe that it is the quality of time rather than the quantity of time spent with children that is most important. The phenomenon of American mothers devoting so much time and energy to child rearing is a relatively recent one in our history, and many experts believe it is not necessarily a healthy situation. Women who live through their children, just as those who live through their husbands, tend to become a drag on those they love. It is hard for this kind of woman to give her children enough freedom to develop independently, and some kind of rebellion is often the result. Furthermore, no one can deny that children want to be proud of their parents, and this can happen only if parents have a good measure of dignity and self-respect. Women who are proud of themselves as people and who are successful and accomplished in some area other than the usual household chores can usually evoke pride in their children. On the other hand, a selfless, devoted, but uninteresting, half-alive mother—almost a nonperson—does little to merit the approval and pride of her offspring. In the long run, her "unselfishness" can become destructive to both her children and herself.

Does this mean disregarding families and their rights? What about the children who get second-best care while their mother goes to work? What about the husband who has to fix his own dinner after a grueling day in the competitive world? What about the man whose career is limited because his wife refuses to move? These are rough situations, and yet the answer is uncategorical: If any person does whatever will make him or her happier or more fulfilled, the people around that person will benefit. If any person restricts his or her own desires and needs repeatedly, or if that person takes an action because of feeling forced into it, he or she has to become a bit less happy, a bit less fulfilled, and the people around that person will undoubtedly suffer.

## JOE AND BETTY

Let us take an example of a situation that raised the questions above. In the case of Joe and Betty Thompson (names are fictitious), it might seem at first glance that the selfish action of the wife caused *undue* hardship on her family. Every corporate wife is a member of a family, and any change in her will upset the equilibrium. Who is to determine whether the change is undue or is worth the disruption? All family members must determine it for themselves. But if the primary change is in the wife, as it was in Betty's case, it is she who must take the major responsibility for her own life.

Betty is a friend of mine from high school days. She and Joe met during college and married immediately after they both graduated. Betty taught school two years while Joe got his MBA at Stanford, and shortly thereafter, strictly according to the plán, she got pregnant. Joe progressed steadily up the corporate ladder, and Betty felt content with three children and a home in the suburbs. Betty says, "I don't quite know when my life began to change, but I gradually realized that I was drinking too much. I at first dismissed the thought of alcoholism because many women in my neighborhood did the same thing—morning sherry and afternoon cocktails instead of coffee and tea." She remembers feeling very lonely and vaguely angry at Joe, but at the same time guilty. "What did I have to complain about? I had money, a good-looking, successful husband who loved me, bright, healthy kids, and most of the time I even enjoyed playing the corporate wife. I always thought I did that act pretty well, and I never minded spending lots of time entertaining for Joe and being entertained for business reasons because that was my main source of fun. What the hell, I was keeping our family up with the Joneses and doing what everyone expected of me."

When her children were eleven, nine, and six, and she herself was thirty-five, Betty began to hear about consciousness-raising groups and was persuaded to try one by her neighbor. This experience changed her life. Her husband says she went "crazy" for a while; Betty says she was really shaken up by the realization that there was so little left of *her*. "After I had been in the group about six months, I read about a course at the university for teachers of children with learning disabilities. It was held in the evenings; Joe and the children agreed that it was a good idea. But, to everyone's surprise, I got hooked; I did extremely well in school, and landed one of the few openings in the university's exciting new program for handicapped children. I really agonized a few days over what this might mean for my family, but the choice was clear. I had to take it." She felt she was coming alive.

Have the kids suffered? "Yes, in many ways. I am not home to greet them after school and had hoped to find a grandmotherly woman to substitute. But the only person I was able to find was a high school senior. The kids like her, but I will have to find someone new next year when the girl goes off to college. There is a cleaning woman one day a week, but she is unreliable, and even when she comes, there is a lot left for me to do in the evening. Consequently I'm not very available to help the kids with homework, but I try to leave weekends free for family activities. The kids complain about things not getting done but are learning to pitch in more themselves. On the whole, I think they are doing fine, and they seem to be proud of me. I cried when our six-year-old told me she had made a speech in school about how her mother helps handicapped children."

For Joe, the change has not been so easy. One night each week Betty has parent conferences, and when she asked him to take over at home that night, he exploded. It was a major fight, but Betty insisted and Joe began to see how important it was to her. Now, on the night that Betty is away, Joe usually takes the kids to McDonald's, and they all seem to enjoy it. However, Betty wonders lately why so many of Joe's business trips occur on that night, and she thinks another major confrontation may be coming. There have been other hassles over household chores, but when Betty remains rational (she says this is not often easy) and adamant, Joe usually gives in.

The worst crisis in their marital equilibrium came recently when Joe was offered a promotional opportunity in another city. "I was depressed for days, but finally told Joe I really did not want to go. He knew it anyway, and told me I was probably ruining his career. We tried to explain to each other our own feelings, and finally Joe said that this job was not exactly what he wanted anyway. The next day he told his superiors that the timing was just not right for a move because I was so new in my job and needed to remain at the university to complete my master's. Joe's boss said he understood, but Joe thinks he read something different on the boss's face." Both Joe and Betty wonder what will happen now. Will he be passed over for the next promotion? If he is offered the "right" job in another city next time, would they be able to reconcile their different needs? Betty has never said it to Joe, but she wonders if their marriage could even end over an issue like this.

No one can argue that there aren't hardships for Joe because of Betty's new life. But there are also benefits. "I knew for a long time that Betty wasn't very happy, but I didn't know what to do about it. Now she's a real person again; we're much closer. There are times when I would like to have my less complicated wife back, but I feel grateful that she never went the alcoholism route, and I certainly find life with her more interesting these days."  .

Clearly in human behavior every action has a reaction. Nobody is promised a rose garden, and no family is invulnerable to stress. Wives who have taken the role of flexible, unselfish peacemaker may not have created many visible or discernible waves. But if this course has been chosen at the expense of more self-satisfying options, the problems have to pop up in other areas. These other kinds of trouble spots may not appear to be connected at all. Often they crop up as somatic illnesses which are never quite cured and never quite understood; migraine headaches or vague back problems are common examples of this. Sometimes the problems get drowned in just a little too much alcohol or temporarily buried with pills that lift "up" or let "down" as needed. Often they appear in overly rigid attitudes about the children or a poorly masked need to live vicariously through the kids. Sometimes a chronic depression takes hold. Sometimes activity becomes a god, and the woman cannot exist without frantic and frenetic activities. In any case, those around her suffer in a way that is hard to quantify or deal with. The loss and pain to her family has to be greater, more prolonged, more subtle, and therefore more unresolvable than any struggle in which a child has some hard knocks, a husband has to fix his own dinner, or a man has to face some rough decisions about his marriage vs. his career.

If a woman has come, through some pain and struggle, to know herself and her needs honestly, she has a pretty good sense of what fits and what doesn't fit. It can be said again that the hardest work any person can do is know himself or herself, but once that process is firmly established, a woman can never again be an object to be molded only by the forces around her. Everything she hears, everything she sees, everything she perceives has to be examined in light of who she is and where she is going in psychological terms. If something, or someone, or some experience can be mulled over, integrated, and made to fit with what she is as a person, it is ego-syntonic. And that process, going on constantly and with some awareness, has to be the happiest, most comfortable way to live. On the other hand, if a relationship or an attitude or a decision is ego-alien, it eventually will not work.

Women tend to be masters at accepting, going along, living vicariously; and American corporate wives might very well win the prize for the most flexible, the most accepting, the most selfless women in the world. The wives who have really been able to integrate this behavior into their character structure do not end up in therapists' offices. The ones for whom this behavior is ego-alien become patients and/or deteriorate into a state where they are only half-alive. The world has taught them that this is the kind of life that will make them happy, but somehow that message never got through to their guts—to their inner selves. And so it is pretty important, even if it is painful, to be honest first of all with yourself about what in your life is ego-syntonic and what in your life is ego-alien. That is part of being selfish.

## LONELINESS AT THE TOP

My survey of chief executive officers' wives—women who are at the very top of the corporate hierarchy—indicated a special problem of loneliness and isolation for them; and this would seem to dictate a special need on their part for selfishly guarding certain relationships, for taking firm stands when it seems as though they are allowed few friends. The women I interviewed repeatedly spoke of their difficulty in maintaining social relationships.

Mrs. T. A. Wilson (Boeing) said they used to have a large circle of friends, mostly Boeing people, who would get together for bridge and pot lucks. "Now we only see them at Christmas. When T. became president, all of a sudden no one called. There seems to be something magic about the title of president that changes things. Suddenly, they think you're Mrs. Big. I don't like that because I've never felt that way about myself, but other people seem

185

to get uptight." She added, "It's also very difficult to plan ahead for a party. It's frustrating because at the last minute T. might be busy or have to leave. Consequently, we don't entertain very often just for fun." Mrs. Wilson compensates with bridge, which she loves, and her relationships with "two great neighbors."

Laverne Phillips (International Multifoods) finds also that relationships within the company are difficult. "We have never made them our best friends. If anything came up, if a person had to be let go, if there were other problems in the company, perhaps friendship would get in the way. We are friendly with all the people in the company, but not inseparably."

Kathleen May (American Can) adds the dimension of time and energy: "When you get to this point, I'm sorry to say, you don't have a close circle of friends. There are very few Saturday night parties. Our weekends are quiet because our weekdays are so busy. There is energy and time for just a limited number of things of a personal nature. Now that we are approaching retirement, we may be sorry; but that's the way it is. I sometimes see old friends in the daytime, but there is never enough time. You have to husband your energies. There is just not time for everybody. Besides, the higher up you get, the wiser it is not to have your social life with anyone from the company. Everyone is tired anyway, but it is better to keep social things separate. Especially at conventions, the wives fan out to contact customers rather than talk to each other."

Her husband, William F. May, adds that "the time demands of business these days are greater rather than lesser because of what I call the killing externalities. A man has to worry about so many other things besides running the corporation. Husbands have less and less time to spend with their wives."

Asther Yogman (J. E. Seagram) is aware that "there are some women I am not to get friendly with. If there were complications in the company, if the man had to be let go or anything like that, my friendship with the wife

186

could be a problem." On the other hand, there is some clinging together. Yogman adds almost poetically: "Like the political wife, the common ground is loneliness. The political wife is always in the public eye; the corporate wives know to huddle together. Visit any business gathering or convention—the coffee and brandy groups are still separated."

The loneliness of these women at the top is special, and they certainly are entitled to special kinds of selfishness in an effort to protect some relationships for themselves. However, the points they make are in some degree applicable to all corporate wives. There are constraints on all of us regarding friendships within the company; there never is enough time to devote to personal liaisons; most corporate wives are expected to talk to customers at conventions rather than to meet their own needs. If those who aspire to the top positions have some idea of the increased loneliness there, perhaps they can make more effective efforts to build relationships now. Perhaps certain kinds of selfish behavior now would guard against any more loneliness than is necessary.

## BEING SELFISH; NOT ACTING SELFISHLY

Perhaps it is important to differentiate here between what I would call being selfish and acting selfishly. Putting oneself first does *not* mean that hurting others is the goal or necessary consequence. Sometimes the people we love must be hurt in the process of our own self-fulfillment; but if a woman is insensitive to the people around her or hurts them purposefully, we are talking about another kind of problem.

For example, if a woman goes to a convention or business meeting with her husband, she may as well face the fact that she is there precisely as an extension of him or because of him. If she goes there to bitch about his rotten boss or his many business trips, if she announces that she can't stand ladies' luncheons and won't go to an-

187

other one, if she pays no attention to her appearance or arrives at every activity late, she is a great liability for her husband and makes life unpleasant for everyone else. It would have been better for everyone if she had stayed at home.

Behavior that is motivated by hostility and deep-seated anger must be sorted out from actions that are specific and justified. The example above is not simply of a woman meeting her own needs first, but is rather a situation of hostile, destructive, selfish acting out. Any corporate wife who takes verbal pot shots at her husband's boss, flirts uncontrollably with her husband's competition, gets falling-down drunk at a company party, or refuses to discuss her husband's work with him, is not just putting herself first. She is out to destroy her husband, and any decent relationship they might have as well.

Hopefully, the idea that a wife can, and even should, be as self-involved and selfish as her husband is increasingly accepted. As Corky Miller, merchandising consultant and independent woman, puts it: "I have to choose what works best for me. I enjoy being my own person and yet being married. My field is full of successful women who work seven days a week, but couldn't possibly maintain a marriage. This is true for men too; I know men who are terribly important and successful, but they are all work; their families come last. I do not choose to have that kind of relationship, but I do need to have all the things that my work gives me too."

Both corporations and corporate wives should recognize the irony in a situation where selfishness is both desired and condemned. The corporate wife is often picked because she is dependent, but she is scolded if she is too fearful and inadequate. She is admired if she is selfless, but if she shows the effects of loss of self-esteem, she is considered a burden and is called emotionally immature. This ironic and tragic situation is beginning to be seen for what it is, but putting additional changes into practice is never easy.

188

The most difficult, nitty-gritty problems, as always, are in tricky emotional areas that are the hardest to talk about. One example of these is sex. Partners may be able to allow each other freedom or "selfishness" is almost any area, but sex is, for most people, the most loaded area of all.

Although the subjects of my *Fortune* 500 survey were sophisticated chief executive officers and their seemingly worldly wives, there were strong indications that personal freedom in sexuality is a no-no to this group. However, some younger corporate wives are admitting new awareness of sexual possibilities for themselves. Many of them are curious about the concept of open marriage. It seems that corporate wives,whose consciousnesses have been raised about other things, are beginning to ask interesting questions about what their place is in our very sexual world.

Our values have changed a lot in recent years, and the media are full of talk about a new sexuality for women. There have been some shocking and drastic developments: Birth control and liberalized abortion have made pregnancy much less of a threat; several famous women have gained attention for their decisions to have children out of wedlock; divorce hits one of every two marriages in some parts of the country; it seems as though everyone from the famous movie star to the fat suburban matron is bragging about her latest affair.

Whether or not there is much sexual acting out by businessmen, the stories and expectations are still rampant. Many people expect that businessmen, who travel a great deal, have a right to sexual activities away from home. In some situations, the executive's sexual activity may even enhance his image of power and virility. Expensive prostitutes and complicated sexual liaisons have long been provided as requested for certain types of businessmen. It is not uncommon for men to become sexually sophisticated outside the home, but perform conventionally at home to avoid suspicion and misunderstanding. One man whom I know only slightly got drunk at a party one night and "confided" to a rather large group that he was getting divorced because he forgot to pretend he was still naive. He got carried away a couple times with his wife, and tried some "tricks" he had learned from other women. She got suspicious that he hadn't just read about those things in books, started to watch him more closely, and eventually found him in bed with another woman.

On the other hand, impotence is also a fairly common problem for middle-aged executives. Often their energy has been diverted to other things, or they have been "burned out" by the pressures of the business world. Even some men who are fairly virile with other women complain of being impotent with their wives. Sometimes their wives react with anger and demands; sometimes they are relieved to forgo the sexual part of their relationship. Many couples use sex as a weapon, or they learn to avoid it completely because it is too painful.

Nevertheless, sex is still very much part of the executive's world. Several very proper, dedicated businessmen have said that much of the conference room, executive lunch table humor is no different from locker room atmosphere in college. Women that pass by may still be rated on a scale of ten to one; jokes with double entendres are still popular.

While the businessman takes some pride in his image as a sexual animal, what has been the sexual stereotype of the corporation wife? She might be described as attractive, but not sexy; friendly, but not flirtatious; interested in sex, but never aggressive about it. She would generally be expected to accept any evidence of her husband's affairs if they are handled discreetly; but any liaison she might have could be grounds for divorce. She is expected to behave "properly," and to be a passive and receptive participant in marital sex only. If she accepts the corporate party line, the wife probably considers sexual adventurousness one of the successful man's prerogatives. But any sexual desires she might have are largely denied. She closes her eyes to temptation, and tries to shut herself off from sexual feelings. Some women can sublimate those desires to such

190

an extent that they are never apparent; others seem to become increasingly frustrated, strident, and sometimes angry.

In essence, there is considerable ambivalence and conflict at all ages and at all levels of the corporate ladder in attitudes about sex for the corporate wife. The message to the liberated corporate wife seems to be: Watch out! Be careful about expressing ideas that could be held against you. Evaluate your audience. Although there may be increasing admiration for businesswomen who have "liberated" ideas, you are not seen in the same category. You may be as selfish about your sex life as you want, but you must be discreet. Decide what the stakes are and predict the possible reaction before you take the risk of exposing yourself—either literally or figuratively—in the sexual area.

One woman I interviewed was open about her sex life, and she said she risked telling me only because it might help someone else. Cassie was from a socially prominent family and had led a rather privileged life. Her husband, twenty years her senior, had been a business associate of her father's, and their very romantic, exciting affair resulted in his divorce from his wife of many years. Bill was drawn to Cassie because of her vitality and joie de vivre, and he knew her life would probably continue to include other men. At the time of their marriage Bill was executive vice-president; he was slated for the presidency and felt secure enough in his position not to "instruct" Cassie about her behavior. They were wined and dined as newlyweds by the top executives of the corporation, and Cassie, in her nervousness and naiveté, bragged honestly about their open marriage. "There were quick put-downs by other wives for almost everything I did after that, and the men made some snide remarks to Bill about his little hot number. It became clear that I was considered strange and bad by these people, but I was determined to live life my own way. Within a couple of years Bill did become president, and now I'm not particularly concerned about my image, but I was just damn lucky that I married a man so close to the top. If he had

191

been a junior executive, both of us might have been ostracized and his career adversely affected. I certainly would never be that open again with people who aren't my closest friends."

How does Bill feel about these experiences? Cassie said, "He's kind of angry about them, and kind of angry at me. We've had a few rows about it, and we just don't talk about it anymore. I want nothing to do with those stupid people he works with, but I force myself to go to a few functions during the year. The way we live is comfortable for us. But I am constantly reminded that his business associates are more square. I guess in some ways that is driving a wedge between us."

In summary, a corporate wife should be selfish and put herself first; she should be true to herself and meet her own needs first and foremost. To say it another way, both partners in a marriage should care for their own growth and fulfillment. Neither should make inordinate sacrifices for the other. Women who allow parts of themselves to slip way suffer from a very special and painful kind of loneliness. To be out of touch with one's inner self, to diminish past sources of pleasure and gratification, is gradually to denigrate the quality of living. Although wives in general, and corporate wives in particular, are discouraged from any real autonomous activities, the healthiest women are those who fight this prejudice vigorously—and selfishly. Increasingly, corporation wives will insist on personhood and will go searching after it in every possible way. Hopefully, in the near future, it will no longer be fashionable for any woman to participate in her own undoing for the sake of others—whether those others are husbands, children, or corporations.

It is also suggested, however, that the corporate wife learn quickly when to make compromises to get what she wants out of the system. It is not possible for a wife to integrate the ideas of "liberation" and "corporation" without a resounding crunch once in a while. When the two ideologies crash head on, as they must from time to time, something's got to give. Another word for that kind of give is called compromise. These compromises are as varied as the women themselves, but they are always choices. The ideal compromise, of course, would be one that both husband and wife can agree on, since both are so intricately involved in each other's life. But in the final analysis, if agreement is not possible, you, the corporate wife, must make your own choices, must assess the risks this involves, and must learn how to take responsibility for your own life.

# 8

# Figure Out the Benefits for You

If a corporate wife stops to consider all the demands on her, the lack of appreciation and compensation for her role, the hypocrisy in some of the ways she is used, she might be inclined to wonder whether she should play the game at all. She might think, "If I am really a free, liberated person, why should I choose to perform as a corporate wife?" And she *should* think, "What's in it for me? Am I getting enough out of this situation to make it worthwhile?"

The function of corporate wife would not have existed as it has for so many years if there were not tremendous benefits in it for most women. As Kathleen May (American Can) says, "How else would I ever have lived in three big cities, had lots of interesting travel [American Can has companies in thirty-one nations], met so many interesting people, and enjoyed such excellent compensation?" Many of the other women interviewed also emphasized the contacts with people. Grace Wilson (Boeing) put it this way: "Even in the past year, we have made several lasting friendships. If the executive and his wife travel, it becomes a small world; you know that you will be seeing these people again at other meetings."

Corporate benefits do not have to be the only thing in your life; there is no good reason why a woman should not be able to have some of the best of both corporation and liberation. Obviously, this involves a basic assumption that there are tremendous benefits for a woman in independence and freedom to grow as a person. What we should take a closer look at is: What are the additional benefits to her from the role of corporate wife?

The first trick is to sort out the healthy parts from the sick ones. Each woman has to do that in her own situation and has to be able to resist vigorously the things that are demeaning to her. But beyond that, each woman must weigh individually what the advantages are for her, and she should be consciously aware of the trade-offs. As some very wise philosopher once said: "You don't get nothing for nothing." Or, in the current vernacular, "There's no such thing as a free lunch."


## THREE STAGES OF THE CORPORATE WIFE'S CAREER

Kanter's explication of three stages in a corporate wife's career progression are useful in thinking about benefits.[1] These stages overlap to some extent, and they are not applicable to all corporate wives, but their general applications are apt for most women. Just as the function of corporate wife differs at each stage, so do the benefits look quite different during each period.

*The technical phase: handling exclusion/inclusion.* This is the phase where husbands have premanagement or early management jobs, when husbands are away from home a great deal, and any involvement from the wife comes in the form of technical assistance or personal support directly to him. Husbands are most concerned during this period about whether they can carry out the technical aspects of their work. The wives, at this point, form an anonymous mass, with little direct connection with the organization.

There are often more problems than benefits during this period for the corporate wife. Her husband is seldom home, has little energy left for his family, and she feels a communication problem with his jargon-laden company culture. Many wives try for a while to assume the role of assistant, but even the educated ones are unable to grasp the details and nuances of their husband's work, and they feel shut out. Confusion and tension around the issue of inclusion/exclusion can be hard on a marriage and the company is often blamed, with the wife becoming bitter and angry.

If husbands and wives both succeed to some extent at communication during this period, and if the wife realizes that her role must of necessity be limited, she can grow. More often, however, women at this stage give up the assistant's role for that of hostess, in which they have some independent territory that they can manage and be praised for.

Some women do see the lavish dinners to which they are occasionally invited as exciting and uplifting; they are home most of the day with babies and housework, and the chance to get all dressed up for a big night out is a thrill. Others, however, see these affairs as meaningless bribes—getting the little wife out of the kitchen so she won't feel left out.

Perhaps the biggest benefit during this stage is a steady income and fringe benefits like health insurance. Roles during this stage may be quite divided, with the wife totally in charge of the household. Wives may share to some extent their husband's dreams and ambitions, but their direct benefits are few.

*The managerial phase: handling instrumentality/sentimentality.* As a husband enters middle and upper management, the wife's role is shaped by her husband's involvement in company social networks. As he becomes enmeshed in the informal personal and political structure of the company, the wife's tasks involve her more directly in a social network of other husbands and wives. As the uncertainty factor increases in the husband's career, the visibility factor increases in the wife's. Since managerial performance can be assessed quite arbitrarily, nonability factors such as trust, loyalty, and fitting in well become increasingly important. Sociability and entertaining, much more private matters during the technical phase, will now receive official notice and scrutiny, often taking on political importance.

In her dealings with people, the corporate wife must now chart a course between instrumentality and sentimentality. She often must choose either the predominance of true feelings in a relationship, or the manufacture of relationships for image and manipulation purposes instead. Many wives at this stage realize that friendships are no longer a personal matter, and old friendships may have to be put aside—for example, when one husband comes to outrank another. The public consequences of relationships make it difficult to have anything but superficial friendships within the corporate structure; at the same time, so much time and energy must go into corporate entertaining that there is little time and energy left for other relationships. Entertaining people you don't like and having to look consistently cheerful and positive can lead to real duplicity in relationships.

This is the stage too at which wives can make or break their husband's career. Whether formally or informally, she becomes part of his evaluation. The company may have no formal wife-screening procedure, but unavoidably she gets looked over. She can benefit her husband's career by making important social connections, or she can damage it by acting like a shrew, showing off in front of other wives, pushing her husband's advancement too hard, discussing company business inappropriately, or being too outspoken or critical.

If the wife opts for sentimentality in relationships during this phase, she has probably hurt her husband's success and cut off her own source of support and satisfaction. Thus, she has no choice but to calculate. Perhaps the most successful maintain the pretense of sentiment even in the most instrumental dealings. In exchange for all this hard work, they then acquire some power and public importance, which is not otherwise available without a career of their own. Their satisfaction and benefits personally come in the recognition that they have an important role, even at the expense often of superficiality and loneliness.

Concomitantly, the opportunities grow during this phase for financial rewards, travel, meeting interesting people, and enhancing social skills. However, if these come at the expense of honesty with oneself, meeting one's own needs, and maintaining real communication with others, they can be empty rewards indeed.

*The institutional phase: handling publicness/privateness.* This phase occurs when the executive gets to the top of an organization or has a position where he must represent it to the world. The wife of the chief has an official role to play in the company's diplomatic system: official hostess, link to the community, mobilizer of other wives, and public relations person. The wife may, at this point, join her husband as a visible and recognized team. However, just as her role at the top becomes more rewarded and rewarding, her life also becomes more controlled. Her private life is constrained, and she has little freedom to refuse participation. Both she and her husband have less and less privacy; the distinction between work and leisure becomes blurred. At the top all friendships may have business meaning. Wives suppress private beliefs and self-knowledge in the interest of public appearance. Their volunteer and charitable activities are used to generate useful business and political connections; even their volunteer world is stratified to some extent by their husband's position.

At the top, people face nonroutine and unpredictable situations, and thus, personal trust and knowledge become especially important. The character of the company's leaders is a determinant for many decisions; wives are important here because they offer a glimpse of the leader's private being. Wives must fit the correct image and confirm the impression that the leader is trying to give. Part of the task of the wife at the top is to make an event seem personal and warm. As an instrument of diplomacy and a critical part of her husband's image, the corporate wife will hide her own opinions to preserve a united front, and play down her own interests and abilities to keep him looking like the shining star.

The corporate wife's power in this phase can be considerable, and she also has the benefit of high income and interesting experiences. However, as the description of her "ideal" role indicates, her existence can be pretty shallow. Not only is she constrained and limited, but the demands on her are heavy. The benefits are lovely, but if she gives up her personhood in the process, they can be quite worthless.

## MONEY, TRAVEL, AND PEOPLE

Assuming that the corporate wife manages to straddle both worlds, assuming that she manages to hang onto her independence and freedom, she can benefit from many shared opportunities and rewards. Although the benefits in every corporate wife's situation are idiosyncratic, there are several generalities that can be recognized.

First, executives' wives usually do well financially. Even if they are not directly paid and do not have the direct sense of earning a salary, most share handsomely in their husband's income. Many even manage the family finances because of other demands on their husband's time, and some have been able to parlay savings into substantial wealth. At the very least, corporate wives as a group have more financial security than most other groups of women, and their way of life shows it. By the time their husbands reach upper middle management, they are well dressed, able to afford the latest styles; those who wish are coifed by the city's most expensive hair-dressers; their homes are the showplaces of the area; their children attend the best schools; they belong to the best country clubs; they can buy practically anything they want. Very few women could afford this way of life without an executive husband. Even though opportunities for women in high-paying jobs are a bit better than they used to be, women still know instinctively that their chances of achieving affluence on their own are pretty dim. Whether financial success means, to a particular woman, ostentatious spending or simply security, it is a rather large part of any executive's appeal. Very few other occupations offer such substantial incomes to the middle manager and above; and probably no other occupation offers the spectacular possibilities for financial reward at the top. Even the highest paid physicians earn only as much as they can produce in the hours they want to work. Even the phenomenally paid entertainers and sports stars can usually attain those salaries for only a few years.

Corporate wives, along with their husbands, do have the worry of whether it will all last. The business world is mercurial, and executives are fired every day. Some men lose jobs for predictable and understandable reasons; other men lose out as scapegoats or because of misplaced loyalties. Especially in times of economic recession, there is always the possibility that income could cease. But there are usually good severance arrangements, and the fears of job loss are probably no greater in this field than in any other. The exposure may just seem greater since the higher the stakes, the higher the risk.

Besides the financial advantages of a good salary and benefits, there are all kinds of experiences and fringes for the corporate wife which are at least partially company-financed. Corporate wives have a right to complain about the amount of time and energy they spend entertaining and being entertained, but one almost never hears them complain about the food they must eat or the places they must go. In contrast to the politician's wife who must endure endless rubber chicken dinners in Elks Clubs or church basements, the corporate wife has usually been to the best restaurants, where she can order anything she wants. Most corporations are quite generous about entertaining any semblance of a client in the most gracious way. It is certainly a joy to go to the best restaurant in town and order filet mignon and cherries jubilee without even looking at the right-hand price column. Few women feel free to do this when the money is coming out of their pockets, and few people are able to enjoy a third party's paying so often.

Even if the corporate wife entertains at home, putting in many hours of preparation time, she is usually reimbursed sufficiently to buy the best quality meats and other ingredients, and to hire whomever she needs to help prepare and serve. To many other women who entertain purely for social reasons, this seems like a fantastic luxury.

It is not entirely clear how it has evolved that business entertaining so often requires the presence of wives. It is even less clear why so much business travel includes wives at sales meetings, conventions, industry affairs meetings, new facilities' openings, and many other functions. From a purely economic standpoint, especially in recessionary times, it would seem that the extra expense of transporting, housing, and feeding wives is wasteful indeed. However, the custom persists and probably will continue for two primary reasons: Many executives feel lonely away from home and like their wives along for company; but perhaps more important, the wives seem to insist on going. Often lonely on their own, with no separate goal or direction in their own lives, they are eager to travel as extensions of their husband.

This, of course, presents problems for the wife whose own activities and priorities may conflict with business travel. But even for these wives, there are tremendous benefits in semiforced travel. Most corporations choose desirable locations and good hotels for their meetings—if they don't, everyone complains. The resort areas like Hawaii, Bermuda, Florida, Arizona and Puerto Rico are common, especially when a company is in good financial times. And even though many activities at these meetings are mandatory, the wives usually have plenty of free time too. If she wants, a woman can always sneak a few hours alone for a good book, some extra sleep, shopping, or a swim on a secluded beach. Furthermore, it is very common for the executive and his wife to schedule a vacation immediately before or after such a meeting. What other couple, except those in business, can have air fare to a choice location paid for, have all the details of their trip worked out efficiently by someone else, and probably get a discount at one of the better hotels as well because they represent a large, important group!

Whether the travel is a vacation, semivacation, or hard-working meeting, most wives go because there are great benefits in it for them. The trips to Podunk, Idaho, or a dull association meeting may be required once in a while, but they are certainly compensated for by the more glamorous kinds of travel. Whether it is because they are more affluent or because they have more business opportunities, corporate wives are usually better traveled than other women. They tend to be more sophisticated about seeing other areas and generally more aware of the whole world.

In addition to sampling the best restaurants and hotels, corporate wives often have opportunities to meet the most interesting people. If her husband is at a high enough level in the company, the wife will be aware of how closely that business is tied in with other aspects of the community. She may have found herself at a dinner sitting next to the mayor, a legislator, judge, clergyman, director of a charitable organization, entertainer, writer, or just a person who has a fascinating hobby. Of course, if she has something to offer herself besides her role as wife and mother, these contacts can be even more stimulating and useful.

Through the company, a wife may also have access to innumerable kinds of entertainment. Most companies hold tickets for football, baseball, basketball, hockey, and any other locally popular sporting events, as well as opera, ballet, theater, repertory, and concerts. Even if one is entertaining the dullest customer and his even duller wife, it isn't so bad if the evening includes orchestra seats at a great musical comedy. And it is certainly no secret that seats not used for customers are sometimes appropriated for friends or family. This is a precious benefit indeed, and one that is often envied by nonbusiness friends, especially when tickets to a particular event are very scarce. The liberated woman who resents having to attend a sporting event with a customer, for example, might compensate by asking her husband to arrange next for an opera she adores.

By being married to an executive, a woman also is entitled to other fringe benefits, such as excellent health care coverage and resources. Most corporations have good general health insurance policies, and some offer exceptional opportunities. Edward Donley (Air Products and Chemicals) said his company is experimenting with a special preventive program by which they hope to demonstrate cost effectiveness. "We have become aware that any problem in one person tends to also create a problem in the spouse. And whether the sick person is our employee or the spouse, that becomes a problem for the company as well. This includes physical problems, alcoholism, and psychological troubles. We have just embarked on a program by which we think we'll be able to demonstrate a benefit to the company if good preventive measures are taken. If males are aware that they can prevent heart attacks, if wives are aware that they can prevent cancer, it will probably be cost effective for us. If the wife of an executive has cancer, there is a cost to the husband but also to the company while the wife goes through this trauma. Both executives and wives will be getting education and free medical exams at appropriate intervals. We probably will publish our results in some business journal."

There are also many benefits for a woman who basks in her husband's reflected glory. I have already said that a wife who has *only* this kind of vicarious existence is in big trouble. But for a woman who is secure in the knowledge that she too has accomplishments, there can be tremendous pleasure in seeing her husband's success, hearing the accolades bestowed on him, and witnessing the respect and admiration he has from others. After all, he chose her above everyone else to share his life; he still chooses her to relax with when he leaves that other world; and she has a certain specialness because of him. Being part of his world gives her opportunities she would not otherwise have. His accomplishments are not hers, but her life is better because of them.

## EVEN MOVING HAS SOME BENEFITS

One other whole area that must be examined in terms of benefits is that of moving. Many a corporate wife who has just been through the trauma of an unwanted move would be hard pressed to find any advantages here, but there are some.

First, corporations must have some awareness of the difficulties in moving, because they usually take measures to make it as smooth as possible. They make an effort to cover the costs, and most families do not suffer financially in a move. Packing is professionally done, and the individual wife finds she has leverage with the moving company because of the possibility of other business if her move goes well. A growing number of companies also assist in house sales; some actually buy the old house, others make payments until it is sold; some will cover any loss from the sale; most will pay any fees or commissions incurred in selling. Allowances are usually quite liberal also for meals, motels, and house-hunting expenses. It is not uncommon for a company to incur expenses upward of $5,000 in an executive move. For those wives who don't want to move, these financial consolations are of small value. But to the wife of a physician who wants to move his practice or a teacher who wants to relocate, they would be enormous. People in other occupations are almost forced to stay in one area if the astronomical costs of moving are not paid.

In terms of benefits also, some women find that they get tired of a house or neighborhood after three or four years, and a move is welcome. They enjoy redecorating about that time and are happy to have a convenient excuse for buying a larger, or more grand, or just a different house.

For those who are able to see change in terms of opportunities, a move can be a very exciting challenge. Change of this magnitude is not an easy situation for most corporate wives, but part of the human condition seems to be adaptability. It is amazing how frightening a new experience may seem at first; but there follows a period of adjustment, and certain new things work out to be even better than the old ones. This "adaptability" in extreme is not healthy; the desire for constant change is just as pathological as the inability to change at all. But the ability to face a new situation—quite alone—and manage despite the fear and loneliness can be an exhilarating experience. It makes a woman aware of her own inner resources. It makes her feel pride in her ability to cope, and gives her a feeling of mastery over the environment. She may still long for the relationships she left behind, but if she can survive without them and not be dependent on them, there is a feeling of strength.

One of the real difficulties in moving is that a wife is so dependent on the relationships within her nuclear family. She cannot really take friendships with her, and old relationships that may have been a great source of emotional support in the past are not available now. Consequently, she is especially dependent on her husband—the reason she moved anyway—and this can be a dangerous situation. This almost pathological dependency is not fair to either person, but it is hard to avoid. Without friends or other diversions, a wife may become preoccupied with her husband and may demand all kinds of things from him emotionally. If the marriage is in trouble, or if her husband is insensitive to this, it can be devastating. As one woman I interviewed put it, "You are so alone anyway. But if there is trouble between you and your husband, you are as alone as alone can be."

On the other hand—that is, on the benefit side—if the relationship is intact, this can be a very strengthening experience. After all, the husband is in a new situation too, and he and his wife have an opportunity to get to know each other in a new way. If they can level with each other about their fears and uncertainties, if they can avoid the games of blame, which are so easy to fall into, they can really help each other. For the first few months in a new location they will have fewer social commitments, and they can spend more time alone together or as a family. If each can try to understand what the other is going through in terms of adjustment, they can get much closer to each other and can realign their relationship, hopefully in a mutually beneficial way.

## COMMUNICATION

Because the corporate wife has more of a role in her husband's occupation than most other wives, she does have a special value and can make herself quite indispensable. In a healthy marriage, there develops a close feeling that they are "in this together" and that they share a very important piece of each other's life. In the old, regressive view of the corporate wife, this is a rather one-sided situation; the wife is encouraged to listen patiently to her husband and set the proper mood for him to communicate his worries and tensions. There is little or no emphasis on the need for him to reciprocate. However, if the two can truly be seen as partners, with the corporate wife fulfilling a specific, well-understood role, there can be an important kind of sharing and communication. The corporate wife has the opportunity to take some part in her husband's business world, to get to know his bosses, colleagues, and competitors, to get some sense of the atmosphere in which he operates. If she also knows her husband well and cares about him, she can be extremely useful in helping him subsequently to sort out feelings about people, decisions, or other actions. Her exposure to his world and to the people he associates with during working hours gives her a tool in communicating with her husband about things that matter to him. Other wives often wish they could have more firsthand knowledge of what their husband is talking about, especially in regard to the people he works with. The corporate wife has more reason than most wives to feel she is part of her husband's work and in it with him.

This at least partially explains why rich men's wives are so loyal. As most surveys of affluent people have proved, these women will tell you that *their* marriage is excellent, *their* marriage is happy. They may describe others' troubled marriages, but they would be very discreet about describing their own. Economic imperatives are at work, and they are reluctant to risk the loss of financial power for themselves as well as their family. As unhappy as the couple may be, the husband's loss of job or status would be potentially disastrous for both. As my survey bore out, corporate wives tend to say the expected, proper things. Besides the economic incentives, they have truly been ingrained with the feeling that they are in it with their husband, and that they must protect their image as well as his. Although this situation has its disadvantages if taken to an extreme, one must admire this feeling of togetherness, the working of two people who love each other toward a common goal.


## TIME TO BE ALONE

Although it may seem contradictory at first, the corporate wife who has this togetherness also has the opportunity for a great deal of aloneness and independence. In this way, she has the best of both worlds.

One of the earmarks of a successful executive seems to be a great deal of travel; another seems to be long hours of work. Both of these may mean loneliness to some women, but to the more independent woman they can be great assets. If she doesn't have to cook for her husband certain nights, she can arrange to have dinner with her own friends or catch up on her reading. She can go to meetings or work for causes he has no interest in on those nights without having to explain her absence or her motivations. She can watch whatever TV programs she wants when he is away. She can be a slob in his absence if she wishes, without any repercussions. The corporate wife usually has more time than other wives to pursue independent activities. Instead of resenting her husband's absences, the independent wife may look forward to them—not because she can't stand to be with him, but because this gives her the best of both worlds. When he is at home, she participates actively in his business life; but he is away enough to allow her a life of her own also. How she uses this potential for freedom and independence depends primarily on how she sees herself as a person.


## PERSPECTIVE

One additional benefit in corporate wifedom is that it can get better with time. The worst years are the early ones, when you seem to be trying to impress practically everyone because practically everyone is your husband's superior. You aren't yet sure how to dress, what to say, how to entertain. Your husband is progressing, but there's barely enough money to go around. You are exhausted by babies and small children and endless housework. You feel trapped and find it awfully difficult to look like the relaxed helpmate your husband is supposed to need. You wish desperately for someone who would help you so that you could have some life of your own. Maybe then you could even enjoy some of the benefits of this demanding corporate world. Almost suddenly, the children begin to grow up, the money seems more than adequate, and your husband has progressed to the point where other wives are trying to impress you. You have come to feel more secure about yourself and your abilities, and there is enough time to devote to purely personal interests—a career, hobbies, volunteer work, or whatever. In addition, you have almost miraculously developed what Burger calls a sense of perspective:

> So armed, the cliffs and peaks around you sink to their proper proportions. The fears and anxieties shrink to their true size and disappear from

# CORPORATE WIFE'S LIFE ASSESSMENT

## Advantages/benefits

Circle the number
most appropriate:

5 = totally true
4 = somewhat true
3 = neutral
2 = somewhat false
1 = totally false

1. I feel well compensated financially.

   1 2 3 4 5

2. I value the fringe benefits my husband's job provides.

   1 2 3 4 5

3. I have plenty of opportunity for business-related travel.

   1 2 3 4 5

4. I enjoy the business-related traveling I do.

   1 2 3 4 5

5. I have met many interesting people through my husband's job.

   1 2 3 4 5

6. I like to socialize with most of the people my husband works with.

   1 2 3 4 5

## Disadvantages/drawbacks

Circle the number
most appropriate:

1. I often feel taken for granted.

   1 2 3 4 5

2. I sometimes wonder why I don't get paid for being a corporate wife.

   1 2 3 4 5

3. I resent feeling that I can't express my opinions in business-social situations.

   1 2 3 4 5

4. I find most of our business-social contacts boring or unlikable.

   1 2 3 4 5

5. I get nervous or resentful when I have to go along on a business trip.

   1 2 3 4 5

6. I would much rather be entertaining my own friends than his business people.

   1 2 3 4 5

210

7. His job does not make inordinate demands on my time. 1 2 3 4 5

8. I feel free to express most of my opinions in business-social situations. 1 2 3 4 5

9. I feel I have a separate life of my own without always involving my husband. 1 2 3 4 5

10. If I suddenly found myself a widow or divorcée, I'm sure I could support myself. 1 2 3 4 5

11. If I suddenly found myself a widow or divorcée, I'm sure I would be all right emotionally. 1 2 3 4 5

12. I feel I share equally in communication with others. 1 2 3 4 5

Total _____

If this total is larger, okay.

7. Because of him and his job, I have little time for myself 1 2 3 4 5

8. I get upset when he is gone a lot. 1 ,2 3 4 5

9. I worry about his getting involved with another woman when he travels. 1 2 3 4 5

10. My whole life is devoted to him; I could never support myself. 1 2 3 4 5

11. If I suddenly became a widow or divorcée, I might crack emotionally. 1 ,2 3 4 5

12. I share equal responsibility with my husband for his success. 1 2 3 4 5

Total _____

If this total is larger, trouble.

the horizon. The panorama before you stretches on and on with balance and restraint. We refer to it admiringly, but all too rarely, as a sense of values.[2]

Another name for the same phenomenon would be maturity; my own husband calls it mellowing. Almost without exception, corporate wives do agree that the situation gets better with time. Whether it is due to age, or experience in the corporate structure, or a combination of both, the wisdom and maturity that usually come after a few years in this role result in a woman's being more able to be simply herself. If she doesn't get too caught up in the demands of the second and third "phases" of her corporate wife career, she will realize that she can have some of both worlds. She becomes more confident in whatever her choices are as a corporate wife, and somehow the whole thing becomes more comfortable with time.

Regardless of the time phase you find yourself in at this point, you might try to assess your own degree of comfort by figuring out the advantages and disadvantages in the chart provided. There are no right or wrong answers in this list, but honest answers are required. What will evolve is an indication of your value system, and the degree to which your life as a corporate wife fulfills your values or needs. If, in adding up the numbers, the advantages outweigh the disadvantages, you are in pretty good shape. However, if the disadvantages outweigh the advantages, you have some important work to do.

## TOWARD A JOINT PERSPECTIVE

We cannot leave the subject of benefits without touching on the benefits that accrue to a man from his wife's liberation. Just as a wife must assess what the benefits are for her in the corporate wife role, it is partly her job to help her husband see how much he will benefit if that is not her *only* role. Many men these days don't need any convincing. But those who cling to traditional roles for emotional reasons, for those who have been turned off by the harsh, negative publicity that has accompanied the women's movement, could benefit from some gentle persuasion as well as some hard facts.

The economic benefits of a wife who chooses a career are fairly clear; she adds income to the family resources, and her husband knows she can earn a living in the event of his loss of job, death or divorce. Emotionally, a man is usually relieved when his wife's happiness or unhappiness is no longer dependent solely on him. Her independent pursuits might even result in important business contacts for him. Furthermore, an independent, resourceful woman is usually more interesting to live with, and most husbands like to feel proud of their wives. There are many, many other benefits to a husband whose wife is independent, but hopefully he will find these out for himself. In the meantime, if he is convinced that there are benefits in the situation for him, his support and encouragement will be an invaluable asset. Just as many men in our survey said that their attitudes about women were shaped by their wife, many women said that the cooperation of their husband had been invaluable.

A liberated woman can find an awful lot of benefits in also being a corporation wife. Similarly, an executive may not be very stimulated by living with the traditional corporate wife, but if the same woman also has some independence and liberation, there are greater benefits for him. If both partners communicate their needs and desires clearly and can also compromise as the need arises, there is a good chance that they can have the best of both worlds and have to give up neither one. The corporate wife who takes a good look at the benefits for her in that system can meet the demands of her role with less resentment and with more feeling of power and control over her own life.

# 9

# Try to Separate Bitterness and Hostility from Justified Anger

Various studies have proved that women are notoriously unable to handle angry feelings. Most women have been raised to "make nice" and have been taught that shouting and disagreeing and confronting are quite unladylike.

Women are not alone in their difficulty with angry feelings. Men too have a hard time using anger constructively. Many men swing between rage and compliance, and many find the whole range of emotions in between quite puzzling to handle. Nevertheless, most men have been given "permission" as children to fight, to be angry, or to fly into rages. The fact that most boys are raised to deny sentimental or soft emotions, and have difficulty with tenderness and vulnerability, is as handicapping for them as the difficulty with anger is for women. Hopefully, both of these sexist situations are changing, but there is still a lot of reinforcement in our society for both men and women to maintain their traditional positions.

The reinforcement for the corporate wife to stay in her place is enormous. If she is an attractive, compliant, helpful, noncompetitive, unaggressive person, she will probably receive a lot of compliments from other executives as well as their wives. On the other hand, if she has controversial opinions and a great deal of independence, she may be branded a troublemaker; and if she refuses to move or entertain, she will probably be ostracized.

The course of least resistance for most corporate wives is to accept their role as extension of their husband and repress or swallow any resentment or anger about their place or lack of place in the world. Does this mean that most cooperative, conciliatory corporate wives do not have angry feelings? To the contrary—it is more likely that the anger has been directed inward or has been diverted into other emotions such as bitterness or general hostility.

Recently, after I had made a seminar presentation at a community college, the hand of an attractive young woman down in front shot up. She said, "I feel like you've been talking directly to me. I was just married a year ago, and we moved here from Chicago because my husband was transferred by his large company. I had hoped and planned to go to law school, but I see now that it would be impossible. We will have to move many times in the next twenty years. Even if I could somehow get through school in one place, I couldn't plan to work for any law firm more than a short time. I would constantly be having to take the bar exam in a new state, and I would usually have to start from scratch in a new law firm. Those are too many obstacles, and I just can't see any change ahead. For the past year I've been sinking deeper and deeper into depression, and I'm more and more hostile about everything." I asked her if she had tried expressing her disappointment and anger to her husband, and she said, "Yes. He didn't understand at first, but he knows that I come from a family of professional women, and he always knew I wanted to go to law school. He is finally accepting that this would be a rotten life for me, and consequently, it could be a rotten life for him too. We are in a couples group now, and we're beginning to talk about maybe going into business for ourselves." This woman recognizes the differences between specific anger and generalized hostility. She sees the beginnings of something she doesn't like in herself and is trying to stop it.

When women are unable to express anger directly, they tend to change in one of two ways: (1) They blame themselves for feeling angry; they feel guilty and gradually become less and less alive, less and less vibrant or resourceful. (2) The anger becomes like a simmering disease, spreading to all areas of life, making them sour and bitter and hostile.

Either of these processes may occur so gradually and so spontaneously that it is hardly recognized until it is almost too late. A corporate wife who knows how to play the proper role may be able to hide what is happening to her from most people, but certainly her family will feel the effects. And any woman who deals with anger in this way is really committing slow emotional suicide. A half-alive person or a bitter, hostile one is not very much good to herself or to others. Either way, she is really existing rather than living. How sad that the alternative—direct expression of justified anger—eluded her or was somehow not acceptable!

## LIKE POLITICAL WIVES

Good analogies can be made between the politician's wife and the wife of an executive. They both must be ready to move, entertain, and look right at all times. There is very little area in which they can develop their own interests; they must always be in their husband's background. Among any group of politicians' wives or corporate wives can be found a large percentage of bitter, hostile women. Myra MacPherson's recent book *The Power Lovers: An Intimate Look at Politicians and Their Marriages* documents the incidence of depression, alcoholism, resentment, and bitterness. These qualities may be masked and hidden from the casual observer, but they

217

are unmistakable to those who know the politician's or executive's wife well. Some would say that these women have every right to feel resentful and hostile. They have been sold a rotten bill of goods, and they have no real forum to protest. The pressures on them to conform are tremendous.

Some of the instructions given to political wives are almost unbelievable. Just five years ago, the House Republican Campaign Committee told the spouses of some Republican congressional candidates: A good wife never appears in public without being extremely conscious of how her every action might affect her husband's political fortunes. She should never put herself into a position in which her photograph might be taken while holding a cocktail glass or cigarette. And of course, she should never drink liquor in a public place where it could embarrass her husband. She should never chew gum. She should never yawn. She should never offer someone a limp or flabby handshake, but she should guard against a steely grasp that might be interpreted as unladylike. Her hair should be done frequently, in an attractive and conventional manner. She should not wear too much perfume. And she should salute the American flag in a particular way.[1]

Although the corporate wife's orders may not be written, they are often equally stringent and structured. There are films that some companies use to teach wives how to dress, how to entertain—"always be charming, gracious, prepared"—and how to provide "a happy, tranquil home, a haven from the workday 'battleground.' "[2]

Thankfully, both politicians' wives and executives' wives have made some strides in breaking out of their molds. The *Wall Street Journal* recently reported that wives' worries are making it harder to recruit candidates for Congress.[3] The Senate GOP Committee had stated that publicity about sex scandals makes women leery of letting their husbands run for office. In addition, more wives now work, and they resist moves to Washington that would disrupt their careers. There have also recently been publications from George McGovern's wife and Eu-

218

gene McCarthy's ex-wife detailing the less attractive aspects of their roles. Nevertheless, the wives of our president and vice president, Rosalynn Carter and Joan Mondale, are still engaged in full-time but totally unpaid jobs. They have both received much public attention for their work on behalf of the country, and perhaps this is enough for someone in such a powerful and visible position; but is it fair that they receive no salary and have no official recognition? What if, by some miracle, a president was elected whose wife had a career of her own?

The wife of one U.S. diplomat noted in print that she must work very hard while stationed overseas at her unpaid job. She is a doctoral candidate with a limited time to finish her dissertation, but she said, "I hardly have time to do my research since we must entertain all the time. Cocktail parties are important because this is when a lot of information is passed on." She added that the wives of Japanese diplomats who learn the language are paid for the time they spend entertaining and speaking with people in their host country, but no other nation pays the spouses of diplomats.[4]

Many women would feel that such a system is not fair to them, and a buildup of resentful, hostile feelings is really a terrible burden. It is like unwanted but necessary baggage which weighs you down. It is certainly not a useful tool in any constructive way. It does not help you to accomplish any changes—either in yourself or the world around you. On the other hand, anger that is direct, pointed, focused can be a fantastically constructive tool. Whereas bitterness tends to make you an object, justified anger makes you a force in the environment to be reckoned with. A little righteous indignation is long overdue among both political and corporate wives. A sense of independence and the feeling that they are in control of their own lives will make them more alive, more interesting people. Reasonable anger when certain things are demanded of them unjustly is a must.

But how can a woman rid herself of these burdens of bitterness and hostility? How can you respond with appropriate anger at the specific situation rather than disappointment and bitterness at the whole world? First, you must know yourself well enough and be honest enough with yourself to admit what has happened to you. You must recognize that you have developed a particular way of looking at the world and at experiences, but it is important for you also to recognize that your behavior has been learned. Obviously, behavior that has been learned can also be unlearned. Also, you should know that your reactions are not neurotic and unjustified. You probably can recite a long list of injustices or experiences that have made you feel this way.

Understanding the motivations of others and of yourself can provide the key. There are basically two things to understand.

First, you just happened to have been raised in a social system that has been unfair to women; but that is not really anybody's fault. Although it seems easy to blame this chauvinistic system on men, that is not very helpful because men have been victimized by the system too. Certainly the economic benefits in using corporate wives to get two employees for the price of one have been enormous. And many men have needed to dominate their wives to salve their own insecure egos. Clearly, also, most men who have had all the benefits of a master-slave marriage would be hard pressed to give them up—unless they become aware of other consequences or other alternatives. The corporate wife who feels victimized should make some effort to understand the culture in which her husband was raised also. If you can see him as a product, even as a victim to some extent, of a social system, he may seem like less of an ogre, and the world may seem a little less oppressive.

Second, the corporate wife who has become bitter should take some responsibility for her reactions. True, you did not feel, as it was happening, that you had much choice; but each woman does have some choice about her reactions, and the women who have acted, rather than simply *re*acted to things that were happening to them, have usually emerged from the corporate battle with less bitterness and less resentment. Again, if you can accept the fact that you have choices and can take the responsibility for your actions, change is quite possible and almost easy. The difference between a woman who acts and one who primarily reacts can be the difference between an appropriately angry woman and a bitter, hostile one. Most women would agree that life is a pretty difficult struggle when everything is seen from behind a veil of resentment and bitterness.

## THE IMPORTANCE OF HUMOR

If a woman can somehow separate these two kinds of emotions, she can certainly deal with specific situations much more clearly. If you are generally seen as a person who is not hostile, your negative reactions will be listened to and respected much more. If you get some real perspective on what things are fair to you and what things are unfair, some of the corporate demands and corporate game-playing can be almost humorous. Some of the prescriptions that people try to place on you are really so ludicrous and ridiculous that your anger might genuinely be coupled with some lighthearted humor. A mature woman who has a strong sense of herself probably learns gradually when it is most effective to use pure, unadulterated anger, and in what situations it is more effective to tinge that justified anger with the humor in the situation.

One chief executive officer's wife responded to my questionnaire by writing across the face of it: "I'm not going to answer these questions. I'm divorcing the lousy bastard if he doesn't join me in a commune. Peace!!" She also chose to identify herself. Is this anger? Is this humor? Sounds like a pretty strong combination of both. At least, it sounds like a woman of action—certainly not a victim. A woman who can separate general hostility from specific anger should be able to deal effectively even with situations that test her tolerance to the limit.

Jackie Guinn, a bright, attractive woman whose husband Chet is vice-president of sales for Longview Fibre in San Francisco, described a beautifully typical example. "I think we have worked out one big problem which all corporate wives encounter too often. You have just started a new, complicated recipe, and the phone rings. Guess what; he won't be home for dinner; so and so is in town. After a few years of almost having a stroke, I really let go—banged the receiver down so hard, the phone nearly came off the wall. Needless to say, the next evening there was a little more than chitchat over our martini. However, I explained—into his good ear—that the banging didn't really do any harm; it did do me a world of good. So that has been our solution to a very sticky problem. You will know my husband; he's the one who holds the phone at arm's length after five P.M."

You can even force yourself to be amused at the ridiculous way corporate wives are pictured in the media. Despite the very definite effect of the women's movement on most aspects of the media, the "ladies' magazines" are still full of articles such as "Your Happiness and Your Husband's Ego."[5] They contain statements such as "to armour your husband against his intensely competitive world, to make him happy and better equipped to make you happy, give him the gift he needs most—build up his ego." Nothing about gut-level, honest communication, even when it may mean disagreeing with him. Nothing about the equally difficult demands and pressures on wives, and the right to expect support from a husband as well as giving it to him. Only the assumption that wives are naggers and criticizers and must be taught to take the pressures off their husband, appreciate him, and listen to him endlessly.

222

I hope we will never again see advertising like the United Airlines' "Take Me Along" campaign of a few years ago. The tune was catchy, but the message was extremely demeaning: the little wife is sitting at home aimlessly and would be just thrilled if her big, important, executive husband would offer to take her along on his next business trip.

Business publications tend to deal seriously with the role of wives only when they get out of line or cause some kind of trouble. In his book *Up the Organization,* Robert Townsend has only one thing to say about corporate wives: "The worst wives (from the standpoint of the effect on their husbands) in my experience are the overly ambitious ones. They seem constantly after their husbands to make more money. They don't understand that money, like prestige, if sought directly, is almost never gained."[6] Nothing about the best wives. Nothing about what husbands don't understand in their wives.

Similarly, another management report mentioned the problems that wives of executives exhibit.[7]

1. They are prone to drink too much.
2. They are often domineering.
3. They are poorly informed.
4. They may be mentally underdeveloped in comparison to their husbands.
5. They tend to be resentful toward the firm for taking away their husbands.
6. Traveling husbands may result in lonely wives, deterioration of their sexual life, and possibly promiscuity on the part of the wives.

Nothing about whether the demands on wives are fair or realistic. Nothing about the possible need for some righteous anger when there is little understanding of their role.

Most corporate wives also hear this line of thinking constantly from other corporate women. It is especially hard to handle when this comes straight from the mouth of the president's wife or the wife of the chairman of the board. But it is really not much cause for bitterness. It is somewhat funny to think of wives disappearing so much into the woodwork, to think of women who describe themselves as such nonentities that they are almost nonpeople. The thought of wives' being so undemanding and unassuming is also quite boring these days to both men and women who are part of the real world. And it is almost pathetic to hear it from women who can see themselves only in this way. They are missing so much out of life and have allowed themselves to be such second-class citizens; surely one must have some pity for them. The kind of philosophy these women espouse cannot be harmful to the secure woman *unless* it is applied to her or forced on her in some active way; and then there is room for justified anger.


## FIGHTING BACK

Most independent corporate wives find that they must gently but constantly remind the people around them that they have needs too. When they find themselves doing this with executives or other corporate wives, it often falls on deaf ears. There may be a polite response, but the liberated woman knows she is not understood and is probably considered rather odd. The bitter woman may feel she is on a crusade to change her listener's opinion about women. The appropriately angry woman does not feel like any kind of crusader; she tries to get across that she is primarily talking about herself. And she gets some benefit—some catharsis—from simply expressing herself, even though her opinions may be controversial. She has been true to herself by making her feelings known. If she gets some understanding or some interest from her listener, it is an added bonus.

She might, for example, find herself in a situation

where she is told that it is her job to create a warm environment that welcomes her husband's thoughts and words. It is her job to help him any way she can. "The executive provides the money for maintenance of the family home. His wife provides the mood."[8]

No independent corporation wife could hear this kind of one-sided, unrealistic prescription and not feel angry. It makes her about as adult and effective as a Barbie doll. It makes all kinds of assumptions about roles that don't have to be true. It assumes a very unequal relationship—hardly a partnership of any kind. It denies that the husband should also try to create a tension-free environment and that her need to be listened to and responded to is just as great as his. For the reasons already stated, most liberated women would want to react to this with justified anger. Beyond the cathartic effect, these reactions could possibly be educational for someone who has never given much thought to what these words imply.

I know the wife of a company vice-president who was told by the president's wife, "This is your company as much as your husband's. Whether or not it prospers is your responsibility as much as his." This young woman happened to have a part-time job on a newspaper as well as two small children. Her answer was a polite "I'll do what I can" to the president's wife, but her discussion with her husband that evening was much more direct. He convinced his wife that he understood her feelings; he did not expect her to be constantly available. In fact, he was somewhat offended that the boss's wife did not think he could do the job on his own. They were both able to joke about the situation a little, and speculate on what they might have said if this person were not the boss's wife.

If a woman finds that she is hearing these ideas from her own husband, she should be justifiably angry indeed. She will find his philosophy of their marriage in direct opposition to her own, and some kind of struggle will have to take place between them. Many women who have not been trained to handle angry feelings

225

find it difficult to stand up to their husband's rage or wrath, but more and more women are learning not to back down. Reasonable people will usually respect an honest expression of anger, and will make some effort to understand it. It helps if the angry wife also makes an effort to explain the source of her anger and the reason this particular thing set her off. The corporate wife who is having a hard time getting through to her husband might also remind herself that the alternatives to anger —depression and bitterness and half-life—are terribly self-destructive. Hopefully this will give her courage to go on, even when the odds against her seem tremendous.

The young woman who looked ahead twenty years and saw she could never be an attorney if she was also a corporate wife had some heavy odds against her. She was newly married; her husband was a businessman when she married him; she knew that moving would be their way of life; he seemed happy with his job and was having some success. Some people would say she had no right to disrupt his life this way. Nevertheless, her own feelings were very real; she had been surprised herself by the intensity of her bitterness when she realized she could not have a life of her own. Her persistence in bringing this into the open will, in the long run, be much healthier for both of them than a lingering, festering bitterness underneath supposed acceptance. In a situation such as this, there are many alternatives, even though none of them is perfect. Their marriage could end; her husband could ask to stay in one place, at least for a while. Their tentative plan for him to go into business on his own is just one other alternative; but the important issue is that they care about each other's feelings, and they could not possibly have a happy marriage if one of them totally subjugated herself or himself to the other.

If your anger is validly based, if there is truly something unfair and demeaning to you in the situation, if you are able to communicate your anger effectively, you will most likely emerge with a feeling of resourcefulness and control over your own life that will be quite exhilarating. Successful experiences with handling anger directly will build on each other, and gradually you will find yourself more and more comfortable with those feelings and more and more constructive in the way you use them.

## MOVING IS SPECIAL

The corporate wife has many sources of anger—unfair demands about entertaining, her husband's refusal to let her take a job, unreasonable responsibilities left to her for raising the children or managing the household, or any of the many other questionable tasks given to the corporate wife. But, in a very specific way, corporate wives should examine their reactions about moving. They should honestly question whether they are overtly going along because they don't feel they have any choice but are covertly channeling angry feelings into depression or general bitterness.

Frequent geographical moves are usually the way of life for the corporate executive on the way up. My survey indicated that there is some difference among companies as to how much moving is required, and there is also more moving in certain specialties, such as marketing, than in others. Nevertheless, it has generally been assumed that any executive who refuses to move has probably put the brakes on his upward mobility in that corporation. Most wives would be very reluctant to take responsibility for sabotaging their husband's career, on which they themselves are so dependent. They instead go along—denying any feelings other than acceptance, and probably diverting their anger and resentment into less recognizable forms.

There is just beginning to be significant examination of the effects of moving on women. In the very important study done at Yale, the researchers found that moving is often a strong factor in a woman's depression, but more often than not, the woman herself is

227

not even aware of this as a cause. Her hostility has been turned inward and has become depression. She has been so programmed to accept this as part of her role that she cannot allow herself to face her feelings honestly. The Yale study found that "most depressed patients are not hostile during psychiatric interviews or with strangers."[9] Indeed, they are able to mask most negative feelings. Depression, once considered an illness of menopausal women, is now common in women of all ages from all economic and ethnic groups, and research shows that certain kinds of mobility are often a causative factor.

Moving in and of itself is not bad. In fact, many women experience excitement in the change and are able to see moving in terms of new opportunities. But the stress involved should not be minimized. One cannot move without having to adapt in many ways, and moving presents tremendous challenges to one's identity.

Jackie Guinn says, with a smile, "What's worse than being asked for a local reference and having to admit that the only person you know is your real estate agent." But she adds, in a more serious vein, "The husband is challenged—I hate that word; the wife and children have to adjust—another baddy."

In an article euphemistically called "The Power of Positive Moving," the disruption of life-style is described: "The major casualty is invariably the unemployed mother whom we find amid the packing cases, the kids at new schools, the husband at a new job meeting new people, while she sits alone in a strange house waiting for a psychic Welcome Wagon that never comes."[10] And as one highly mobile executive explained in a *Time* magazine article, nomads purposely avoid any community ties: "We've discovered that to prevent the pain of saying goodbye, we don't say hello any more."[11]

Although most of the chief executive officers' wives I interviewed presented a cooperative, intact facade about moving, several of them also acknowledged the difficulties.

Laverne Phillips (International Multifoods) had lived in Cleveland all of her life until seven years ago. She had raised her family there, had many friends and relatives there, and still had a son in high school when the move to Minnesota came up. "I went along because the new job was a challenge for my husband, but I can see how difficult it would be if you have to move over and over. So much depends on the attitude of the wife and mother. The gal's attitude is so important for the rest of the family. It took three or four years for me to reestablish myself here. Now I am too involved again. I always felt secure and was never concerned, but the transition did take time."

Martha Smith (Copperweld Corporation) has made four moves and acknowledges that they haven't all been by choice. "I am grateful we haven't had to move more often. It is harder on kids to move than most people want to recognize. My kids adjusted because they could see there was not much alternative. My orientation was basically a positive one. In a business situation, you realize that the whole family is going to benefit by moving."

However, when you are on the move frequently, you cannot have very deep roots in any one place. You cannot have more than very superficial impact on the community or any group of friends. Your ties with your extended family must be loosened when you don't see them very often. Even money doesn't help very much in establishing meaningful connections with a community or a group of people. Money cannot be used to buy your way into most groups; in order to have status or power or authority in most groups, you have to be around awhile —sometimes for generations. Some people find that they can exist very well without this kind of community involvement, but for many corporate wives, it is just that— existing. By contrast, it is a feeling of rootedness, of involvement with the community, of meaningful relationships with friends, that turns existing into living for most of us.

Although it is reasonable to think of moving in terms of opportunities, one cannot deny that there are losses. The losses for skilled and professional women may be significant as they search in vain for similar or equal positions, but the losses for the housewife with small children are also painful. Men too experience losses in a move, but the executive is usually welcomed into the new community through his work, and he almost always makes the move with more feeling of purpose. A man who works does not quickly develop friends, but he immediately has a circle of acquaintances with at least their work in common. Any woman who does not work will probably find it much more difficult to develop relationships. The common denominator for women with young children seems to be an interest in the children's activities. The PTA or the local swim club may be the best way to strike up conversations, but these are not confidences, and the people may or may not ever become friends. Both men and women often find church an easy way to break into a community, but churches, like all organizations, have their hierarchies and their testing systems.

Women, who are culturally more prone than men to rely on relationships, often feel a strong need for someone outside the family to talk to. When a woman is on the move, her old friends no longer quite fill the bill. As time and distance separate them, there is less gratification from even a long phone conversation. Many women move with the feeling that they will maintain these precious friendships, but gradually feel them slipping away, almost against their will. New relationships are not yet trustworthy, and certainly the woman does not want to be known as a parasite on her new acquaintances.

In general, people who move go through a period of aloofness, which masks their anxiety about whether they will really be accepted or will fit in. There is no way to shortcut the testing period to determine which acquaintances, if any, will become friends. This process can last for varying lengths of time, and the corporate wife during this period is really in transition. The old friendships no longer feel comfortable; the new relationships are a bit suspect and awkward. In many ways she is quite alone, quite alienated from what may at other times be a primary source of gratification and pleasure.

The pressure on the small family unit of husband, wife and children during this period is tremendously intense. Without gratification from other relationships, the nuclear family members may demand outrageous and impossible things from each other. They may unconsciously try to consume each other with their needs and their emotions. They may unrealistically look within the family for reestablishment of their identity. This turning upon each other of family members is a dangerous and potentially explosive situation. If the corporate wife does not recognize it for what it is, if she does not force herself to look outside her family for gratification, she will probably become increasingly bitter and resentful. After all, she has moved because of her husband, but he is busy and preoccupied with learning a new job. She has probably coordinated the move around the needs of her children, and yet they do not seem to understand her or appreciate her. She feels let down by the only people she really cares about because they can never really replace her friends, her community contacts, and her feeling of rootedness.

If the corporate wife can focus angry feelings and express them directly when unfair demands are made on her, it is unlikely that she will sink into bitterness and hostility. If her husband is too concerned with his work and uses that to escape from the chores of moving, she can tell him how that makes her feel and can make reasonable demands that he share these thankless tasks. If her children make constant demands on her because they too are missing their friends and identities, she can point out what is happening and refuse to be their doormat. If she needs her husband's business contacts to help reestablish herself in the new community, she can push him to help her find a job or introduce her to the proper people for membership in volunteer committees or whatever. She can tell him that she is not married to his job. She can declare loud and clear that even though it is a prescription for the executive's wife, patience is *not* her middle name. This appropriate use of justified anger might simply be called assertiveness; it makes her a force in the environment. On the other hand, bitterness and hostility can easily become the "baggage" of the victim.

The denial of, or defense against, all of these feelings can result in a state called anomie by the sociologist Emile Durkheim. Anomie is truly a feeling of disorientation, uselessness, purposelessness. Even hostility and bitterness are preferable to this state, but it is not hard to see how anomie develops in a corporate wife who feels rootless and alienated. She may have experienced moving many times, or she may have gone through the process just once. Whether her reaction is rational or irrational doesn't really matter. What matters is her feeling that there is no point in involvement; why should she try to make friends? Why should she put herself out? Why should she risk being hurt again? Why should she care about herself or anyone?

An executive who recognizes this state of mind in his wife may initially find it quite acceptable; she doesn't bother him and she doesn't really seem sad or depressed. But she has really committed emotional suicide, and if his mobile way of life continues, she will probably never recover. He may not know it initially, but he will be living with an invalid for the rest of his—or her—life. If he is a man of any introspection, he will probably take some responsibility for her anomie. Most probably, he will eventually come to wish that she were bitter or hostile, or even vicious. How much better yet if she had been able to express her anger at the way of life both he and she chose. How much better if she had not felt she had to adhere to her traditional role. How much better if she had refused to accept the excessive renunciations that moving required of her.

A woman in one of my seminars said that she had moved to Seattle five years ago after almost twenty years in California. She had gone back to school there to get her teaching credentials and had worked the final eight years there in an exciting elementary-school program. Nevertheless, her husband saw an excellent opportunity in Seattle, where he also preferred the quality of living. "I agreed, but I gave him an ultimatum; I said now he would have to promise to stay with me the rest of his life because he had taken away my source of support and all my meaningful friendships. There is no way that I could get another teaching job in this market; my children are grown and are no source of support for me; and I am not the type who makes friends easily." How did her husband react to her ultimatum? "He accepted it. He knows I'm right."

It is not very pleasant to contemplate this woman's dependence on her husband, when she had worked so hard for independence in California. And it is not very romantic to realize that he must stay with her regardless of what may happen in both their lives. But her assertion and her anger are valid, and she made a reasonable pact with him. It is certainly better than underground hostility; and it is far preferable to anomie.

## RISKS AND REWARDS OF APPROPRIATE ANGER

Expressing anger, even when it is clearly and totally justified, is not without risks. The biggest risk, of course, is the loss of a mate; but most liberated women could tolerate that risk. The executive who puts obstacles in his wife's way will and should be the primary target of her justified anger; and this of necessity becomes a risky situation. But it is terribly important for the corporate wife to see her husband's actions for what they are. For example, if a wife's independence includes getting a job, the executive will probably not be threatened by the challenge to his earning power as a lower-class man might be. But he will most likely resist the loss of her free time to travel with him or entertain for him or devote herself to his needs. These kinds of prejudices on the

233

part of men are ingrained from childhood and are especially strong in executives who are used to being waited on by secretaries and other underlings. They can best be handled by the corporate wife honestly, expressing how these things make her feel, and by standing firm in her assertiveness to be as complete a person as she can. Most men will thus be helped to identify their unconscious prejudices and will even respect their wife's anger.

On the other hand, some corporate wives, in facing their husband's resistance, will see that their man is motivated by insecurity and fear. This kind of man may be terribly afraid that his wife's freedom will bring her to his level and will make him less of a man. A woman who sees this for what it is has a difficult task. She may be able to convince him herself, or through counseling, that her separate identity need not diminish him. She may even be able to demonstrate gradually some benefits for him. But if it seems clear that he would rather deal with her neurotic behavior than her honest anger and assertiveness, their relationship probably should not continue. To stay in that relationship would be extremely self-destructive on her part.

There is beginning to be slight recognition in corporate circles that there is some value to the "ornery" wife. A woman who does not simply adapt on demand, a woman who does not simply accept all that is asked of her, is probably also a woman who has pride and character. She is probably also someone who can think more clearly and who can make more critical judgments. Those qualities are beginning to be respected in a corporate wife because they are ultimately a help to her husband. They allow him to grow also in small and unsuspected ways. The woman who can be ornery or justifiably angry from time to time does not tend to burden herself and her husband with pervasive bitterness and hostility. The woman who has learned to recognize the differences between these emotions has a head start in relating to her husband and the world.

# 10

# Be Willing to Take Risks

It is an integral part of our social system that women are dependent on men. To quote Gloria Steinem: "There is still the assumption that a woman is not a complete human being by herself . . . We have to consider the ways in which we are man junkies."[1]

Most corporate wives could be accurately and succinctly described as man junkies. They are reluctant to explore alternatives for themselves largely because they are so afraid to take risks. They have been conditioned to view their future and the futures of their children in terms of their husband's success, and a more independent stance seems terribly frightening. They are, of course, reinforced by the whole corporate structure wherein their dependence is an economic asset; and, in many cases, the system is abetted by their husbands, whose insecure egos are threatened by their wives' assertiveness. However, as all successful people have had to learn, our self-esteem is largely of our own making, and self-esteem almost never comes without taking some risks. It can be said in very simplistic terms: In order to go forward, we have to pick at least one foot up off the floor.

A woman who decides to buck this well-entrenched system by living through herself rather than through her husband faces some pretty formidable odds. The powerful corporate structure labels her different, strange, a suspicious character, and perhaps even a little bit crazy. Other corporate wives are awed by her or threatened by her and tend to ostracize her. Her own husband may not understand her and may resent the inferences his associates make. Other men may put her down when she tries to talk to them on their own level, or may think she is on the make because she is interested in them as people. Because there are significant benefits for the corporate wife who stays in her place, there are concomitantly significant risks for the corporate wife who does not accept the traditional role.

## THE MARRIAGE COULD END

The biggest and most frightening risk is that the marriage itself will end. For many women, the mere thought that they might have to make decisions, if not support themselves, is enough to keep them quietly subservient and immobilize them completely. Many of these women married young. The wife may have worked at a menial job just long enough to put her husband through school and get him launched on his career. She happily looked to her husband as the breadwinner and sought to elevate her social and economic status entirely through him. She correctly evaluated the special advantages men have in our society. She put all the effort she could into "catching" the right man; and then she stood by his side and waited for him to provide the comforts and upward mobility that are part of the American dream. Only after several years of marriage did she become dimly aware of the power struggle going on between her and her husband. Only reluctantly does she admit even to herself that the money her husband makes has other meanings besides just financial ones. Only in neurotic ways, perhaps, can she begin to expose her loneliness, disappointment, boredom, and fears.

These women may wonder about equal opportunities for themselves and may begin to wish for a more equal partnership in marriage, but the possibility of losing that marriage seems to leave them with nothing. They are totally unprepared to face life without a husband; almost any amount of distress seems better than being alone. If a woman knowingly shakes up the equilibrium in her marriage, she must accept responsibility for some kind of consequences. If she tries her damndest to keep the status quo, she probably feels the chances are better that her marriage will survive intact.

But this kind of thinking is full of fallacies. Specifically, every wife should know that she is always just one second away from being alone anyway. A sudden heart attack or an automobile accident could make her a widow tomorrow; a relationship with another woman or simply a dissatisfied, reevaluating husband could make her a divorcée overnight. To allow herself to remain totally dependent on her man and on her marriage is to put herself in an extremely vulnerable position.

The displaced homemaker is finally beginning to receive the help and attention she deserves, but until recently she was a nonentity. She may have served many years as somebody's wife, but she is probably not eligible for welfare or social security, and she is untrained or too old for entrance into the labor market. Jill Ruckelshaus, who served as White House adviser on women's affairs under the Nixon administration, says that only about 44 percent of divorced mothers are granted child support, and fewer than half of them ever collect a cent. She knocks the fairy tale expectation of brides' living happily ever after, and says, "That wasn't a pedestal we were on; it was an isolation booth. What we were doing all those years doesn't count when a woman's displaced and finds she's no longer part of a serene backdrop for the rest of the family, but a star, responsible for finances, for all."[2]

In several of her regular columns, "Using Your

Money," Martha Patton has encouraged women to gain financial knowledge and independence, and she has been especially critical of the "Marabel Morgan mentality."

> Nowhere in her book does Marabel Morgan suggest that a wife should have any idea of or responsibility for family finance. She puts down any possible professional interests and prepares the woman to do nothing more than pamper a dominant husband. Nowhere does she suggest that an intelligent partnership is possible. Nowhere does she warn women to prepare for possible widowhood. [Yet Marabel Morgan has] one of the busiest and most successful careers it is possible to imagine. Now come on, Marabel, let some of the other girls have a try at these goodies.[8]

Although most women equate marriage with financial support for the rest of their lives, there is nothing in the contract that guarantees or even suggests this. Once a woman can get it through her head and into her gut that there is simply no *safe* way to operate in this world, she can probably face the ultimate risk: that the marriage itself may not survive. It seems clear that the loss of one's marriage is undoubtedly much less of a risk than dependent women believe. Nevertheless, some marriages do end when wives assert themselves or insist on certain changes, and corporate wives should be able to entertain that possibility.

If the corporate wife chooses to remain in her vulnerable, dependent position, there are several possible prescriptions for disaster. Death and widowhood is the first possibility. Your hard-driving, stress-laden husband is a likely target for a coronary, for alcoholism-related liver disease, for tobacco-related lung cancer, or even for suicide. There may be some consolation for your life of indignities if he dies early, and you inherit his money. Finally then you may discover that his money also means real power for you, and you may find ways to enhance your own self-esteem through that money and power. But, more likely, you have never learned how to use that kind of power anyway, and you would probably continue in your role as victim of male bankers or brokers or executors.

The second possible disaster is divorce. It is not at all uncommon for middle-aged wives who neglected their own education and growth to be shelved for younger, more interesting replacements. Divorces for people in their forties and fifties are occurring at an alarming rate, as both partners are evaluating the meaning of their lives. Unfortunately, a common pattern is still the helpless, depressed corporate wife who thought she did everything right and seems to have no idea what hit her. Whereas corporate executives in the past would have avoided divorce because of repercussions on their advancement, they are now finding that divorce is much more acceptable. As my interviews with the *Fortune* 500 chief executive officers indicated, this is the one quasi-moral area that seems to have loosened up.

Top managers vary, of course, in their attitudes according to their own personal experiences. But as one young bank vice-president put it, "Our whole top management would have to be canned if divorce were not accepted. The first one a few years ago was the senior vice-president. Then a whole slew of others followed. It seemed like when one high corporate officer got a divorce, there was a rash of lower executives who did the same thing. It was almost as though these men were waiting for a leader to prove that divorce would be condoned."

There probably are as many executives who want divorces because of *non*assertive wives as there are those men who want splits because their women are too assertive. One study of women who are married to "stars," done by Pamela Uttal at Sarah Lawrence, concluded: "The best way to hang on to a husband who is dynamic and successful is for the wife to be dynamic too."[4] Uttal found that very few successful husbands would like their

239

wives to do less outside the home; several husbands thought their wives should be doing more. Her sample of forty who returned her questionnaire is small and not necessarily representative, but the husbands were all very successful men, and most were business executives. Of the twenty-six women more than forty years old, six had full-time jobs; four had part-time ones; four were full-time volunteers; seven were volunteers part-time; three described themselves as professional artists; and two said they were in college. Of the 14 women under 40, four were employed full-time; three worked part-time; two said they were students; and five left that question blank. When the thirty-five women who said they had their own activities were asked if they felt guilty about devoting so much time to them, about half said no because their schedules were contingent on their husband's; a quarter said they did as they wanted and didn't feel guilty; another quarter, whose schedules were contingent on their husband's, still felt guilty. Were these wives interested in their husband's career? Seventy-eight percent said yes; and 63 percent said their husbands talked to them about their work. Thirteen of the women were in psychotherapy or psychoanalysis. Most of the women who said they were married to "stars" thought their fathers had been "stars" too. They were emphatic that their husbands supported their activities outside the home, and in many cases their husbands had urged them to initiate those activities. Uttal's main finding was that "a wife had better be dynamic and have her own identity if she wants to hold a man who has star quality."

In the old days when divorce laws were more stringent and divorce was seen in terms of villains and victims, a wife might have been able to hang onto a husband who wanted out by threats of reprisals or various kinds of emotional blackmail. But in these days of no-fault divorces and increasing moral acceptance, any wife's chances of hanging onto a husband who really wants to go are pretty poor.

# THE EMOTIONALLY DEAD MARRIAGE

In some ways the third type of disaster that can befall the vulnerable corporate wife is worse and more poignant than the other two. It is the dead, meaningless marriage. It is sad but true that many middle- and upper-middle-class corporate marriages are marriages in name only. The ability to communicate has been lost or perhaps never was present, and the two partners are a study in alienation. They are alienated not only from each other, but also from their own human core—their own personal uniqueness. Both of them have probably been affected by the corporation's demands for conformity. Long ago, they probably gave up willingly—but painfully—their playful, childish, eccentric tendencies in favor of the solid, mature behavior that would be more "appropriate" for the rising executive and his wife. The corporate pressures helped to put them in a conservative mold and essentially put negative value on any creative, nonconformist qualities.

Many of these dead marriages, then, are the sum total of two emotionally dead people. Both of them may choose to continue this arrangement because of the corporate suspicion toward men who can't control their private life, as well as for other reasons. They may both be so emotionally tired and indifferent that alternatives seem beyond their grasp.

But this picture of unresourcefulness, unfortunately, more often fits the corporate wife than her husband. While he at least presumably has some meaningful work to keep him alive and stimulated, she too often fills the vacuum of her life with busywork, and is estranged from meaningful human interaction. The chance to spend time alone is a marvelous freedom to other more resourceful people; to her it is a terrible burden and a curse. She leads essentially a housebound life; her children are either grown or otherwise not meeting her needs; and she has long ago abandoned any hope of accomplishments for herself.

It is a terrible tragedy to feel trapped in a marriage

241

so full of frustration and loneliness. Whereas loneliness might be tolerable when one is single, marriage is supposed to provide the opposite feeling. Most people have unrealistic hopes about great happiness in marriage, hopes that are gradually abandoned as they become more mature. But to have these hopes cruelly and utterly dashed —to have to accept the knowledge that you are truly lonely within the marriage—is a very bitter pill to swallow. Seidenberg puts it well: "The toll that the dead and empty marriage takes in human misery is incalculable. The marriage is preserved at the expense of the parties involved. The social tragedy imitates the medical irony —the operation was a great success, but the patient died."[5]

The ability to be alone, after all, is something that we all should strive for; the fear of being alone is something many of us struggle with. We are raised in clumps, in groups, and great emphasis is placed on how sociable we are as children, how popular we are with our peers, and how well we get along in our families. To be away from others becomes a scary thing, and aloneness becomes confused and synonymous with loneliness. But, as Anne Taylor Fleming writes, aloneness is an accident that, if one is to be at all happy, must be survived. "We share each other's beds somewhat freely not out of boldness but out of timidity, out of the fear of being alone . . . What we need instead of soul-searching sessions are classes on how to be alone: Aloneness 1A, Intermediary Aloneness, Advanced Aloneness. The great joy of these new classes is that attendance would not only not be required, it would be forbidden."[6]

Recognition of a dead, meaningless marriage can lead to much more aloneness, but as Fleming indicates, this just might end up meaning much less loneliness.

## ASSESS YOUR HUSBAND'S ABILITY TO RISK

In the light, then, of these disastrous possibilities for the marriage anyway, most women can gain enough courage to take certain risks. If a woman has assessed accurately the person—that is, husband—she is dealing with, she probably has at the outset a good idea of how much of a risk she is taking by upsetting the equilibrium. If the marriage is in bad trouble anyway, her assertiveness may be, and probably should be, the catalyst to end it.

The man who is practiced in hiding his feelings and who virtually never talks about them will find it difficult to change. It is a big risk for many executive husbands to open up in the feeling area. As family counselor Jerry Walker puts it, men may not be ready for equality in the world of emotions, which has customarily been identified with women. "It is just a conjecture, but women may be able to move into a world of harsh competitiveness with more ease than men can learn to express emotion. In the interchange, as he sees it, she gains and he loses."[7] The open and honest expression of feeling, and the sharing and understanding of their wife's emotions, may be too much of a risk for a few men. Their egos and their facades may be built on such fragile turf that the invasion of real feelings into the system could cause the whole person to crumble.

On the other hand, a corporate wife's assertiveness could be an eye opener for an executive who has been up until that point an expert at denial and sublimation. If the marriage is in fairly good shape to begin with, it can almost be guaranteed that her assertiveness is well worth the risk. A reevaluation and reassessment of their life together may be in some ways painful, but the outcome will have to be more honest and therefore better. Emotional growth for one and hopefully both of them will eventually reap tremendous benefits in their relationship.

It is important to emphasize that not all husbands are equally hard or easy to deal with in such matters. It may take considerable guts and strength of character for a woman to insist on personal recognition from the man in her life. She has, after all, been steeped in a culture that denigrates women and gives the power to men. When she tries to take some of that power from her husband and claim it as her own, she is going against very difficult odds.

243

## WITH WHOM AM I DEALING?

| My husband is _____ (qualities, characteristics) | The risk, if I want to change the equilibrium, is _____ (low, med., high; of what kind) | This suggests that my strategy should be _____ |
|---|---|---|
| 1. | | |
| 2. | | |
| 3. | | |
| 4. | | |
| 5. | | |
| 6. | | |

But when that husband also happens to be a well-paid, well-respected corporate executive—a bona fide authority figure—she has her work cut out for her. Obviously, many executives, despite their status and power, do not take themselves seriously at home and are really not so difficult to deal with. But other men in these positions can be quite overbearing, and the way a woman deals with this kind of heavy-handed husband will help to determine the caliber of risk.

It is probably safe to say that the risk to the marriage can be minimized if a woman follows one basic rule: She must be straight with herself and talk always from a feeling level. In other words, her focus must be on how the situation makes her feel rather than an accusatory focus on what her husband has done wrong.

A woman named Mitzi came into therapy feeling hopeless about her marriage and asking for help to begin again on her own. She had asked her husband to get therapy with her, but he had adamantly refused. When I asked her to role-play her conversation with her husband about professional help, it went something like this:

MITZI: I am sick and tired of your lack of involvement in our marriage. You come and go as you please. You don't give a damn about my feelings. You're always too busy to talk to me. It is useless for us to try to live this way anymore. The only possibility I can see for us is to get a professional opinion. Maybe someone else can straighten you out.

TIM: No way. I don't need any shrink telling me what to do. The problem is all yours anyway. I'm perfectly happy with the way we live. You go and get help if you want to; I don't need it.

Mitzi was asked to repeat her words as though Tim were saying them to *her,* and she was able to see how accusatory she had been. She tried it again a few days later:

MITZI: I wish I could explain to you how concerned I am about our relationship, and how much I would like to try to make things better for us. I guess I've been pretty hard to live with these last few months, but I've felt so shut out of your life lately. You're so busy, and I so often wish we had more time to talk. I feel awfully lonely sometimes. And I wonder if you don't feel lonely at times too.

Tim's response this time showed that Mitzi had hit a nerve; he often felt lonely too, but hadn't felt able to talk to her for a long time because she seemed so burdened with her own feelings. They talked about wanting to recapture some of the closeness they had once had, and Tim agreed to come into therapy with her. The risk of opening up was considerably minimized once Mitzi started to talk from a feeling level and indicated her own willingness to work and to change.

But even if the ultimate risk, the end of the marriage, materializes, most women can console themselves with the fact that there is seldom any situation where divorce means financial destitution or the loss of a reasonable custody battle.

In terms of money, one would not deny that a divorce means financial losses. An executive's ex-wife is no longer entitled to share equally in his income. But there has almost always been an accumulation of some assets, and the courts are still quite lenient in the financial settlements they give to wives. At the very least, alimony is seen as a kind of termination pay, or a temporary fund that allows a woman to gain or regain marketable skills. In some cases, alimony is a very generous payoff. The risk of real financial distress for the corporate wife who "loses" her marriage is almost nil.

Similarly, the woman who wants custody of minor children almost always gets it. Custody is beginning to be looked at more in terms of which parent can truly provide the better environment. In fact, increasingly today, the problem is that neither parent wants the responsibility of custody. But the woman who says she is afraid to risk her marriage because she will lose her children is really

246

talking nonsense. As a general rule, she still has the upper hand here too.

## THE RISK OF FAILURE OR SUCCESS

One other frequently immobilizing risk is that a woman will somehow fall on her face; she fears that she will strike out independently and then fail. It is almost easier to endure all kinds of inequities silently than to face the possibility that the alternatives may not work out either. To assess this risk, you should be hard-nosed about determining the realism of your goals. Obviously, a high school graduate who sees liberation in terms of becoming a famous brain surgeon is doomed to failure. And there are various gradations of that theme. It is realistic to expect that a job will meet many needs: The income will provide a new sense of independence; the associations with co-workers will provide stimulation; the learning process of a new function will be gratifying, and there should generally be some growth involved. But a job will never solve all of your problems. It can never substitute for a good marriage, or make you totally happy, or make you into something you are not.

There are particular hazards that face a woman re-entering the job market or returning to school after many years of absence. Many women tend to forget that there is rigorous competition in the marketplace for all the good jobs, and many are prone to give up at the slightest sign of rejection. Many books have been written about how a woman can get back to meaningful work. A current, excellent one is Richard Bolles' *What Color Is Your Parachute?*, which provides many ideas as well as references. Indeed, women are really fortunate today to have so many experts and services at their disposal for reentry. But the decision of any woman to get back into the world on her own merits—not just as someone's wife—is a truly awesome one, and should not be taken lightly.

Nevertheless, if this kind of independence and as-

247

sertiveness is approached seriously and wisely, the risk of failure is really very small. Any woman who sets her goals realistically and seeks a reasonable place for herself in the outside world can get what she wants. You may have to compromise along the way. You may have to reassess your goals periodically. You may have to work at it harder and longer than you had anticipated. But you will certainly not end up—if you are mature—with a sense of failure. To the contrary, you will undoubtedly be buoyed up by the changes in yourself and by your newfound sense of growth.

There are, of course, a fair number of people—men as well as women—who fear success as much as failure, and who cannot allow themselves to succeed. Matina Horner has written about this phenomenon in women whom she tested between 1964 and 1971, and others have documented its existence since then. It seems that many women are affected by the societal stereotype that views competence, independence, competition, and intellectual achievement as qualities basically inconsistent with femininity. Consequently, they become fearful that success in achievement-related situations will be followed by negative consequences, and they inhibit their performance or level of aspiration.[8] The fear of success can be as disabling as the fear of failure.

Such a woman may be aggressive enough to land a good job, but she will immediately find herself in trouble with co-workers and superiors. She repeatedly puts herself in positions where she feels mistreated, and she especially sees herself as victimized by men. Her energies go into these struggles rather than into her work, and she is a perfect target for openly chauvinistic males. Her ambivalence about success-failure may be quite hidden, even to her, and she will be repeatedly disappointed. She is constantly overreacting to supposed slights and constantly looking for a cause. The risk for her in pain and disappointment is a considerable one unless she gets some help with her problems. But the risk for her in the traditional role is also great, since her neurotic fears will undoubtedly surface in some other ways as a housewife.

248

# THE RISK OF REPUTATION

Sometimes women feel that their stable, middle-class reputations will be risked if they become too assertive. They value the security they have, especially with men, for fitting in so well; independence or liberation could jeopardize their image within the corporate world. Indeed, some people will be angry at them, will be threatened by them, will make fun of them for being so different, so pushy.

Women executives face the problem daily of different behavior standards for males and females, and some of the same principles apply for corporate wives. Dollie Cole wrote the following indictment about the odds against businesswomen, but the term "businesswoman" could be interchanged with "corporate wife."

### Double-crossed by the double standard

A businessman is aggressive; a businesswoman is pushy.

A well-dressed businessman is fashionable; a businesswoman is a clotheshorse.

He loses his temper because he's so involved with his job; she's bitchy.

He gets depressed from work pressures; she has menstrual tension.

He's a man of the world; she's been around.

He's confident; she's conceited.

He drinks because of excessive work pressure; she's a lush.

He's a stern taskmaster; she's impossible to work for.

He's enthusiastic; she's emotional.

Geographical considerations also come into play when one thinks about the corporate wife's image or reputation. Probably a woman can get away with things in a large eastern city that she could not in the Midwest. Several of the people I talked with emphasized the special problems of living in a small town. Asther Yogman (Seagram) said, "In a small town, the corporate wife has to behave the way I do at conventions. I'm the hostess, I have to remember everyone's name, I have to smile at everyone (even the elevator operator), and not offend anyone. The small town wife is more exposed."

Martha Smith (Copperweld Corporation) says she can usually remain fairly anonymous with a name like Smith, but when they lived in a small town, she became well known. She remembered a particular incident. "When my husband became vice-president, I went into a jewelry store to buy him a new pen, but the salesman knew who I was and kept trying to sell me a nine-hundred-dollar watch instead. If I felt like wearing jeans and a T-shirt, I couldn't go downtown there. I had to be so careful of how my image affected other people."

Edward Donley (Air Products and Chemicals) spoke of the "small, insular, conservative community in which we live. Our company's reputation is at stake. We would urge firmly that any public deviation from the norm be discontinued. Divorce is much more acceptable than it was ten years ago. And extramarital relationships are not as rigorously opposed as they used to be. But anything like that must be done in a very discreet way."

Certainly a woman's reputation will be affected negatively with some people when she becomes stronger and more assertive. But there is also the risk, and the real possibility, that she will be increasingly admired and respected in other circles. As there is more acceptance of liberation for women in general, corporate wives will obviously not have to worry so much about the prejudices of the key people they are dealing with.


## SYSTEMS MANAGEMENT FOR CORPORATE WIVES

Another risk or fear that women experience is the concern that they will not have enough time and energy to go around. When they don't have time to do household tasks as compulsively as they once did, they are afraid they will look and feel inadequate. If her husband and children are not hovered over and taken care of quite as much as they once were, the wife is afraid she will appear uncaring or neglectful.

It is true that when a new activity or new direction is added, something else has got to give. It is also true that a liberated corporation wife who balances many priorities must have an abundance of energy. But a lack of energy is very often associated with chronic depression; by contrast, the stimulation of a new interest can increase one's energy tremendously. Many women take special time and find ingenious ways for filling up their "energy bucket." Both men and women often say that the more they do, the more they can do.

The risk that change will upset the family's equilibrium is great; the risk that this will be a detrimental or negative upset is small. A woman who sets out to make changes in herself will have to restructure her priorities. The schedule that she may have clung to for years will have to be discarded. There will have to be an adjustment period. But the new balance that emerges will most likely be healthier for both her and her entire family.

In general, the risks of women who want to buck the traditional corporate wife system are smaller and smaller. The future for women as a whole looks bright. There is increased consciousness among all groups of people about equal rights and equal opportunities for women. Even though these new ideas are often not put into practice, there is at least intellectual awareness that women can no longer be shut off and shut out. Rigid sex roles and rigid definitions of masculinity and femininity are slowly disappearing. Women are proving themselves to be equal in intelligence with men. Certain myths of male superiority are being questioned and challenged. The situation for women who want a different place for themselves than they have had is an optimistic one. There is even some movement to applaud husbands who give special support to their wives. It was refreshing to see the husbands of Anne Armstrong, the former American ambassador to Britain, and Margaret Thatcher, the leader of the Tory

Party, singled out by a newspaper reporter for their sensitivity and thoughtfulness in support of their wives.[9] As the reporter said, this makes one believe that men really are inherently equal.

Much of the risk for the corporate wife who also wants independence lies in her perception of the situation and the odds. As the following hypothetical exchange suggests, she must learn to assess problems accurately, choose among alternatives appropriately, and learn to live with her decisions:

> POOR WOMAN: Lord, is it true that to you a thousand years is like a minute?
>
> LORD: Yes, that is true.
>
> POOR WOMAN: And is it also true that to you a thousand dollars is like a cent?
>
> LORD: Yes, that is so.
>
> POOR WOMAN: Then Lord, could you give me a thousand dollars?
>
> LORD: Yes, in a minute.

Furthermore, a corporate wife who decides to start taking more risks should understand the nature of change and the resistance she might encounter:

> There is nothing more difficult to carry out, nor more doubtful of success, nor more dangerous to handle, than to initiate a new order of things. For the reformer has enemies in all those who profit by the old order, and only lukewarm defenders in all those who would profit by the new order, this lukewarmness arising partly from fear of their adversaries, who have the laws in their favour, and partly from the incredulity of mankind, who do not truly believe in anything new until they have actual experience of it.
>
> —Machiavelli, *The Prince*

Women who choose not to fit into the corporate wife mold may have to risk feeling quite alone at times. There are many people who stand to profit from the old order. However, things are changing, and they will not be alone forever. Although these women will be laughed at and deprecated in some circles, they will be listened to and admired in others. Hopefully the areas of receptivity are growing. Certainly the groups that have been instrumental in making changes are not giving up; they are continuing the militant fight for women's rights, and the ranks of their supporters seems to be growing.

It should do without saying that, in order to take risks, you must have certain convictions about the benefits. But the willingness to take risks also assumes that you have a fair amount of security within yourself. A risk, by definition, is clearly never a sure thing. It always means that you must be able to live a little dangerously, that you must be able to go a little out on a limb. Insecure, frightened people can never chance this. On the other hand, secure, mature people find that life is not very exciting or gratifying without risks. Plodding along safely is pretty dull—"You never get nothing for nothing."

How does a timid, dependent woman get the courage to take risks? How does she become convinced that, to use the old cliché, "nothing ventured, nothing gained"? We have already discussed several important steps toward identity and security for a woman within herself. But beyond that, it is practice in risk taking that provides its own rewards. Unless you take risks foolishly or neurotically, you will find that you have few losses and many gains. The ebullience and success you feel in having taken one risk will push you to take another. If your risks were extremely calculated at first, you will probably have to think them through less each time. Taking risks will become more natural to you, and this process will be amazingly freeing. (The Risk Assessment Profile may be useful.) With the ability and willingness to take risks,

Describe one risk you took each day, one time you went out on a limb, one time you did not play it safe.

What did you profit or lose? Did you assess the situation accurately? Did you have realistic expectations?

Day 1—

Day 2—

Day 3—

Day 4—

Day 5—

Day 6—

Day 7—

Day 8—

Day 9—

Day 10—

you are truly an independent person. Your control over your environment is vastly increased. Your sense of power in risk taking makes you a much more interesting and alive human being.

# 11

# You Always Have Choices

The idea that everyone has choices in every situation, at any time, in any place is a hard one to sell to many people, especially women who have been raised to think of themselves as not being decision makers or choice makers. Nevertheless, this concept of choices is the essence of freedom for all human beings. It is the core of what we have come to call liberation for women.

Part of the difficulty in convincing people that they have the ability—as well as the right—to choose is the responsibility and visibility that choice implies. A woman who simply lets things happen to her is protected from the possibility that she may make a wrong choice; she is able to hide somewhat from decisions that may be difficult and is therefore less vulnerable to overt stress and burdens. A woman who makes it clear that her husband is the boss and looks to him for her happiness can live vicariously and get many pleasures without having to "get her feet wet." She also has an easy target to blame if her husband messes up or if her life is somehow not happy.

The usual reaction to the concept of choice is disbelief: Sure, I have a choice about whether I go to a PTA meeting or go shopping. I maybe have some choice about whether to take a job or not. But what choice do I have over my husband having a heart attack? Or my son getting lousy grades at college? Or my daughter marrying someone I don't like very much? Or my husband and me being hit by a drunken driver on our way home from a Saturday night party? Or the company ordering us to move to a new location? The fact is that these situations may not involve choices of action, but they very much involve choices of reaction. And on the basis of analyzing well, and being very conscious of those reactions, you can then make various choices of behavior. In other words, you certainly cannot control the whole world, and you clearly cannot control other people. But many different kinds of reactions are possible, even to events that often seem calamitous and overwhelming.

The choices of reactions to the kinds of events mentioned above are many. To name a few: You can deny the whole situation or repress it (at least until the feelings pop up some other way). You can accept the situation stoically, figuring that the other guy has all the cards anyway. You can accept the situation angrily, letting the feelings simmer and fester, or perhaps lashing out at the most available target. You can accept the situation resignedly with the knowledge that you have control only over your own life and cannot control anyone else. You can try to effect some changes in the situation by telling other people what to do. You can try to influence change by making your feelings known—for example, a daughter might be more influenced about her fiancé by hearing her mother's honest expression of feeling than by being told she is stupid and wrong. You can make threats about what you will do if a situation does not change. You can rebel totally and refuse to be involved further in a situation. You can turn to alcohol and/or drugs. You can even commit suicide. Or you can use your sense of humor and sense of perspective to get through many a rough situation.

By way of illustration, let us examine several aspects of life that almost every corporation wife must face. The tendency is for most women to accept whatever circumstances seem to hit them in these areas and let their feelings show only in subterranean or sabotaging ways. These situations, at first glance, may not seem to involve many choices, but, on closer inspection, it becomes clear that making choices and taking responsibility may be the most important part. In fact, the ability to make choices and take control of your life in these areas may at times be even more important than the choices themselves.

## TIME MANAGEMENT

The first, almost global choice the corporate wife must make is how she fills up her time. If you do not wrest control of this from all the people around you—husband, children, friends, and relatives—it will seem that your time is completely occupied with things you *must* do, and you will feel that there is little or no room for choice. As was said by several women I interviewed, the priorities change as children grow up, but when children are small, there seems to be no time for anything except corporation and family. One midwestern CEO's wife, who asked not to be identified, said, "We have six children and one of them has recently been diagnosed schizophrenic. Maybe I go to one function a week that is *clearly* for business; but the others—church meetings, charity things, luncheons of various kinds—those things are really business too, and I don't feel I could say no. My children are mostly grown now, but it seems like they still are always asking for things. And our schizophrenic son will always be a big concern for me. He is in special programs, and of course we can afford help, but it seems like I still have to do most of the legwork and most of the transporting. It doesn't look like I'll ever have time to just sit around and look after myself."

Granted the number of children, the age of children, and special problems with children, such as retardation or emotional or physical illness, determine to some extent the priorities of the corporate wife (and, hopefully, of the executive as well). But to allow these demands to usurp all of your time is to abdicate responsibility for your own life. That too must be seen as a choice—the choice of letting your children or husband take up every minute of time and every ounce of energy so that it seems as though there is little self or little selfishness left.

Many women do this when their children are young because it seems the only way. Certainly the pressures on a young corporate wife and mother to conform to this pattern are heavy, and the reasons for this kind of lifestyle may be totally valid. But, even in these years, you must recognize that there are alternatives. You have to be aware that some women under similar circumstances are making different choices—and that you have a responsibility to think of your own needs and pleasures too. Young wives and mothers are so accustomed to being the organizer, the spectator, the scene setter, the pacifier, the authority pleaser that they frequently end up doing for everyone but themselves. A young woman who says she does not have a minute in her busy day for herself is in big trouble now and will probably be in even bigger trouble a few years from now. These are the years when behavior patterns are becoming set and when family members are adjusting to certain role expectations of each other.

Commonly, the pattern for corporate wives is a period of child- and home-centered activities, and then a traumatic change as children grow up and become more independent. In many cases the self-sacrifice that was connected to children in earlier years becomes even more particularly attached to the corporation, as women accompany their husbands on more and more business trips, attend more and more charity luncheons, and are more and more dependent on their husband's business life to provide them with excitement and stimulation.

Whether the woman in her middle years fills her time with boredom and busywork and tries to live even more through her husband, or whether she involves herself in new and exciting projects and thereby enters a whole new period of growth, is really a matter of her choice. Her changing sense of perspective in her middle years—and, hopefully her hard-won maturity—should open up many new options and interests for her. If she has had some practice as a younger woman with how she fills up her time—and has not simply felt directed by the forces around her—the opportunities now that children are grown can seem virtually limitless.

Another area of expanding choices in how a woman fills up her time involves her behavior at business conventions or conferences. Until recent years a woman who went with her husband to such a meeting had the choice of filling her days with playing bridge or coffee-klatching with the other women. If she was not very happy with the bridge/fashion show variety of ladies' activities, her only other choices were to stay in her room or go and complain about the program. Thankfully, the picture has been drastically changing in recent years, and women are being offered more choice in "ladies'" activities at business meetings than ever before. Besides the usual things, women are now able to play tennis or golf, shop on their own, listen to a speaker on some subject usually thought to be of interest to women, or even stay in their room with a good book. One of the primary components, of course, of intelligent choice in such a situation is that you must approach the alternatives with an open mind. If you can avoid prejudicing a group activity, you can usually find some interesting person or some kind of fun in any group of people.

The most exciting change in programming for women, however, is the invitation for them to participate in heretofore "men's activities." At many company or industry meetings these days, fascinating speakers are brought in and workshops are held on a wide range of subjects. Women are often invited to attend as well as men, and it is gratifying to see how many of them are

261

jumping at the opportunity. Certainly this is an area of programming where women can exert a great influence. There are many ways to indicate your preferences to the people who are planning activities for women. Most of these people are anxious to have the ideas of the group and can handle *constructive* criticism. The emphasis on choice should and can be communicated to the planner in many ways.

Laverne Phillips (International Multifoods) told me she is proud of having been "instrumental in many of our organizations in getting the wives to sit in on the sessions. I am pleased to see more and more of them attending and therefore conversing more knowledgeably on current topics." When I asked her how she accomplished this, she explained, with a mischievous smile, "With charm, lots of charm. Seriously, I did it by praising wives who went to the meetings and praising the people who happened to be in charge. If any husband told me how much he had enjoyed a program I had not been invited to, I would tell the person in charge how much the women would have enjoyed that program. I would ask, if we promise to be quiet and sit unobtrusively, if we could sit in on a particular session.

"Very often I would meet with a kind of smiling resistance at first. You know, it isn't always the older men who are threatened. I found that the men in their forties resist quite a lot. Bill [Mr. Phillips] feels they aren't quite as secure as the older men. They are already threatened by younger men, and they might be more threatened by wives who could talk intelligently on the same subjects. The men in their middle fifties and sixties —especially the top executives—usually seem quite happy to have their wives sit in."

Are the wives allowed to participate in these meetings?

"No, the wives keep their mouths shut. They have not really been invited to participate. The time is just too vital for a wife to pipe up and ask a question. Maybe they would have an opportunity later to ask something if the speaker stays afterward. For example, we recently had the minister of oil of Iran as a speaker. The wives all had the feeling that this was pretty important. Maybe a wife would feel knowledgeable about something, but she is not an employee of the company."

I asked Mrs. Phillips when she began to work on this change, and she said it started six or seven years ago. "In addition to these large meetings, my husband has a meeting of the top management team and their wives once a year. It is a three-day retreat type of thing. Every evening there is a dinner and a speaker—economists, psychologists, futurists. The next morning there is a question-and-answer period with that speaker. At first the whole thing was amazingly resisted by the younger VPs, and the wives of these men resisted by not attending in the morning. They chose to play tennis or golf instead. But they found that in the evening other wives were conversing more intelligently, and they began to attend too. In addition to the yearly meeting, there is a quarterly one-day meeting. There is always one speaker from the company, and the wives feel free to ask any questions they want. Furthermore, Bill also spends one session with the wives and answers all kinds of questions. We're finding that the wives are starting to suggest speakers."

When Mrs. Phillips was asked why her husband takes an interest in involving the wives, she said, "He feels that if they're involved, if they understand what's going on, they will be better able to help. Bill has always felt free to confide in me; he knows I'm not going to tell it further; and I think I've been able to help him."

What if a woman could not attend because of career conflicts?

"That would be okay. I am very, very active civicly (Art Institute, symphony, church activities), and there are times when I can't attend meetings. But I try not to let this happen very often because I want to keep getting invited."

In many ways, from Laverne Phillips' description, her husband's company is a very progressive organization. And it seems that in her charming, determined, but gracious way, she has played an important part in making it so. One could argue with the extent to which wives' time is used by this organization, but at least there is real consideration of their part in the process.

In more and more companies the women who sit in on convention meetings are less and less reluctant to participate. I have personally heard corporate wives ask intelligent questions that expanded the level of discussion. For example, I once heard Betty Pilsbury, whose husband is an Indian Head, Inc. vice-president, and who herself travels widely running workshops as a Girl Scout National Board member, ask an important, incisive question at an industry meeting. The vibrations in that predominantly male audience were of acceptance and respect for her. However, at other times, one can interpret the looks around the room to mean annoyance that a woman is taking up time, as well as surprise that she could ask anything so intelligent.

Hopefully, future involvement of women in these meetings will mean full participation and not just observation. This also presumes that women will be informed on relevant issues and appropriate in their verbalizations. Wouldn't it be exciting if some of these wives, who are at meetings with their husbands because they have an interest in the company and in the work, could even be invited to share with the group some of their own special areas of expertise and interest that might be peripherally relevant! More and more corporate wives, especially those in the younger age groups, are going to be having interesting careers of their own—which brings us to the next major area of choice.

## EMPLOYMENT

One of the questions routinely asked of the chief executive officers' wives who were interviewed was whether they were acquainted with corporate wives who had careers or jobs. The answer was usually "no," but many quickly added that they felt it was partly a function of their age group. A few said they might do it differently if

264

they were younger. Some, like Laverne Phillips, said they considered their volunteer responsibilities even heavier than a nine-to-five job, but they allowed that those volunteer activities gave them more flexibility than a job or specific career would. And it is that availability or flexibility that their husbands and the corporations seem to demand. Those who did know corporate wives who were also career women mentioned occupations like painting, sculpture, interior decorating, and travel representative, wherein the hours are quite elastic and controllable.

Work has traditionally been an area where corporate wives would deny any possibility of choice. The average corporate wife might say that she would love to get an interesting job, but how could she? She doesn't have enough education. It seems like a million years since she held any job at all; probably nobody would hire her. Good household help is impossible to find and outrageously expensive. She has to be available to her husband for frequent out-of-town trips and spur-of-the-moment entertaining. Besides, who would do the cooking and shopping and organizing and chauffeuring and bookkeeping work that it takes to keep a household running smoothly?

These are all real problems, but they also have real solutions, most of which include compromise of one kind or another. The problems are countered by all of the possible reasons that a corporate wife might choose to take a job even though the odds may seem to be against it. One reason is still money. The corporate wife may be less needy financially than most other American working women; nevertheless, her income may provide the extras that her husband's salary can't quite cover. Couples are very much affected by the high cost of living these days, and many of them are opting for the upward mobility that two incomes can buy. As a recent article in *Business Week* states, "These women enable their families to exchange the overdue bill from Sears for the charge account at Bloomingdale's, the Chevy for a Cadillac, the weekend at the shore for a month abroad."[1] In 1976—the latest count—63 percent of the 9.6 million U.S. families with incomes of more than $25,000 had a working husband and a working wife, compared with 42 percent of the 1.2 million who earned that sum in 1967. Many of these couples have become affluent, conspicuous consumers; but many others, especially those whose children are high school and college age, feel that they simply need both incomes to survive.

In the process, something generally good seems to happen to marriages. Most sociologists feel that "the dual-income family offers broader roles for husband and wife, equal participation in family matters by both mates, and an end to the negative image of the working wife . . . The two-income family has become a chance to grow all around."[2] The sense of financial independence the corporate wife's salary gives her may be as important emotionally as it is economically.

Although most corporate wives may not work primarily for the financial benefits, they are increasingly going that route for the other benefits work provides. This usually has more to do with establishing identity than almost anything else. As Sigmund Freud put it so succinctly: "No other technique for the conduct of life attaches the individual so firmly to reality as laying emphasis on work: for his work at least gives him a secure place in a portion of reality in the human community."[3] Men have always been identified largely in terms of their occupation, and this standard is increasingly applied to women as well.

This has been the situation for some time in other countries such as Sweden and the Soviet Union. Women in the Soviet Union occupy all kinds of "male" positions and have all kinds of social expectations as well as supports (such as good day care facilities) to hold jobs outside the home. One American woman traveling in the Soviet Union had to adjust quickly to the question, "What kind of work do you do?" But most American women are not very well prepared to deal with these questions.

One can argue whether work should indeed be such a huge factor in establishing one's identity, but we live in a real world where this is fortunately or unfortunately

266

true. The low esteem in which the non-earning woman is held is shown in the estimates by banks and insurance companies of what her services are worth: approximately $13,000 a year for a work week (according to the Chase Manhattan Bank) of 99.6 hours.[4]

The fact that work also provides meaningful contact with people is no small part of its attraction. You often hear corporate wives complain of loneliness; their husbands travel constantly, or work long hours, or are preoccupied with work even when they are home. Certainly work relationships are not always "meaningful" ones, but they are likely to be more so—more focused and more stimulating—than gossiping with a neighbor or appearing at functions as a mere extension of your husband. Corporate wives may have many acquaintances in the business network, but real friends and meaningful relationships are harder to come by, and work is one possible source that most corporate wives have traditionally denied themselves. As men have known for years, work can provide a sense of identity, financial security, friendships, intellectual stimulation, sexual sublimation, and even sexual gratification.

One CEO's wife (who later asked not to be quoted on this) suggested that many career-oriented wives are younger women who are married to successful men considerably older than themselves. On the reasons for this, she speculated: "They didn't grow up, so to speak, with their husband's careers as we did. Their husbands had it made when they married. The wife was accepted because of her husband's position, which we all know. When the wife starts out from scratch, she feels she had a part in it. Not that she is responsible, but she feels more secure. The ones who marry men in top positions feel they need more for themselves. They seem to feel they have to prove to someone that they have something on the ball."

If the phenomenon of young career wives married to older successful men is indeed true, this woman's explanation may be one of many. The career orientation of these women may also stem from the fact that they are not expected to put so much effort into their husband's career; these husbands have already made the big time. Neither do they suffer the effect of being "burned out" by their supportive efforts, as their older sisters might have been. They do not have so much invested in their husband's career and may have more energy left for themselves. Possibly they get more support for independent functioning from their husbands, who are secure and no longer struggling, and who are less threatened by their wives. It is quite possible that work, for these women, combines the ingredients of the woman's youth with her husband's predetermined success.

One of the very real reasons why work has not seemed a viable choice for corporate wives in the past has been the career limitations for women. Many corporate wives have correctly assessed that their own chances for making it in certain fields, of rising to the top of the corporate or any other occupational ladder on their own, were pretty poor. Therefore, educated and bright as they may have been, they put all their energy and resources into promoting their husband's career. They accepted the American system and sought to make it to the top through their man.

Now the picture has drastically changed. Fields that were previously closed to women are opening up, and female executives are being actively sought. It is a truly exciting time in our history for a woman to be making an occupational choice. Interesting jobs are now a more realistic choice than ever before. The revised Executive Order No. 4, which became effective in April 1972, has precipitated radical changes in the employment of women. The order includes regular audits and affects all companies having government contracts if they have fifty or more employees and do $50,000 or more contract business per year. It emphasizes all kinds of equal pay and opportunities for women, including the right of women to advance to executive and managerial levels in business organizations. Consequently, women are being offered top-level, especially "visible" jobs that would never have been open to them before. In all, job choice and economic independence is now a really viable option for women.

This is not to say that the picture has totally changed. The statistics are only slightly improved in recent years. "A woman will earn only 60 percent as much as a man with the same qualifications . . . Women with college degrees earn an average of $9,000 a year, only slightly more than a man who dropped out of high school."[5] This is also not to say that some male executives are not still putting obstacles in the way of women. But a reasonable number of other executives will admit that they may have been forced into doing themselves a real favor. Certainly a woman who can reap financial and psychological benefits from a position in the outside world can't help but enjoy and appreciate that productive, capable, recognized, and rewarded part of herself.

Another job choice for women who eschew the full-time career for various reasons might be part-time work. Increasingly, employers are meeting demands of women for jobs that are less than full time, or jobs with flexible hours; interesting experiments are being tried such as splitting a regular full-time position between two women. In many ways, part-time work is attractive to both men and women; it allows time for child care or entertaining and other things we all wish we could do more of. But corporate wives who insist on an interesting part-time job or nothing would be wise to consider the realities: The job market is an extremely competitive situation. Other employees will resent part-time workers and will probably be threatened by them. The most interesting jobs will probably not be available on a part-time basis because the important worker will need to be available when others are. Thus, part-time work is a choice that is more available to women today than ever before, but it involves compromises just as full-time work does.

It is hard for many women to give up motherhood in order to have successful careers; it is equally hard for other women to give up careers in order to have families. There are no simple answers, but several facts are pertinent.

First, as of March 1976, almost half of mothers with young children were working—49 percent of all mothers with children under eighteen were in the labor force, working full-time or part-time, or looking for a job. These statistics from the Labor Department compare with 9 percent in the labor force in 1940, 27 percent in 1955, and 35 percent in 1965. The most dramatic change has come among women with very young children. Among the 14.6 million working mothers in the labor force, 5.4 million (as of 1976) had children under six years old. Between 1960 and 1976, the proportion of working mothers with children under *three* rose from 17 percent to 34 percent. Forty-six percent of the 61.7 million American children under eighteen in 1976 had working mothers.[6]

Also pertinent is the fact that women who are well educated and can get interesting jobs are choosing to have fewer children. The impact of effective birth control is a relatively new phenomenon in our history, and there has been some fascinating research done on the effects that fertility limitation has had on women's careers and personalities.[7] A study by the Rand Corporation indicates that the expected baby boom of the 1970s has fizzled. The fertility rate for poorly educated teenagers has not changed much, but the rate among well-educated working women is low. The higher salaries of women have made childbearing more expensive, and the new employment rate of women has reversed the relationship between births and economic cycle that previously was based on mostly male employment. It seems that as long as the nation prospers and employment opportunities for women remain good, births and fertility rates will remain low.[8]

On the same side, there is evidence from several long-term studies that gifted women who follow careers are happier than those who don't. A fifty-year study of seven hundred gifted women was begun by Stanford University psychologist Lewis Terman in the 1920s and has been continued by researchers Pauline Sears and Ann Barbee at Stanford. The participants are now in their late fifties and sixties, and there is a very significant difference in happiness between the women who choose to be "income workers" and their counterparts who opted for homemakers' lives. The study says that 79 percent of those who followed careers, with or without children, are highly satisfied, while less than 20 percent of the homemakers expressed high satisfaction with their path. Women who classified themselves as both income workers and heads of households had the highest satisfaction rate of all—92 percent. These women had IQs of 135 or better as girls, and three-quarters of the sample group had children. In general, those who were married and had children were happier than those who did not have families.[9]

Some other facts are also important to recognize, however: Women who have the highest success in jobs, as rated by salary level, also work the longest hours. A study done by Heidrick and Struggles, international management consulting firm, found that women who are corporate officers must plan to work long hours. Women earning less than $20,000 average forty-four working hours weekly; those earning $20,000 to $40,000 devote forty-eight hours; those making $40,000 and above average fifty-seven hours each seven days. Only 31 percent of the women officers surveyed had children.[10] These figures make it clear that real success in a job cannot be had without some trade-offs; it is not easy to be corporate wife, mother, *and* executive.

Furthermore, one must realize that the best choices do not just happen; they involve career planning and political awareness. Susan Broz Ogden, MBA, an assistant professor at Seattle University who also runs frequent seminars for women in management, says she is constantly urging women to do more planning. "I once asked a group of thirty-five mid-level managers how they got their first real job. Twenty-nine responded that it was a case of chance or luck or knowing someone (usually a relative). Only six had consciously chosen their companies beforehand, and only one out of thirty-five had ever done any long-range career planning before choosing a position. Men spend a good deal of time and effort

271

at this, but most women spend more time buying a new coat than they do evaluating their own career paths. A woman once told me that she knew a lot of women who have been working twenty-five years and still see themselves as temporary employees. People have a tendency to get where they are planning to go. If women set up specific career signposts, they will be able to see just how far and how fast they are moving—or if they aren't moving. If the signposts don't move, they will be able to do something about it."

One social worker I know had risen to a middle-management position in a state agency before she and her husband decided they wanted a couple of kids. When she was pregnant with the first child, she negotiated a transfer to a part-time position in a training unit. She went back to work six weeks after the delivery, but when I talked to her a few months later, she was dissatisfied. "I can handle the hours all right, but I miss the decision making and the prestige of my old job. Now that I'm no longer in management, people don't treat me with the same respect, and I don't have nearly as much satisfaction from my job."

About the same time she was considering a return to full-time work, she became pregnant with her second child. She decided, rather than overextend herself, to interrupt her career for a while, and she quit. Now she is really unhappy, and wonders about her other choices. "I've tried going to seminars and taking a continuing education course, but it is really hard to keep up. I've found that people even treat me differently now. For a while after I left, my friends in social work kept me informed of things that were going on, but now they seem to think there is too much of a gap. They ask me about my babies, but they don't ask my professional opinions anymore. I'm having a real struggle to still see myself as a professional."

This woman has no easy solutions; there are massive problems for her in all possible choices—full-time work, part-time work, career interruption; but the important factor is that she does have choices:

272

# CHOICES OF DUAL-CAREER COUPLES

The kinds of compromises that a career woman who is also a corporate wife has to face were detailed recently in the *Wall Street Journal* article titled, "For Married Couples Two Careers Can Be Exercise in Frustration."[11] The writer notes that many couples today "have thrown aside the basic societal premise that a woman's job is her husband's career and instead have chosen a life that includes both spouses pursuing full-time careers." Some marriages crumble under the pressures of career and home, which absorb all the partners' energy and time; other marriages survive and prosper almost because of the strains. Most dual-career couples find that children make the necessary adjustments much more complicated. Not only are these couples subject to pressures and possible transfers from both jobs, but domestic responsibilities must be divided somehow. While most working couples divide child care duties and household responsibilities that hired help doesn't cover, women typically assume a greater share of these duties. Most women try to do everything well and feel guilty when they can't, while husbands tend to feel little anxiety and guilt about children or household tasks being shortchanged. But they encounter hardships too, especially since "most of their associates have the ready mobility that comes with a joint effort behind one career. At home, many of their neighbors unwind from their workday with a waiting martini. Dual-career husbands often don't have these career or domestic comforts; they may have to fend for themselves." Most businesses are neither concerned about nor equipped to deal with dual-career problems, and therefore, the article concludes, these couples find little help in making their compromises and/or choices.

The sheer logistics of child care and household management demand difficult choices every day for dual-career couples. How much income can be diverted to pay housekeepers, babysitters, day care centers, after-school activity centers, and how much can they lean on the volunteer help of friends, relatives, and neighbors? Who takes care of emergencies, and how? Since they don't have a large quantity of time with their children, how do they make it quality time? Who does the minor things that make life easier, like calling the plumber and buying toilet paper? How do they apportion their limited emotional strength to each other, children, and friends?

Susan Ogden, who herself is part of a dual-career marriage and also sees many women like herself in her management seminars, says, "Even if the husband gives lip service to the idea of joint responsibility, in reality it is the wife who has the greatest work-load and greatest responsibility. The stress on her is both physical and emotional. The physical part is the sheer amount of manual labor it takes to keep a family running—the washing, cleaning, ironing, cooking, and shopping. The emotional stress has two elements: First are the psychological pressures of continually trying to coordinate two or more busy lives. Even if the wife is lucky enough to have a good support system with housekeepers and/or parents, these also add to the pressure of scheduling and rescheduling. I know one female assistant professor, finishing up her Ph.D., who says, 'I have six children and I am frankly glad I don't have a husband, since I simply don't have enough time for him, the children, and my career.' "

Ogden adds that the second kind of emotional stress most working wives and mothers face is guilt. "I have yet to meet a working mother who doesn't continually suffer strong feelings of guilt that somehow she isn't doing enough for her children, husband, family, job, and even the local PTA. Until our culture changes, or until women stop feeling that they must be superhuman individuals, the pressure of maintaining dual-career families will continue to take its toll on the American working woman."

If a corporate couple has dual careers, there is surely no way to survive without mutual support. But these employed women, as a *Business Week* article states, should be able to count on their husbands being "dependable for the obvious reason that [the men] chose this way of life as consciously as their wives did. If they had preferred homebodies and/or childlessness, they would have married someone else."[12]

## THE CHOICE TO MOVE UP AND/OR OUT

Another major area of choice in which corporate wives certainly should share is the decision about upward mobility in their husband's career; and these decisions often include choices about physical or geographical mobility as well. Many women would say they have no choice at all here, and in reality, many executives would not involve their wife in these decisions. But in a real marital partnership, there would be good communication as to the pressures and competitiveness of upward striving. Ideally, husband and wife should both participate in decisions that might involve longer work hours, more traveling, more responsibilities, and more pressures. Although a liberated woman should be the first to acknowledge that the final decisions about a man's career belong to him (just as she must take the ultimate responsibility for her own life), she certainly has an important part to play here. Her choices include: encouraging his competitive spirit and helping him every step of the way; suggesting that he relax in his job or maybe even take early retirement; and a whole range of possibilities in between. Her choices in the area of occupational mobility too should be responsive to his needs as well as her own and will obviously depend on all kinds of circumstances; but the point is that the corporate wife should be awakened to this as an important area of choice.

The geographical moving so prevalent in corporate life has already been explored and is often difficult to think of in terms of choices. The company attitude may be "take it or leave it"; there may seem to be no alternatives. My survey showed that the average number of moves an executive and his family might have to make in a twenty-year period is four, and this number rises dramatically in certain specialties, such as sales. Most chief executive officers who were interviewed expressed annoyance or anger about wives who made moving difficult.

Bill May of American Can described a man who made two international moves but whose wife caused havoc each time; this executive's usefulness to the company is now diminished and he is headed for a lower position. "A man's refusal to move is not held against him in that location, but it limits my ultimate plans for him. If a woman objects to her husband's hours or travel or the place where they are living, I usually get it indirectly. But the Peter Principle sometimes works well—some people are moved down to lesser jobs and are very happy."

Kathleen May is generally in agreement with her husband: "Usually moves are a step up the ladder; usually a man doesn't get that chance again. If he refuses because of his wife, he gets seen as weak—not putting the almighty corporation first. If his wife is going to stand in his way constantly and be a millstone around his neck, he is not somebody that a big company can depend on, even though he might have something to contribute in a different way."

And yet no one pretends that moves are easy. A few people relish change and are glad to escape certain areas and people, but for most executive families, moving is a wrench. The roots, the emotional stability, the secure identity of the old area are not easily reestablished in the new home. Increasingly today, couples are deciding that they won't go through this, and companies are being forced to deal with it.

A recent *Time* magazine article titled "The Immobile Society: Is America Settling Down in Middle Age?" suggests that the great national game of musical houses is slowing down. Companies are having to eliminate many executive transfers around the country; the spokesman for one company said, "We are trying to slow down the revolving door." Why the change in attitude? Why the sudden feeling that maybe the job doesn't come first? Some analysts attribute the change to women. "Women

276

always thought of going along as a wifely duty. Now they are saying, 'Wait a minute; it's my life too, and my children's lives.' Working wives have an even greater say in the decision, especially if they hold a middle- or high-level job that cannot easily be matched in another city."[13]

One executive recruiting firm, Gilbert Tweed Associates, reports that one in three male executives contacted these days say they can't move to a higher paying job because the dislocation would interfere with their wives' careers or studies. In more and more cases, the firm has to find a spot for the wife too.[14]

At least one research study, which looked at 714 young, white, college-educated wives, found that moving is a real detriment to a wife's career. Of those wives in the sample who were employed in 1964, 88 percent who did not move interstate were still employed in 1968. However, only 75 percent of those who did move because of their husband's upward mobility were still employed in 1968. The conclusion is that, among young college graduates, geographical movement is unfavorable to the wife's continued participation in the labor force, and it probably interferes with the development and achievement of occupational goals among women.[15]

While more and more couples are choosing not to move, temporary separations are another option. A *Fortune* article about Robert C. Wilson, head of Memorex, detailed all the changes he has made in his career as a "turnaround man." At one point, Mrs. Wilson and their girls decided to remain in Syracuse. "The family had been separated before. The girls were teenagers by then, and Mrs. Wilson felt that she had to make a decision about who came first, the husband or the children. She found moving to be a wrenching experience. It took her a year to settle into a new community, the children longer. There came a time when one more move was simply too damaging. Today she says she can't remember whether the family has moved thirteen or fifteen times." She finally joined her husband in California, but by that time they had been separated for five years except for short visits back and forth.[16]

In some cases corporate wives play a major role in the decision not to move, to move only to certain areas, or to have a temporary separation. In some cases they play a minor role. Probably in more cases than we will ever know, the wives are blamed for refusing to move by husbands, who dare not admit their own preferences to their bosses. Essentially, corporate wives who may have in the past believed they had no options about moving now should be thinking in terms of many choices.

## CHOICES ABOUT MARRIAGE AND SEX

One other important area of choice that is increasingly being faced by corporate wives is whether to stay in a bad marriage. Women who might have in the past felt totally bound because of the children or the appearance to the corporation are now seeing that divorce is a real possibility for them. Even those who choose to stay in unhappy marriages have all kinds of arrangements as possibilities, and they now have more outlets for feelings than would have been thought of a few years ago. Continuing in an unequal marriage, where the wife has grown much more than the husband, *or* where the wife is ill-equipped to keep up with her successful husband, is now only one of many choices.

Sex, or the lack of sex, in a marriage now has more meanings than ever before. A couple may be totally faithful to each other; they may keep trying but one or both may be unsatisfied sexually; there may be no sex in the marriage but both may remain celibate; one or both may meet sexual needs or desires outside the marriage.

The corporate wife may try to deal with her loneliness through increased sex or through total denial of sexual desires. Although sex for many middle-aged, conservative corporate wives is still the conjugal Saturday-night-with-lights-out routine, the possibilities for other women in the sexual area are vastly expanding—except for one factor: Discretion must always be an integral part of any choice in this area for the corporate wife. As

278

my survey indicated, any sexual choice other than traditional marital fidelity includes some risk or some loss if she is not utterly discreet.

Your marriage can remain the same, or end, or change. Your sex life can remain the same, or end, or change. Just this simple fact can open up new vistas and give a new sense of freedom. As one corporate wife said at a seminar, "When I felt I didn't have any choice but to stay with that bastard, I felt so trapped and angry and bitter. Once I realized I could make it alone if I had to, I decided we should have separate bedrooms as a first step. That was a shock to my husband; I guess he thought he was the only one who could take a step like that. Now I think he's a little bit worried about what I might do next. I really don't want a split from him, but I sure needed a little breathing space. I'm finding that there are a lot of possibilities between total dependence and total independence."

## PAY ATTENTION TO WHAT YOU CHOOSE TO FOCUS ON

These are just a few of the specific choices a corporate wife has, but concomitantly important is the concept that a person should always pay attention to what he or she chooses to focus on. You might say that this is a sophisticated way of describing "the power of positive thinking," or "the rational approach to living."

In almost every situation in life, there are positive aspects, negative aspects, growth aspects, self-destructive aspects, rational aspects, irrational aspects. Most of us have stock, conditioned, almost programmed responses to situations, and we can learn a lot about ourselves if we pay attention to the ways in which we tend to respond. This requires taking a step back from our own behavior and gaining more objectivity and perspective about ourselves, but it can be easily done with a conscious effort and a little training.

One of my weekend groups included a thirty-three-year-old woman whose corporate executive husband had just left her for someone else. This wife was quite attractive, bright, articulate, and was obviously getting a lot of attention from male members of the group. But she was in tears for the whole first half of the weekend and talked repeatedly about her lousy self-image and her sense of failure. As the group got to know each other better, a warm sense of camaraderie developed, and there was a real sense of fun, enjoyment, mutual discovery. One could see pleasure on this woman's face at moments when she wasn't aware of herself, but as soon as the discussion got around to her, she seemed to put on her tired face and pained expression. It was pointed out to her in several circumstances that she chose to deny her pleasure and concentrate on her pain. In fact, she insisted on coming back to her suffering over and over again. This knowledge was like a bolt of lightning to her. She had choices within her own responses to focus on; her choice of focus helped to determine other people's responses to her; she really had considerable control over her own happiness : unhappiness ratio.

In all of the areas like moving, entertaining, communication, sex, and employment, there are many choices of focus. One corporate wife might focus mostly on the problems and difficulties; another might tend to focus on the solutions or the compromises; another might even focus on the opportunities. Consider, for example, the woman whose husband travels a great deal in the course of his job. On one end of the continuum, she might concentrate on how lonely his absence makes her, how much responsibility this dumps on her, how hopeless it is to travel with him because he is never available and she is left alone in a strange city. On the other end of the continuum, she might tune in on how much more interesting his travels make him, how much she enjoys the freedom to pursue independent activities (or just do nothing) while he is away, how broadening the travel is for her too when she can appropriately accompany him.

Similarly, the woman who finds herself at a convention, uninterested in the planned activities of the day, can focus on several things: She can bitch to everyone within earshot; she can find a confederate and blab all her troubles to one person; she can find alternate activities for herself; she can go to the activities anyway and try to get her "kicks" from involvement with other people; she can lobby in whatever appropriate ways she can find for a change in this program or the next one. Essentially, her choice of responses is the first step; but the second, perhaps equally important, step is her awareness of what it is in that situation that she chooses to focus on.

The reactions and responses of a woman in these kinds of situations are not isolated, haphazard, hit-or-miss variables. They usually form a pattern that is part of her character structure and which, if understood, says a lot about how she deals with life. As just one kind of measure, it is important for you to assess whether you tend to focus only on your own needs and desires, whether you tend to focus primarily on what other people want or think of you, or whether, more ideally, you put both aspects in perspective. Without the important focus on yourself, you will evolve into a victim—almost a nonperson. But without also being very aware of others, you will find yourself out of touch, alienated, unable to communicate with your husband and other people.

The importance of choice and of paying attention to what you choose to focus on can be emphasized for everyone, but it is especially important for corporate wives, who are primarily seen as extensions of their husbands, whose behavior and activities and attitudes are pretty well prescribed by the corporation, and whose opinions are generally not sought and usually not valued very much. The recognition of choice can change the way a corporate wife looks at herself, and it will almost certainly affect the way others see her as well.

# 12

# Six Who Defected

One option always available to men and women in the corporate world is to leave it. This usually happens in one of two ways: Either the executive decides to take a different type of job, or the wife decides she has had it and gets a divorce. There are other kinds of departures from the corporate system such as retirement, husband getting fired and being unable to find another corporate position, widowhood, an unwanted divorce in which the wife sees herself as victim. But in these situations the element of choice is minimal.

The interesting comparisons come from people who "had it made" in the corporate structure but still opted to defect. These men and women are able to weigh both sides; they are in the somewhat unique position of having experienced two different ways of life. This is not meant to suggest that they are thus totally objective. The fact that they have chosen another route leaves them with some need to defend that choice; there is a human need to justify our actions. Nevertheless, we can learn from those who compare the corporate wife's role with another way of life.

These are the stories of two couples who left large corporations to start small businesses of their own, and two divorced women, whose present circumstances evolved largely from their distaste of the corporate wife's role.


## EVE AND JEFF

The Martines are an intelligent, handsome couple who have been married eleven years. Eve is Hawaiian and petite, thirty-three years old; Jeff is thirty-seven, and was raised on Mercer Island, Washington. They met when Eve was a student at Seattle University; Jeff had completed the University of Washington, a stint in the navy, and an extended trip to Europe, and had just started as a salesman for Pacific Air freight "at the lofty salary of $475 a month plus car." Jeff says, "I was twenty-five, had fooled around enough, and felt nervous about that. I felt I was way behind the pack, and was anxious for the opportunity to work as hard as possible."

Shortly before their marriage Jeff was transferred to Denver as district manager, and Eve willingly joined him there. She easily got a high school teaching contract, and they stayed less than one year before a bigger district managership took them to Atlanta. They stayed just ten months in Atlanta, where Eve also taught high school, and then moved on to New Jersey for a year and a half. New Jersey was the only place they both disliked: Jeff says, "The Newark airport was always a mess—tough unions and all kinds of crime, but it was important from a career viewpoint to get experience there." Eve describes her feelings as follows: "I'm not sure whether it was because I was expecting a baby, and missed the warmth and camaraderie of friends and family who could share the experience with me, or because I just didn't like living in New Jersey. It was at this point, however, that we became foster parents to a teenager I'd taught in Georgia. I suddenly had a whole set of problems to worry about with a foster daughter and a new baby. There isn't really a substitute for a husband and family living, but with as much as I had on my hands, the problem of Jeff's being gone much of the time was at least deferred."

Jeff admits to working very long hours; they agreed that he averaged one day off per month. "No question about it; I was an inadequate husband and father. It wasn't that I didn't care. I was just totally consumed with my job; I didn't have much energy left for my wife. In that kind of business I could never relax. I often got calls in the middle of the night, from everywhere in the country, and almost everything was an emergency. I don't think I was eager just for the money—I sincerely believed in the company. It was an ego trip, a very exciting thing. I had friends all over the country; I felt I'd earned a good reputation; I felt unique; I was from Seattle and knew the guys who were running the show personally. The company had become Airborne by this time, but we were still small; there were many problems and setbacks. I felt I was really necessary and making a contribution. I knew I would not like the stereotyped corporation, in which people cared only about their own careers and not the company, but this was different. It was a heady thing. We all worked very hard, but the company took care of its own—a kind word now and then, and you never had to ask for a raise."

Eve adds, "When I was pregnant with Malia, and we were in New Jersey, I was worried about my father in Hawaii, who was mourning my mother's death. Jeff's boss offered to send me once a month or so to Hawaii, or he would have transferred us to Hawaii if we had wanted. They were very paternalistic in the best sense of the word." What responsibilities did Eve have for entertaining? "We entertained our own people, but generally things were not stratified as I imagine they are in other corporations. I never talked about these things with other wives. It was simply indicated to me that we would be frequently moved."

Six months after they bought a house in New Jersey, there was a "call from heaven" offering Jeff the manager of sales planning job at the Seattle headquarters. "I became

285

an itinerant preacher of the corporate gospel. We had forty or fifty offices around the country, and I visited most of them—recruiting, helping out, trying to encourage everyone."

His time off now advanced to perhaps two days per month. In 1973 he became vice-president of marketing.

Eve says, "It bothered me more that he was out of town so much than it did when he was just working long hours. Jeff would say he was gone about ten days per month; I think he was gone about three weeks out of four. But I always had my fair share of other problems; our second child, David, was born in 1973, and I also became surrogate mother to my brother and sister after our parents died. That seemed to defer our own personal problems again."

Did she ever wonder if all those hours were necessary? "Our system has always been that if he says something is necessary, I don't question it, and Jeff does the same with me."

But in 1975, after several agonizing months, after having become VP at age thirty-three and having been told he had a limitless future at Airborne, Jeff decided to leave. "Even when I was enjoying it the most, I never thought I wanted to do this all my life. I never really enjoyed working with trucks, government regulations, and other things in that business. My original immature goal had been to be able to retire by the time I was thirty-five; and maybe I could have made a lot of money. But the guy I worked for was just a couple of years older than me, and there were at least three others at my level who wanted to be president. I decided I didn't want that kind of responsibility even if it was offered to me.

"Somewhere along the way, also, I learned that either the corporation's philosophy as I saw it was superficial, or else things had changed. I had been all over the system as a corporate apostle; I'd gotten very close to many of the people, and we'd shared a lot. But as the company grew, much of what I said became obsolete. There were new layers of management; we had an overdose of MBO [management by objectives]; line managers could fire anybody and promote anybody; there was no recourse. I totally disagreed with management on that issue, and I felt two-faced. Things were not as I had represented them to be. My enthusiasm collapsed, and although there was real growth in earnings, all the fun things were gone in the sense of honest relationships with people. If I complained, I was accused of being a soft shoulder. I felt a sense of intimidation, but couldn't change my attitude or my behavior.

"Perhaps the catalyst was my dad's death. He had always kept me from becoming a self-important egomaniac. Now after he died in 1973, I reflected on what kind of father he had been to us. I saw myself at my son's age, and recognized I was not the father he'd been. I started to rethink my personal priorities. At some point the rising family concern and the dropping corporate zeal intersected.

"One other experience drove home the point. We had used at Airborne a sales training package that was behaviorally based. Once we brought all the salespeople to Seattle and found out we had a lot of stiffs in the company. We learned that human nature leads everyone to hire those who are less likely to threaten us, and this process creates serious problems as it repeats itself several steps down the line. It had unquestionably happened to us. We started a new form of recruiting in which we looked for early patterns of behavior that could be seen continuing into later life. This had nothing to do with sex, race, or education; but the relationships during early family life proved to be important with terrifying consistency. I interviewed hundreds of people, and contrary to my initial prejudice, found the theory almost totally valid. As I looked around, it often seemed like I was one of the few who'd had a normal, good family life, and I could recognize the great advantage this had given me. At the same time, I had to confront the fact that I was being a mediocre parent myself. Someday somebody will interview my kid, and what will he say?"

The process was not an easy one for either Eve or Jeff. "The president of the company offered us a month in

287

Europe to think it over, but I couldn't accept because I knew I'd feel obligated. Thankfully, Eve has always kept us in the black financially, so I wasn't worried about money." Eve adds, "Money and investments was my job. Money equaled freedom. I think we had a mutual desire for some change, for more time together as well as with our children. Jeff also wanted independence, which corporate life doesn't afford. He really wanted to try his hand at being captain of his own ship."

But how did she feel about such a drastic change? "Other women who have been in the situation where their spouse wants to seek independence and fulfillment know it's very difficult, if not impossible, to deny this desire. I can sail my own boat, but I can't sail somebody else's. If we could afford it, that luxury of freedom could be had. We were at a good age, he in his mid-thirties and I in my early thirties, so we thought we'd give it a try. I'm not as inner directed as Jeff, but I'm good at picking up the pieces and making them okay. My past personal history proves that I'm a counselor. I have a lot of respect for Jeff, and he's also given me lots of compensation. I was amazed at the amount of money Jeff had been willing to spend on my teen-aged brother and sister because of me, and all the trips we had made in the middle of the night to help them out."

Jeff says, "I didn't think very hard about what I was going to do until I left Airborne, but I'd always been fascinated by printing, which I'd learned from my father, and I had bought some of the printing at Airborne." Eve adds, "He had a remarkable urge to do something with his hands; he needed something more tangible."

A significant signal was the $300 printing press Jeff bought Eve for Christmas six months before he quit. "From the marketing point of view, printing is a primitive industry. I thought, since I'm a great marketing genius, I can do better. But we spent an incredible amount of money getting things started. I was ignorant as hell."

Eve interjects, "What we really did was to embark on the process of learning a trade. Jeff had his interest in printing, and I had some interest in money management,

288

so we pooled our resources and started off on our adventure. Don't think, however, that I did not have real concerns about how we would make a living. I did not have the financial comfort in my background that Jeff had."

Their new business is called Realty Supply Company, and Jeff has worked hard at it from the beginning. "But it's been like a hobby too. I wondered at first if I would get tired of it, bored with it. Once the word got out that I'd left Airborne, the phone started to ring with other corporate offers, but I knew that was not what I wanted. I believe that which we enjoy doing we're likely to be good at, so I went upstairs one night and wrote, 'What's important to me.' I sort of gave myself an in-depth interview— what my strengths are, what the red flags are, what I really like to do. I feel very fortunate; I have gotten an option most people don't have—to pick a niche for myself. I started what I enjoyed most—printing and selling, and I want to keep it small, at least by Airborne standards. I look forward to more time with my family. I own it, so it cannot be sold out from under me; I cannot be fired; it is an expression of myself, something I can be proud of. Frequently in the corporate world you hear two people talking to each other as though they are corporations. It sounds like a silly conversation; I wanted to relate to people as people. Printing is one of the few industries not dominated by a few vast concerns—and the people in it tend to be individualistic."

What are the drawbacks for Jeff? "I have to fight my own weaknesses. Everything exists in magnified form; my weaknesses are much more exposed. I'm fairly effective in dealing with people, but sometimes I'm too anxious to serve; I bend over too far. These traits are more visible now."

For Eve's part: "My life has become much more complicated. I went from a suburban housewife, with a history of doing almost anything to make our life successful, to a woman very much involved in a business. I am no longer the wife of Jeff Martine, vice-president of marketing and sales; I now must say that I am the wife of a printer. The business has evolved into a totally consuming project. The challenge is much greater than either of us had expected; hopefully so too will be the rewards. But I get most depressed when I worry about money. I see life as a progression. Family is very important; relationships are very important; but there should also be financial progression. I came from little; my father had less; and I expected us to progress financially without having to dip so far into savings. We've made some money at real estate, and we've both taken dives on the stock market. Perhaps it is significant that we cashed out our Airborne stock; the first thing we did in a sense was to get rid of it forever. That was my impulse more than Jeff's—cutting the umbilical cord; saying it's behind me now—water under the bridge."

Eve usually works at least six hours each day in the business, and says, "Our lives are completely intertwined. The time we spend at work is shared. It's a totally different trip from being the wife of someone who works for that amorphous thing called A CORPORATION. It is ironic, perhaps, that Jeff is actually spending as much time working now as he did at Airborne; he often goes back to work after dinner, and usually works Saturdays and Sundays. But interestingly enough, I don't have the same resentments I felt when his corporate job took him away, because it's my business too. The stakes are higher now as it's our stake."

Does she miss the security of his corporate job? "There is a great deal of politicking and maneuvering in corporate life, and even the most adept sometimes find themselves out due to changes out of their control. So I don't think that our situation is any less secure than it was when Jeff worked for a corporation. In this case, we're making our own security. I enjoy the work I do. The only part I don't like so far is not having a big fat income. It's also very different taking care of yourselves vis-à-vis health insurance, life insurance, taxes, etc. They're called fringe benefits, and now I know why. I'm getting a very meaningful education, the hard way, learning about these things, plus accounting and bookkeeping."

When I asked Jeff how he sees Eve's role now, he

said, "She's like my boss and my board of directors. She scans everything, and it may be a good thing because I am sometimes impulsive. But when I was at Airborne, I could come home and not say much about work if I didn't want to; now we have to explain things to each other. This is difficult when things go bad, but overall, we are infinitely closer. We fight our battles as we go; before we only touched orbits from time to time."

What about entertaining now to get or keep customers? "The market we serve doesn't expect or have time for entertaining. It is an unsophisticated industry. After all, nothing is really sold; things are bought. The salesman goes out and finds needs and ways to fill them, but if you don't want the product, nothing can make you buy it." They both agreed that, more than ever now, "we do only what we want to do with customers, and spend our time with those we want to share our time."

Jeff summed up some of the enormous change in their lives this way: "The corporation is like a jealous mistress. I don't think I could work for one and still be a decent husband and father. What is comical and tragic at the same time is that this status thing is really so unimportant. I found out after I left Airborne that, one, my friends didn't know what I did anyway; two, if they knew what I did, they didn't care; and three, what I'm doing now doesn't make any difference to them either. On another personal note, I found that once I could no longer deify my boss, I had a stronger need for religion. Everyone needs a boss. I've also become more conservative regarding government; I really feel those taxes now; and silly government spending makes me livid. One of the dangers to our society is the increasingly large scale of organizations. It is easy to forget where the money goes; taxpayers' money becomes 'federal funds.' This—our small business—is extremely real; it is a total commitment in dollars and in many other ways."

Now the difficult questions: How would Jeff feel if Eve had a separate career and were less available to him? "It would have been okay when I was with Airborne. Eve has talked of going to law school, and I've supported

291

that. But I couldn't have managed these last couple years without her; she's a big part of this business."

And could Eve have gone on being an Airborne corporate wife without complaint? "I don't think so. My own problems diverted me at times, but I made a lot of sacrifices. Our new life has its cons as well as pros, but the change has been good for us, and we have great expectations."


## RAE AND BOB

The Miles are an attractive, energetic couple in their early forties. They have been married sixteen years, and have two children—Steve, who is thirteen, and Alison, who is eleven. Bob worked for IBM for fifteen years before leaving in January 1973 to start his own business. He is a third-generation Los Angeleno, and says that he had no intention of migrating north, but his IBM career gradually took him farther north, and they have been happily settled in the Seattle area since 1968.

After college and graduate school, Bob began marketing training with IBM in Santa Monica; he went from there to San Diego. "Then, because I was the only bachelor in the group and junior on the totem pole, the manager convinced me of a career opportunity in Portland. Rae and I met there in 1961, and I was there eight years."

Rae says that their life during those years was that of newlyweds. "We weren't management; our social life was smashing; we were all young and in the baby-making stage. Almost all our friends were IBMers; we all had nice houses and were involved in decorating them; we were all at the same level in the company although we were twenty-one to fifty in age. I never found such closeness anywhere else. I was working in the advertising department at Hyster—an eight-to-five job; most of the wives worked before they had babies." Did they do any customer entertaining? "That was handled by Bob in the daytime." Bob adds, "Others may have been more social than we were, but IBM is a very high-principled organiza-

292

tion. There were no payoffs; you couldn't drink on company time."

Rae does remember Bob's long hours. "He was expected to work an awful lot. He used to tell me that if he didn't, he wouldn't have a job." Bob says, "They gave us a quota, and you had to work at least fifty hours a week to meet it."

Rae also remembers some constraints on conversation. "I was working on Goldwater's campaign in Oregon, and he was having a very bitter fight there. Whenever we went out socially, most of the people we met were Johnson Democrats, and I remember being told by Bob to cool it." When Bob didn't seem to remember these incidents, Rae said, "Maybe I just felt it. But those were not bad years. Bob was always one of the highest performers, always made more than quota. We were buying a house and thinking about babies; we had terrific friends; mostly it was a big party.

"We did see, during those years, many IBMers who were very transient. The pattern was only two years in each place; the man would come first and pick out five places with a real estate agent; then the wife would come and they'd move into one of them; the wife would have the place completely done by an interior decorator; and everyone knew they'd be gone in two years. They didn't seem to mind, and I didn't think too much about what that kind of life would be like for me."

In 1968 they were transferred to Seattle; the position involved a salary increase, and they wanted the change mostly for Rae. She had been born and raised in Seattle, and it was home for her. Eventually, they both decided they wanted to stay in Seattle, and in 1973, Bob quit.

"There were several reasons as I look back upon it. It was clear that they could hire two young fellows for the wage I was making, so there was limited opportunity. My name had been on the promotion list when we came to Seattle, but somehow, shortly after I told them that I did not want to move geographically, my name disappeared from the list. There was no place to go—so many overqualified guys and no place to put them. There were too many chiefs; half of us had master's degrees. At times life at IBM was super; at times it was unbearable. When the managers were bad, I had a hell of a time; I would come home all dragged out. Incompetency in management made it very frustrating sometimes. Maybe I was different than most; maybe I expect too high quality. But I had always wanted to start my own business; it was in my family; my grandfather and father were independent businessmen."

What was Rae's part in this decision-making process? "I practiced active listening, and we talked a lot. We were also able to reverse and shift when I was having my problems. Bob has tremendous self-confidence; I was more scared than he was. This area was in the middle of the Boeing depression; what if the business was a failure?" Bob reminded her that "my salary had lessened the last couple of years anyway. Computers were being moved out of companies faster than the moving van could move them. IBM was managing our earnings very closely; in a complicated way, they decided what your income would be, and it seemed to be less."

Rae says, "Perhaps the thing that scared me the most was the loss of fringe benefits; IBM's benefits were truly magnificent—cradle to grave. I also thought of missing the Golden Circle; we had gone on these marvelous trips two or three times with other top salesmen and their wives, and the future looked like we might go every year. Actually, Bob was more concerned about money than I was, but it turned out to be a big change in life-style. We never bought anything new for four years —the last two with IBM, and the first two with the new business. We both questioned at times whether we had done the right thing." Bob adds, "It took almost two years before I started to make money. I started ROI Computer Company in January, and it was the end of May before I made my first commission of seven dollars.

"But the freedom was wonderful. Within IBM the managers were subject to such pressure to produce certain things. If today they were producing green lemons, then by God we not only had to sell green lemons, but we had to do it by procedure 34B. And the manner of selling was not always palatable. If you didn't make progress with an account, they would want you to try to replace the manager or go above him. IBM salesmen had a lot of clout for lots of reasons; you could drop hints or put pressure in certain places. The object was to go around him, above him, or get him replaced, but I would not become involved in that stuff. I guess my fault at IBM was that I did not tell them what they wanted to hear." Rae adds that "Bob is very honest."

So how has Rae's life changed in the last five years? "Bob still works long hours. He is often at his desk in the evening after dinner. I served at least a year and a half as his secretary; I did his typing. But I didn't do it well enough, and he always gave it to me late at night, wanting it immediately. That caused a lot of family conflict.

"By that time I wanted my own identity, and I guess I was selfish about it. One alternative would have been for me to get a decent paying job elsewhere, but I had been taking care of a sick child, and I had had it. My university art degree was lying fallow, and I had always wanted to work for an art museum. I had applied two years before to a docent class at the museum, and they accepted me just about the same time that Alison went into first grade and Bob started his business. I didn't want to give up that opportunity.

"I have always had major responsibility for raising the children and managing the household. Bob manages the books, but I write the checks and take care of all the details. I often think how nifty it would be if he could have my responsibilities for six months. Bob could take care of the children and the house, and tell me how organized he is."

What about company entertaining? Bob says, "I have always kept business and home life separate. What I have to do, I usually do at lunch." Rae adds, "Besides, Bob is a homebody; he likes to come home for dinner. I sometimes regret that I don't get more invitations out for dinner. I used to hate those command performances for IBM

295

Christmas parties, but I wouldn't mind a dinner with customers from time to time. In the early years, Bob used to go out with the boys for an evening, and that was business. If he had taken me too, I would have encouraged it. He also took people to the cabin we had, and allowed customers to use the cabin sometimes. But Bob and I aren't party people. About the only regular thing we do is during Seafair each summer; he takes customers on his sailboat for lunch every day during that time, and on the unlimited hydroplane race day on Lake Washington, we both go with customers who have also become social friends."

Bob sums up his new way of life by saying, "I much prefer it. We never have to face another move. My home is very important to me, and I could not move every two years like some IBM people do. The only people who seem to like that life are the ones who don't want to put down roots. The peace of mind to me is extremely important. Within IBM, I'd know I was doing a good job, but it might not have been what they wanted. There was a time with IBM when I was commuting to Olympia every day; I think of the years added to my life by not commuting. And I think what it means to have the BS pressure off me. Now my office is five minutes away from home." Rae interjects that she can call on him in an emergency if necessary. Bob adds, "I can take time to coach my son's soccer team. I am selling used computers and have a lot of business contacts. We still get our fabulous trips, often for association meetings in good places, although we pay for them now ourselves."

Some things are a little more difficult. "When we sought our own insurance, it was very expensive. The retirement program at IBM was super; we have to make our own retirement plan now. Vacations are a problem; I don't take any without worry, without thinking, 'I lost this much or that much.' It is a different kind of pressure; nobody does my work while I am gone. But I am not interested in bigness or status. I am also not interested in training a competitor; if I brought someone into the business, I would eventually either have to give him a

296

percentage, or he would go out on his own. Besides I am raising my partners—my son and daughter."

The absence of IBM from the Miles' lives certainly has brought changes, but the lean years seem to be over, and both Rae and Bob say they are happier than ever before.


## JANET

Janet Wilson divorced her husband—and at the same time, her corporate wife's role—about eight years ago. She was eager to tell her story, but asked that her real name not be used because some of her feelings might be embarrassing to her ex-husband.

Janet was twenty-one and had just graduated cum laude with a journalism major when she married Bill; he had been in the military, and had just gotten his MBA from Wharton. He took a job with a brokerage house in New York, and Janet went to work for a women's magazine. Those were happy years for them; they had the money and the energy to enjoy the big city discoveries; they were both progressing rapidly in their jobs, and Janet looked forward to a very successful career. In fact, the more she worked, the more she began to question her previous desire for children and the suburban housewife role her mother had played. "We had a few hassles way back then about my growing interest in my work. I remember one time when we were planning to go on a Caribbean vacation; I got an emergency assignment, and decided to postpone the vacation rather than confront my boss. But Bill wasn't very happy with that decision, and he sulked around the house for weeks. Another time we went out for dinner to celebrate a raise I had just gotten. I was still making nowhere near what he was, but he had not gotten a raise in over a year, and he was very unpleasant to me that night. It was shortly after that that he began to look around for another job. One of his good friends was with a large international oil company, and it was through him that Bill went to work there. He went into a management training program there with the understanding that when he finished that program in about six months, he would probably be transferred overseas."

Leaving her job was not easy for Janet; she thought she would miss the people more than anything. But she observed that Bill seemed much happier than he had at the brokerage firm, and she really looked forward to living abroad. "When Bill came home with the news that it would be Rome, I was ecstatic. We sold some of our belongings, but the rest were well packed by a professional company, and we set off on our so-called holiday. What a shock that was! I couldn't speak the language and had a hard time learning it; our apartment was infested with insects and mice; the frenetic driving made me afraid to go anywhere on my own; I missed my friends and my family. Some couples from Bill's company had us over, but the women all seemed so dull; I didn't like them very much, and I'm sure the feeling was mutual. Bill was working long hours, and didn't have much patience with me when I complained at night."

What do many couples do when all else seems lost? "We decided to have a child. Tricia was born in Rome, but my parents came over for the occasion, and that helped make it a very warm and happy time. Bill was delighted with the baby, and also made an offhand remark to my parents that now I would not be on his back anymore. When Tricia was a year old, we were transferred to Istanbul. Jonathan was born there, and during those years I was so busy with babies that I had little time to think of myself. But there were still quite a few nights when I cried myself to sleep. I felt very alone and lonely; I wondered why I wasn't able to adjust better; I needed to tell my troubles to someone, but I was too proud to unburden myself to family or friends, and Bill simply wouldn't listen. Those were very bad times for me, and even though I spent all my time with the kids and tried not to hurt them, I think I was a pretty lousy mother. What socializing we did was usually with company people, and whenever we went to parties, I put on my happy face."

When they were transferred to London, Janet felt relieved. "Finally, it was a familiar language, and I decided to try to get some work. I got some contacts through old friends in New York, and I tried to find a part-time job, but there seemed to be so many obstacles—working papers, finding my way around, getting a responsible nanny, locating an employer who would accept me on a part-time basis. Finally, I settled for some free-lance editorial work, but after a short burst of interest from the people I'd contacted, the work stopped coming. I guess if I had beat the bushes a little more, I might have found something interesting, but I didn't have much energy those days."

After only a year and a half in London, they were asked to come back to New York, but the understanding was that it would be a brief assignment, and that they would be off again within a year. This time, Janet decided to stay with her parents in Rhode Island. "Bill lived in a New York hotel during the week and came up to see us most weekends. He was in great spirits; he seemed almost relieved to be rid of us, at least temporarily. He saw a lot of his old school chums; he ate at the best restaurants, and bought some new clothes at Brooks Brothers. He was clearly moving up in the world, and he wanted to look and act it."

What about her? "I felt like I was in drydock. For the first time in my life, I began to use alcohol to help me feel better. Oh, I never got really drunk, but after the kids went to bed at night, I had two or three drinks; and when Bill came up on weekends, I often drank to get myself into bed with him. He was eager to have sex, as always, but I had to have a few drinks to feel anything at all with him; even then, I was far from turned on. But by that time, I had learned pretty well to monitor my behavior around him. I still felt I was pretty lucky to have him; he was good looking and successful; I liked telling people I was the wife of an executive."

They went briefly to San Francisco after that, where they lived in an apartment hotel, and then to Australia, where it all came apart two years later. "I remember standing in the middle of a crowded cocktail party, and thinking, 'What in the hell am I doing here?' Even though I knew most of those people, they were like strangers to me. I hadn't found one friend among the women, and a large part of that, I guess, was my fault. I had found myself talking more and more about the work I had done, and how much I wanted to get back to it. My children were in school full-time, and I had time on my hands. I guess this was offensive to most of those women, who had long ago given up any plans for careers themselves, and seemed so satisfied to be a part of their husband's life. I guess I was putting them down in a way when I wanted something else. Anyway, I felt out of place in that group. I had done my fair share of entertaining and working on committees, but it wasn't enough. I knew that I could never have any meaningful career with these overseas assignments; the culture was different, and I couldn't, in good conscience, promise to be in one place very long."

What was her relationship with Bill like in other ways? "Bill is basically a nice, hard-working guy, but we had become estranged from each other. When I told him I planned to leave, he couldn't believe it at first. We talked like we never had before, and he tried to think of ways to make me stay, but it was too late by then. I knew I just couldn't live that way the rest of my life; he had his work and his feelings of success. I don't mean he didn't care about his family, but we weren't the only things in his life. I felt guilty for a while about taking the kids away from him, but three years later he married an Australian woman with two children of her own."

Janet decided to return to New York, where she had spent her happiest years. Her parents helped her get situated in a small Manhattan apartment. Her children were now eight and six, and she got after-school baby-sitting help. She found a job in a small publishing house, and she worked very hard, reading manuscripts at night, learning the business from anyone who would teach her, inviting people to dinner who could be helpful to her. She admits that she became quite political, and that she found it hard at times to be a good mother too. Her parents and her ex-husband took the kids for most school vacations, and she somehow managed. At this point, eight years later, she is an editor at one of the largest and most prestigious publishing houses in New York, and she makes about $40,000 per year. "I don't live like a queen on that in New York," she says, "but I'm my own boss. The kids are teenagers now and doing quite nicely. I've been close to remarriage a couple times, but I always escaped," she says with a soft laugh. "In one case, I think the man found me too threatening; he wanted a more passive woman. In the other case, I found that there was trouble with the kids, and it would have taken too much time and energy to integrate him into our family." Would she marry another corporate executive? "You may think I'm crazy, but I would like to someday marry again. Maybe it's a need to have somebody when I get old. I would hate to go through all that corporate wife nonsense, but if the executive was a very special man, I might be willing to try under certain conditions. I certainly would not give up my own career, which probably means we would have to stay in New York. And I would certainly question a lot of that stuff I used to accept.

"I sometimes ask myself these kinds of questions: How much accommodation to the corporation is really necessary? How much of it is admissable and when does it become a form of indirect pressure that almost amounts to blackmail? How much can any corporation expect of any employee or his wife and family? Who should draw the lines? These things make me wonder about individual welfare versus corporate power and profit. In exchange for a meal at Lutece, is a wife supposed to readily cancel her evening course? spend three hours on the telephone hunting up a sitter for what could be a kid coming down with the mumps? polish her nails, wash her hair, and dress up? catch the five P.M. train into New York only to sit for three hours with some boring woman or two while their husbands drone on and on about last year's incentive or next year's model? Should anyone have to submerge his or her own identity merely to be a superfluous attachment whose value is symbolic? Frankly, a Big Mac with an intelligent friend who values your opinion on politics or modern art is a better meal.

"I also wonder whether I could find any man who would play the corporate husband role for me. The truth of the matter is that executive women rarely engage in after-hours entertaining, probably because their husbands are not expected to join them. And also those women don't want to do it themselves. They would rather go home and out to dinner with friends, or just kick off their shoes and watch the evening news. I just wonder if all this executive mucka-muck entertaining and convention going is really necessary to progress and the pursuit of profit. Or is it that the corporations have absorbed so much of an executive's life anyway that he doesn't know what else to do with his time, or his mind, or his life? We are all aware these days that material gain is not enough to sustain any human being. More and more people are dropping out of lucrative jobs to live a life closer to their families and to themselves. The saddest thing of all that I have observed is the executives—male and female—who have neither the time nor the energy nor the interest to spend all the money they make. The government is the real winner, or the tax accountants busy building shelters that the tax evader never inhabits—not even spiritually."

Janet makes all these points with the acknowledgment that she herself is still struggling with what it means to be an executive. "But my life as a corporate wife gave me some preparation for what I do not want my life as an executive to be. And I'm still working on how my job affects and will affect my family—one day at a time."


## MARTA

Marta Simmons is also not this woman's real name; she said she is still experiencing the pain of her divorce and would find it difficult to talk publicly. She is fifty-five years old but looks at least ten years younger. She married Tom when she was twenty-five and continued her teaching job for five years after that. Her first child was born when she was thirty, and the rest of her four children were born about two years apart after that. Tom is an attorney who has worked in the legal departments of three major corporations. They have lived in three different cities on the eastern seaboard, and for the last six years of their marriage they lived near Philadelphia. They divorced about five years ago.

"I was your typical corporate wife for twenty-five years. I prided myself on being an excellent hostess and conversationalist. Tom frequently brought out-of-towners home for dinner, sometimes on very short notice. I served on a million boards and did a lot of volunteer work. I pretty much raised the children alone because Tom traveled a lot, and when he was home, he didn't want to be bothered. I always bought the idea that home should be a refuge, so I managed our lives that way. I suspected over the years that Tom had other women on the side, and I personally knew about two of them. When I confronted him about it, though, he said he didn't want to discuss it, and I decided to leave it at that. He was generous with money, and the kids adored him, even though he didn't pay much attention to them.

"The other women always bothered me, and once, about ten years ago, I went into therapy to have someone to talk to about it. I stayed in therapy about six months, but I didn't get much out of it. My shrink was a man too, and every time we discussed this problem, I kind of felt he was siding with Tom. He never said that, but I wondered if he felt Tom's need for other women was because of me—I wasn't attractive enough or sexy enough. We belonged to the Methodist church, and one time I also went to talk to my minister about it. He told me to pray, but I had the feeling he wasn't taking it all too seriously. After all, he knew Tom to be an upstanding church member and a big contributor; I don't think he wanted to get involved."

For the most part, Marta sat on her feelings and continued to do all the things that were expected of her. Maybe she would have gone on like that forever if her friend hadn't introduced her to a little theater group. "This neighbor of mine was a little nutty, but we became pretty good friends, and I liked her a lot. She got involved with an amateur theater group in Philadelphia, and once, when parts were being cast for middle-aged women, she convinced me to try out. I had belonged to a thespian group in college, so this was not entirely new to me, but it had been a long time. At first, I really intended to work mostly in the supportive, administrative end of the group, but somehow I just got hooked on acting. I spent long hours there. My husband complained; my kids complained; they weren't used to having to fend for themselves; but they couldn't make me quit. I got bigger and better parts over the next three years; I had starring roles in two very good productions.

"I also had my first affair in thirty years. He was fifteen years younger than I, and we had a wonderful time. He taught me to play tennis—and many other things. He was an actor who had been divorced long ago, and he had settled in Philadelphia only temporarily. The day that he told me he was moving to Los Angeles, I wanted to die. But some part of me had known all along that it would end and that it was for the best. I pulled myself together pretty quickly, but it was then that I began to think about leaving Tom."

After three months of talking, they both accepted the fact that they had grown in different directions, and Marta decided to head for New York. What about the children? "I decided to leave the kinds with the money. That may sound crass, but I had seen so many friends scraping along on child support, or not being able to collect it. I didn't want them to change their standard of living. By this time, you see, the oldest was twenty and in college; the others were fourteen, sixteen, and eighteen. They know who their mother is; I am still their mother, and they all come to visit me. But taking them with me was just not practical."

Marta enrolled in an acting school in New York, and her days were full, "but I had some very lonely times that first couple years. I used to think about the fancy company dinners, the traveling at company expense, about being the wife of a somebody. Now, I sometimes thought, I'm a nobody. But luckily those days passed, and I began to think of myself as a real person. Tom was always good about giving me money, but it was a happy day when I told him a couple years ago I thought I could make it on my own. I've been doing quite a few commercials, and once in a while I get a part in an off-Broadway play. Who would believe there'd be so much work for an old dame like me. No, strike that. I really feel younger now than I did twenty years ago. That life I led for all those years— the perfect corporate wife: That wasn't me; that was just a facade of me. Sometimes I feel like I wasted a lot of years, but I try not to focus on that; I try to be grateful that I've been able to change, that I'm healthy and still have a lot of years ahead of me. It helps that I have a little nest egg from the divorce settlement, but my security is much more inside me now."

Does she have any interest in marrying again? "No way. I suppose I shouldn't be so categorical about it. I have had a couple relationships with men, and I do like to have relationships that last awhile. But, you know, I'm also finding out how much I enjoy relationships with women; I used to feel wary of other women, but I really am more open to close relationships now. I like my independence; I need space. Maybe it's because I lived in the shadow of a man so long. It's hard to sort out whether it would have been any different if Tom were a physician or an architect. But the corporate life sure took a lot out of him, and out of me too. It's not the kind of life I would choose for my children."


## DEFECTION IS THE MOST DRASTIC CHOICE

The choice these six people made—to defect, to leave the corporate way of life—is a most drastic one, and this is certainly not meant to be a recommendation. Not every couple has the desire or the financial resources or the emotional wherewithal to start their own business; clearly, not every corporate wife has the desire or the resources to divorce her executive husband. Nevertheless, these are options that help to illustrate the totality of the situation.

Sometimes we see things more clearly in retrospect; sometimes we have to get away from a psychological place to really understand it. By sharing their stories, these six people help us to look at new perspectives.

As is obvious from all of these experiences, defection from the corporation does not imply an end to struggles. There may be less moving, less entertaining, or less pressure of a certain kind, but the change is almost always accompanied by less money and less security for a while.

As Jeff Martine says, the corporation is a man's jealous mistress; for the corporate wife, it might be called an unforgiving master.

It is important to note, through Janet and Marta, that the women who defected via divorce never blamed their splits solely on the role of corporate wife. In each case, there was also a crucial ingredient missing in the marriage, and this can be described as communication, openness, honesty. Both Janet and Marta made some stabs at changing their lives within the marriage, but they got little support or cooperation from their husbands. It is impossible to know whether they could have tried harder to get through to these men, but, in any case, communication was extremely important.

You always have options in dealing with the corporate wife's role, and defection is just one of them. But even this drastic change should emphasize that you are never a victim; you are never helpless. You have power to change your own life. If you can establish a sharing, open relationship with your corporate partner, all kinds of possibilities can begin to develop. If you can get straight and honest with yourself and each other, the choices will make sense and will help you both to grow.

# 13

# Learn to Enjoy and Appreciate Yourself

The first and most important step in learning to appreciate yourself is to look inward as well as outward in terms of responsibility. A woman might see the corporation or her own husband or men in general as perpetrators of many wrongdoings, but this need not make them villains. As one woman puts it, "Women don't hate men; some of our best friends are men." They as aggressors have been part of the same system that made the corporate wife passive, submissive, and acquiescent—a second-class citizen—but they too have suffered in the process. In looking at herself, in introspection, the individual woman can find explanations and solutions that will never come by laying responsibility totally on others. In the process, she will undoubtedly find that she is an interesting, complex, growing person and will gain increasing appreciation of herself and her own worth.

Most of us grew up in an environment that was fairly critical of us. Besides our parents' demands and expectations, we had to meet the requirements of schools, churches, police, and other judgmental institutions. These have made us achievement oriented, but they have also produced a lot of uncertainty and self-doubt. Girls especially have grown up in a culture where they were valued less than boys, where they were thought to be less intelligent, less logical, less stable, less goal directed than their brothers. The corporate system has added to these self-deprecatory feelings for women by insistence on conformity to a rather conservative mold, discouraging spontaneity and playfulness, and judging corporate wives by a rather narrow standard. It is the rare woman, let alone the rare corporate wife, who has really learned to enjoy and appreciate herself. Nevertheless, this sense of security or appreciation or enjoyment of oneself can be learned and can stem from a variety of sources.

## THERE ARE NO VILLAINS

One common point for both executives and executives' wives to consider in looking at their situation is that there really are no villains. In many ways the system has been destructive to both men and women. But spending one's energy in resentment or bitterness at men or at the business world is a useless exercise. Certainly the purpose of a corporation is, and should be, in the economic realm. It exists to make a profit. Domestic problems are not the company's concern, and involvement in marital relationships really should be beyond its scope. The use and misuse of corporate wives—often to get two employees for the price of one—has been largely for economic rather than malicious reasons. It is the responsibility of the women involved with these corporations—indeed it is their mandate—to say a resounding *no* when use becomes misuse.

Some people have suggested that corporations might assist corporate wives by providing counseling or paying for courses to update skills. But this, in my opinion, is simply a different kind of paternalism and perhaps a more subtle kind of manipulation or control. What corporations should increasingly be told to do is butt out! If the corporate wife is not on the payroll, she can rightfully refuse to be controlled.

There will undoubtedly be a struggle for many years to come because of well-entrenched patterns of behavior on both sides, but vitriolic efforts to place blame on the corporation are misdirected. As Seidenberg says:

> This situation illustrates once again that the women's struggle, like many others, is not a battle of good against evil, but a conflict of diverse forms each of which has a legitimate claim to be heard. As much as we need and enjoy their presence (to appear as saints by contrast), real devils these days are hard to find.[1]

Similarly, men need not be seen as targets for resentment because they too have been raised and trapped in a system that may not be very helpful or healthful for them either. There is growing recognition in our society that men have suffered in different ways than women have in our unequal division of labor and rewards.

The fact that women are taking on new challenges and responsibilities will undoubtedly be good for women; recognition, power, money, new interests and roles will surely make them more interesting and more fulfilled people. The fact that women are becoming increasingly involved in activities other than twenty-four-hour mothering will probably be good for children. It will avoid the situations where children are burdened by all their mother's desires and expectations; it will relieve the children of the responsibility and/or guilt for their mother's happiness and/or unhappiness. But these changes for women will certainly benefit men too. Men can begin to feel less burden for the financial and emotional support of the whole family; men can begin to relax a bit about the need to feel strong and rational at all times; they can perhaps begin to be more in touch with the feeling level of themselves, and medical experts are sure that this will benefit men both emotionally and physically.

Another source for this process of self-appreciation is an honest assessment of one's marriage. This is considerably easier for the corporate wife today than it was several years ago because of the increasing realism all around us about marriage. In the old days women were taught that a good marriage should be their ultimate goal—their end all and be all. Mr. Right would protect them against all the financial and emotional turmoil of the world, and they would live happily ever after. In the past, when a woman found herself in a lousy, disappointing marriage to an executive who was evidently highly regarded by the corporate world, she concluded something must be wrong with her.

Today we have been helped by the social sciences to understand that marriage can never be any kind of total answer; that one person can never fulfill all of another person's needs and desires; and that a certain amount of disappointment in marriage is to be expected. Furthermore, there is increasing acceptance, even in the corporate world, of divorce as the logical end to bad marriages. Because of this and the many changes in the ways women are now seeing themselves, the corporate wife is more free than she has ever been to think of all kinds of marital arrangements and alternatives. As she becomes more realistic about what she can and should expect from her own marriage, she need not feel so trapped, so victimized, so disappointed. As she relaxes a bit in the knowledge that her husband cannot make her happiness for her, she will see herself as a more important person and appreciate her own capabilities more.

In sexual ways, women are just beginning to get a sense of who they are and what makes them tick. Our survey and others would seem to indicate that corporate wives are slow to catch up, but other information points to tremendous awakening of sexuality for women. *Redbook* magazine received questionnaires from 100,000 women—mostly young, white, middle-class, married women—and reported a striking shift of sexual mores in its September 1975 issue. The results of this survey state that the overwhelming majority of these women no longer sub-scribe to a sexual double standard, and that women have abandoned the role of passive sexual partner. After mar-riage, 31 percent of the women in the sample had had ex-tramarital experience—a third of them with from two to five men. Many women (36 percent) who had never had an extramarital affair said they had a "fairly strong" desire to do so. The majority of women occasionally (69 percent) or often (13 percent) had intercourse while under the influence of alcohol; about 20 percent occasionally or often had sexual relations under the influence of marijuana. Oral sex was an almost universal experience, with 90 percent of those women describing it as an enjoyable experience. The majority of women thought that sex was appropriate "any time."

Another survey of sexual mores, based on many in-terviews and written by a journalist, validates the Ameri-can wife's interest in sex, but it indicates that sex between housewives and their husbands is almost dead. Besides turning to men other than their husbands, it seems that women are preferring lesbianism, masturbation, and even abstinence to marital sex.[2]

These are the days when most women are trying to find out their identity sexually, as well as other ways, and corporate wives probably won't be far behind. There can be a great deal of excitement and pleasure in throwing off the old taboos, the artificial restrictions about sex with which most of us were raised.

I have one friend who went through a marriage and divorce and has just recently announced to her affluent, conservative family that she is a lesbian. She is introspec-tive enough to know that she felt both pain and titillation in their negative reaction. She also enjoys to some extent the curious and hostile stares she gets in public when she is openly affectionate with her lover. Her sexual identity has changed drastically and, to be sure, she is still struggling somewhat, but she is excited about how it feels to be in love with a woman. "It's wonderful to know that my whole life doesn't have to change because of her. I can be myself in a way that I never could with a man. She

311

doesn't make demands that I fulfill a role the way a man would. I don't know if I'll be with her forever, but I really love her just the way she is, and she feels the same about me." Lesbianism would be a huge step for most corporate wives, but one can benefit simply by the consideration of that alternative. As your feelings about yourself and about other women change, lesbianism becomes at least more understandable.

Many women who are not experiencing orgasm have also begun to search after it. While "frigidity" in women used to be common and quite acceptable, most women today want to experience orgasm and are trying to find out how if they don't already know. Sexual therapists are having a great deal of success in treatment with preorgasmic (they say there is no such thing as nonorgasmic) women.

Out of all this rethinking and exploration, some women are finding that they prefer an exclusive relationship with one partner; other women are finding stimulation and growth in experience with several men. The important point is that the rules are now of the individual woman's making; she is finding out what turns her on or off instead of blindly accepting what clergymen and physicians and other experts—mostly men—have told her. As her horizons open sexually, she is appreciating new aspects of herself and gaining new respect for her own sexuality.

Another important factor in the way a woman looks at herself is the tremendous upheaval all around us in the general attitudes about women and women's roles. No one can deny that women's roles are changing and that attitudes about women are being drastically shaken up. Although my survey of men at the very top of companies showed only a minimal response to this upheaval, it is really apparent all around us. For those who still think that women's liberation is just a product of some kooky fringe group, there is much evidence to the contrary. There is certainly still a sizable group of women who want to maintain the status quo, but whether they like it or not, laws are being passed that make women equal. And these laws are changing the practices of employment, credit, alimony, abortion, and many other areas in almost revolutionary ways. Few businessmen, for example, would have predicted five years ago or would have believed even two years ago that they would be spending the time, energy, and money that they now are expending to make sure they are an equal opportunity employer.

Even the impact of age is changing. *Time*'s recent essay, "In Praise of Older Women," says we are experiencing a "welcome, and slightly amazing development. In an almost measurable way, the average age of desirability in American women seems to have risen by a dozen years or more." Young girls, in contrast to women of 35 or 40, seem somehow unformed, incomplete, far less interesting, and sometimes unbelievably ignorant. The changed response in men is attributed to a series of changes in women themselves—the way they run their lives, the way they see themselves. Only older women can have the loveliness that comes from finally having "taken permanent possession of themselves."[3]

This is a very exciting time for women, a truly transitional time; it is a time of great frustrations and great opportunities. In many ways for women the future never looked rosier. Militant women are not backing down and are making great strides; the courts and the laws are consistently changing the way women have been viewed. The rigid definitions of masculinity and femininity are no longer accepted, and the myth of male superiority is gradually disappearing from most areas of life. The fact that the corporate world, especially in its attitudes about corporate wives, is lagging behind need not discourage us too greatly. This too will undoubtedly change with time. The important point is that all this is going on around us, and that it is extremely exhilarating if you can be in tune with what is happening. Whether or not you agree totally with all the changes, you cannot deny that there is a state of flux, of change, of growth for women in general. Being aware of the same conditions in yourself, being open to new ideas and new experience, can significantly add to your enjoyment and self-appreciation.

313

One of the assumptions, of course, of this new equality between men and women is that both partners must be competent and must be able to contribute. Many corporate wives have been so used to being in secondary positions in regard to decision making that it is difficult for them to have faith in themselves and in their opinions. Real egalitarianism in a marriage demands real mutual respect. This kind of respect, and even trust, must be given by husbands to wives but must also be earned by those wives (as well as it should be earned by husbands). In most business situations, there is some kind of hassle in an atmosphere of trust and respect for each other's competence before a good decision is made. A marriage in which decisions are shared calls for the same ingredients.

A top executive of a midwestern manufacturing organization stated the facts about many corporate wives in his organization. (He added that he would be in big trouble if his identity were known.) "Most husbands in this company consciously do not involve their wives in any way with work. Most of those wives are high school graduates, and they are really not interested anyway. They spend their time playing bridge and doing 'wives' ' activities. Their function is to make sure meals are on the table, keep the house clean, and presumably be a sex partner less and less frequently. New York wives are more sophisticated; it is like the 1890s here in the Midwest with women. The men want to keep women in their place. Most husbands here enjoy the opportunity to get away from their wives. You should see some of them!" This indictment speaks for itself and is, unfortunately, too often true. It should be clear that before a woman can expect other people to have faith in her and her judgments, she has to demonstrate competence. She also has to have faith in herself. But how does she develop that confidence?

The problem with an egalitarian relationship is that it assumes relatively equal positions. However well intentioned the couple may be, it is difficult indeed for two people who are grossly unequal in the outside world suddenly to seem equal at home. Consequently, the idea of open marriage is a difficult one for many couples to relate to. There is validity to the statement that two people cannot live in an equal, open relationship as long as the woman is socially and economically dependent on the man. The concept of real and significant sharing in a relationship demands a good measure of independence from both parties. They have to be able to feel they are there because they want to be; they are sharing because they want it that way. It simply is not equal, it is not sharing, if one person feels he or she is there because there is absolutely no alternative.

Obviously, then, in an effort to achieve a more equal relationship, most women will have to find within themselves competence, independence, sound judgment, and a certain kind of emotional security. This may be a real challenge for women who are not used to looking at themselves in this way; but once found, it can make anyone feel very good and very strong.

Economic independence is perhaps one of the trickiest attributes for most women to achieve. Many women say that this does not matter to them, but most women who consider themselves liberated will tell you the opposite. It is just those women who appear unconcerned about economic independence who panic when they are hit by divorce or their husband's death. As long as a woman is economically dependent, it is next to impossible for her to have direct confrontations over problems with her husband. Instead her complaints will tend to be expressed in the form of depression, withdrawal, or hysterical outbursts.

If it takes a period of transitional sacrifice to achieve economic independence, your husband will have to believe that it is worth it. Something that may seem silly to him at first can be explained if it is important to you. As one woman said to her husband when she decided to go back to law school: "I've been pushing while you swing a long time. Now it's my turn to swing."

One further point on the subject of economic independence: If you as corporate wife are the owner or co-owner of a large amount of stock in major corporations, you can assert your economic power by going to stockholders' meetings. Your demands, for example, that women be equitably represented in the executive suites and on the board of directors of those organizations could be powerful indeed. Working toward these kinds of changes in the status of women could accomplish an important task, as well as giving you a sense of economic power in your role as consumer and owner.

## NONTRADITIONAL ROLES FOR MEN

One of the unexpected joys for both the corporate executive and corporate wife may come in what at first appears to be the painful shakeup of role expectations. Many corporate executives hide behind their job responsibilities to avoid household tasks that are repetitive and distasteful. But an increasing number of executives are finding real satisfaction and surprising pleasure in their new responsibilities with children.

There is a sense of closeness with your child that can be experienced in no other relationship; loving and caring for a child is a feeling like no other, which fathers benefit from experiencing as well as mothers. The usual pattern of mother accepting all the responsibility for child rearing has probably been counterproductive for mother, father, and child. The more equitable sharing of both burdens and joys is already being shown to benefit all concerned. When the executive gets a fuller sense of what child rearing means, his appreciation of the "mothering" role will probably be enhanced rather than diminished. The corporate wife can then experience her part in the parenting process in a different way. But she will also be freed up to appreciate other parts of herself as well.

Despite this emphasis on more androgynous forms of parenting, roles in the family for men and women are far from reversed. A recent comprehensive article in *Newsweek,* "How Men Are Changing," says that most men are a study in contradictions. Though many men are committed to the ideas of women's lib, they have serious trouble integrating their new values with reality. Nevertheless, many men are reassessing their priorities, their ideas about success, their notions of themselves as omnipotent husbands and lovers. Even the lip service they are giving to the changes in women is important: the rhetoric can ultimately affect the reality.[4]

The emergence of female executives, and consequently corporate husbands, into the business world will most likely also have its benefits (as well as its threats) for corporate wives. It is quite possible that the still rampant corporate transfers will become fewer as corporate husbands refuse to move, and that it will consequently become more acceptable when a corporate wife says no to a move. It is also possible that demands on corporate wives for entertaining will lessen a bit as it is recognized that corporate husbands are not usually available for this. In addition, it is doubtful whether the practice of "looking over" corporate husbands will be as possible or popular as the practice of "looking over" corporate wives has been. It is doubtful too whether the same conservative, narrow standards will be able to be applied to corporate husbands.

At least one writer, John Molloy, has given some serious thought to "executive husbands." He interviewed several of these men and found them to be a most uncomfortable group. All of the men, even those who were executives themselves, complained bitterly of the rudeness at their wives' business-related social gatherings. "The company people start talking shop, and everybody else is out of the conversation. These men find themselves standing there like dummies or talking to their drinks." Nevertheless, top executives whom Molloy interviewed said they expect an executive's husband to have certain skills, and several said it is only a matter of time before companies officially or unofficially interview them as they now interview executive wives.[5] Hopefully, many husbands will refuse this kind of scrutiny, and the unfairness of it for corporate wives will also be seen. It might then be recognized that the qualities they have looked for in corporate wives are not necessarily healthy ones. If the corporate wife is to be judged at all in the future, she may then be judged on her own accomplishments and productivity, rather than her passivity and submissiveness.

## THERE WILL STILL BE CHOICE

In the future, some corporate wives may still choose to ignore their own identity. They may feel as does Inez Donley (Air Products and Chemicals), "I believe in doing things on my own, but I don't think I need to make a mark on the world. My husband is the boss, even though I feel very capable of making decisions. I want to be able to travel with him, so I don't want to tie myself down to any demanding jobs at home. If I were the head of some organization, I would not be free to travel. We are low-key people; I prefer to live that way, work that way, and entertain that way."

Or they may take the route that has been chosen by Rosemary Heimoz-Kaufmann: Rosie is an extraordinarily bright, capable European woman whose husband, Michel Heimoz, is a Swiss-American financial consultant. Although she could certainly be doing other things, she says with a knowing smile, "Ironing my husband's underwear is about the sexiest way I know of keeping my marriage together."

As this cartoon from *The New Yorker* so vividly illustrates, the corporate wife's traditional role can be one hell of a job! An individual woman's choice may still be the same, but the difference between the present and the future will probably be in the way these statements are received. Whereas traditional attitudes presently are positively reinforced in our culture, and whereas they probably today do not represent a very thorough or honest self-evaluation by these women, they will be looked at tomorrow with more scrutiny. These decisions about a woman's identity will in the future be evaluated more in terms of the choices that are open to her and in terms of her responsibility to and for herself.

Challenging the traditional assumptions is never easy, but corporate wives are beginning to see that it can be done. Although the corporate world is changing very slowly in its assumptions about wives, it _is_ changing—mostly in response to corporate wives and their husbands who think there is a better way and are demanding it for themselves.

The media have begun to focus on executives who are shifting their priorities. An article in February 6, 1978 _Industry Week_ says, "They don't shun high risks in their company life. With the family, though, they seek to control the risks. They want stability, respect, and the love of family members. They don't want to earn it at a distance. They want to spend as much time with their family as possible." The new executive is more balanced: "It isn't that his goals aren't as lofty, it's just that he has concluded that rising to the top might not be his ultimate reward." Business entertaining is less important; many of them reserve home entertaining for a limited number of close friends. Many of them have working wives and share household responsibilities with them. Many of them look for a balanced life-style in their residential environment and are refusing to move. They work very hard, but they do not want to be workaholics. They sometimes sneak away for a mental health day: "They can step back from their jobs before losing part of their nose on the grindstone; they allow time for healing." They value their vacations, and limited use of marijuana for relaxation is not uncommon.[6]

Similarly, *Time* magazine, March 6, 1978, says that as the sixties kids become managers, there are more questions, fewer late nights, and a broader concern for society. Young managers are more concerned about balanced life-styles than their elders, and they are harder to control. They are reluctant to accept transfers to other cities if the moves don't fit in with their personal plans; one reason is that many of them are married to women who also have careers. Kids of the sixties, young managers aged twenty-seven to thirty-five, still hold relatively junior jobs, so their influence is limited, but it is growing. "As their influence rises, they will lead corporations toward more openness and disclosure; more debate before making decisions; more emphasis on selecting, training, and rewarding people, including more women and nonwhites; and greater flexibility in life-styles."[7]

Again, *Time* magazine (June 12, 1978) recognizes the change in "Mobile Society Puts Down Roots; Young executives—and their families—resist the nomadic life." American executives are increasingly interested in things money cannot buy, such as a stable home life, fun and culture. They feel that work isn't everything; you've got to stop and smell the roses along the way.[8]

Probably in reaction to this growing emphasis on life-style, there is a disturbing move by some firms to hire and promote divorced men over married ones. This is in direct contrast to the earlier insistence on marital stability; for some who hire executives, the pendulum has swung to the opposite extreme. As a recent *Wall Street*

*Journal* article puts it, the entanglements of families and the recent resistance to moving has made the single-mindedness of divorced executives very attractive.

"For a growing number of jobs many companies actually insist upon the unattached."[9]

This is truly an unfortunate development, just as both men and women seem to be seeking more balance in their lives. Surely a multi-faceted, broader-experienced executive is a better decision maker than the single-minded work horse. But the attitude favoring single-mindedness is understandable from an economic point of view; if the company can't get two employees for the price of one, they damn well want 100% of that one.

The direction of this trend is yet to be seen. As younger, more balanced executives rise to top positions, there may be more value placed on separation of business and family life. It is also possible that, as divorce and competitiveness increase, the divorced executive will be increasingly attractive. Certainly our societal values are still in flux, and many of our sacred long-held beliefs are up for grabs.


## TAKE CREDIT AND TAKE STOCK

Corporate wives are in no small way a part of this change. The media are not giving much credit to them, but it is about time that they be seen at the front of the parade rather than bringing up the rear. There are still risks and uncertainties for those who choose independence and individualism, but there is sufficient encouragement too. You may have to endure some resentment if you try to change your place in the corporate world. You might even have to go on strike until your husband agrees to renegotiate some of your marital role assignments. But you should refuse to be married to a corporate bigamist— psychologist Mortimer Feinberg's term for men who are married to their job and their wife.[10] Your marriage can be much more exciting and alive if both of you put it in perspective. He must give your relationship the importance it deserves; you must not allow it to be the only important thing in your life.

The advantages of being a corporate wife—the financial rewards, the travel, the new people and experiences—cannot and should not be denied. On the contrary: They should be earned and deserved with appropriate behavior in appropriate situations. But they should never be earned at the price of personhood for the corporate wife. In fact, they cease to be of any value at all when the wife must demean her own importance as an equal human being or deny herself the pursuits and pleasures that are uniquely her own.

The use of a self-appreciation inventory might help you to recognize all the things you like in yourself; it may also force you to find ways of changing the "don't likes" into "likes."

The following story comes from a children's book, *The Velveteen Rabbit,* but I like very much what it says about the process of self-appreciation; and I think the analogy to the changing life of the corporate wife is apt:

"What is REAL?" asked the Rabbit one day, when they were lying side by side near the nursery fender, before Nana came to tidy the room. "Does it mean having things that buzz inside you and a stick-out handle?"

"Real isn't how you are made," said the Skin Horse. "It's a thing that happens to you. When a child loves you for a long, long time, not just to play with, but REALLY loves you, then you become REAL."

"Does it hurt?" asked the Rabbit.

"Sometimes," said the Skin Horse, for he was always truthful. "When you are Real you don't mind being hurt."

"Does it happen all at once, like being wound up," he asked, "or bit by bit?"

"It doesn't happen all at once," said the Skin Horse. "You become. It takes a long time. That's why it doesn't often happen to people

322

# SELF-APPRECIATION INVENTORY

(Force yourself to stick with the spaces provided.)

*Things I like about me:*

1.
2.
3.
4.
5.
6.
7.
8.
9.
10.

*Things I don't like about me:*

1.
2.
3.
4.
5.

*What can I do to change the "don't likes" into "likes"?*

1.
2.
3.
4.
5.

who break easily, or have sharp edges or who have to be carefully kept. Generally, by the time you are Real, most of your hair has been loved off, and your eyes drop out and you get loose in the joints and very shabby. But these things don't matter at all, because once you are real you can't be ugly, except to people who don't understand. . . . Once you are real you can't become unreal again. It lasts for always."[11]

It is truly exciting to know that you can be free and still have the benefits of being married to an executive, to find that you can have the best of both worlds. So few of us are fully alive; so seldom do we have minds really open to all kinds of enjoyment; so rare is it that we really understand and enjoy and appreciate ourselves. It is, however, more than a platitude that you must love yourself before you can really love others. Corporate wives can bring much more to a marriage if they have confidence in themselves, if they bring unique and different interests into the relationship, if they have a strong sense of themselves as equal, independent people, and if they have a feeling of control over their own lives.

But in the final analysis, it cannot be done for the marriage or for anyone else. Liberation, freedom, independence, the ability to make choices—all emphasize the value and importance of the person to herself; all point to the corporate wife as a mature, fulfilled, first-class human being.

With some work, a lot of organization, and maybe just a pinch of luck, you can put it all together as an independent corporation wife.

# Epilogue

# Men of Quality Are Not Threatened by Women of Equality

*H. Ray Looney*

I consider myself a liberated man, and my wife has had no small part in "making me what I am today." But the implications of this are not simple, and the resolution of conflicts is not always an easy process. At least once a week—when her work instead of food is piled on the kitchen table; when the laundry must wait till next week because her exams are coming up; when I see other wives taking shirts and suits to the cleaners while I take my own; when Maryanne refuses to go with me to an out-of-town meeting and I am questioned by associates about our relationship; when I ask her about dinner with customers at an elegant restaurant, knowing most women would be pleased, and find that she is angry and upset—at those times, and many more, I repeat to myself, in a semireligious chant, "Men of quality are not threatened by women of equality."

The real fact is that I wouldn't have it any other way. My wife refuses to accept the stereotype of the corporate wife, and that has caused me problems from time to time, but it has also enriched my life, made it more interesting and even exciting.

My seventeen years as a corporate executive in three large companies has taught me, among other things, that my wife is part of my "package." She is expected to perform in a certain way, and when she does not, eyebrows are raised. When I have made it clear to my superiors, for example, that we could not live in small towns because of career opportunities for her, I believe I have seen genuine surprise on their faces. But perhaps the fact that I value her career has helped to make those restrictions more acceptable. The business world is also beginning to see women like her more often, and our situation may be becoming less of an oddity.

Among our business and social relationships, dual-career couples, or couples were the wife is independent, are increasingly common. Corporate couples have some special facets to their lives, but they are not too different from others in their search for reasonable roles. Lou Methenitis, who is president of a manufacturing company in California, says that his wife sometimes works longer hours than he does; Nancy is a social work supervisor who went back to school after their children were grown, and Lou laughs about being "therapized constantly." Jim Coyne is a cardiologist in New Jersey who encouraged his wife Colleen to go back to her psychiatric social work career (they have two small children); but he now wishes at times that she had less energy for work and more for him. Jan Dray, a psychiatrist in the San Francisco Bay area, moved his household and his well-established practice last year so that his wife, Barbara, an attorney, could accept the position of assistant dean at the Stanford University Law School; he is proud of her accomplishments, but finds that her job forces him into a lot of responsibility for entertaining and care of their two pre-school-age children. Bill Gershell is a psychiatrist in New York whose growing practice and analytic training leave him little time for household responsibilities; yet his social worker wife, Roz, is now embarked on an MBA program

326

as well as a part-time job, and the care of their household and six-year-old son must be somehow divided.

Conversation with these couples often revolves around time constraints and role adjustments, but not one of them would want it any other way. Not one of them would want to go back to the system some of them experienced where the husband went out to "earn the bread" and the wife stayed home in a purely supportive role. Why? Their lives are richer for recognition of the fact that when one person invests primarily in the other, and not in herself, it is boring, and unfair, and a tremendous burden as well.

We are all products of our environment, and the secondary role of women is a part of our history. Most men, at this point, feel some conflict between their emotional and intellectual understanding of women. I personally have ambivalent feelings that go way, way back. I was raised by a very strong, assertive mother, who taught me the importance of all individuals—male or female. But I was also raised in a male-oriented family where I had a brother but no sisters. All-male athletics were the most important activities of my youth, and my father was most proud of me when I excelled in aggressive, competitive sports.

I have been part of a corporate system that seldom puts women into decision-making positions. In the last few years every businessman I know has been conscious of the need to change this, but there is also evidence of tremendous resistance. I attended a corporate meeting a few years ago at which Gloria Steinem was the speaker, and almost every man there found her ideas offensive and insulting. At the same time, most men have now become conscious of discrimination and prejudice in the business world, and the more conscious we are, the more we are able to see. My own secretary, Clarice Campbell, is an example of a very capable, dedicated woman, who would have made a very good executive if she had been given the opportunity a few years back.

However, the changes wrought by the women's movement are not merely an effort to make women equal to

327

men in a man's world. The changes, instead, are a basic questioning of some of the most fundamental values in our society; these issues have to do with power-structured relationships, with control by one group over another, and all the other things that "sexual politics" implies. These changes are bound to have a profound effect on all of us— on our jobs and public lives as well as our families and private lives. In most other revolutionary movements, we could choose to be spectators because we did not have to be involved. But in this reevaluation, a majority of Americans—51 percent—are involved. We may have been able to ignore the blacks and young people, but our mothers and wives and daughters and teachers and secretaries can hardly be ignored. This may be the basic reason why the women's movement appears so often as a threat not only to men but to a large percentage of women as well.

The corporate world has traditionally expected a woman to get her "goodies" through her husband. She is somebody because she is somebody's wife. She is supposed to find her fulfillment in taking care of her husband and children. The goal of her life is to get her man, and then to hold her man by being constantly adaptable, available, and gracious. There has been little recognition that, by being put on a pedestal, patronized, flattered, and seduced, women have also been put in a cage. There has been little attention paid to the possibility that, by their being made totally responsible for the household and so-called nuclear family, women have been made helpless in isolation; the family may have become to them not a fortress but a prison.

Above and beyond all this, however, I think it is terribly important to recognize that the only sense in which women are victims is a sense in which we are all victims. And if we are all victims, then there are no victims. Men can hardly be held responsible for a system that evolved out of what was economically and sociologically feasible. But, now we must be conscious of contributing to a system which maintains attitudes and behavior that prevent our fullest development of potential as human beings. We are all in this together.

Bill Russell, who has turned out to be as eloquent a writer as he was a basketball player, put it this way:

> The way things are now, most men dominate or are dominated by the women in their lives. Domination carries a heavy price. With it comes all the pressure of trying to dominate someone else's life, and the very difficult and serious obligations that go with domination.
>
> One advantage of dealing with a woman who is free is that you become a part of her life and not her whole life. And she's a part of your life and not your whole life. Some men fear that they will no longer be taken care of when women are free. But I think that then men and women will take care of each other on a firmer basis, because they'll be doing it out of strength, not out of weakness.
>
> With liberation should come the best kind of relationship of all—horizontal relationships. When I say horizontal, I don't mean lying down. I mean where two people are on the same level, and they see eye to eye while standing up. If we liberate ourselves, we should be able to meet as equals in partnership—friends.
>
> Some men today are letting themselves be pushed around so they won't be thought of as chauvinist pigs. But such a patronizing attitude just demonstrates their chauvinism. I don't let anyone push me around, male or female, and I try not to push anyone around. If I refuse to let a man insult me, I should refuse to let a woman insult me. If I were competing against a woman for a job, I would treat her like competition. I won't change my behavior just to avoid being insulted, but I will try to be open to constructive criticism.

329

For some, masculinity means that you should be stronger and smarter than anyone, but for me these traits are without gender.

For some, impotence means an assault on their manhood, but for me it just means you're missing some fun.

Some men are reacting to the women's movement as a threat to them. The key word here is "reacting." Reaction very rarely solves problems. Action solves problems. Just as the civil rights movement profited from the labor movement in terms of tactics, so has the women's movement profited from the civil rights movement, using what will work for them. And men should also learn from these movements.

Men have to treat women as individual entities and not stereotypes. But they must also treat themselves the same way, and not feel that they have to fit images created by other people. It's a two-way street. It goes from man to man, woman to woman, men to women, and vice versa. This is not easy because you walk a fine line between being respectful and being condescending.

Men must learn not to treat women as their mothers or daughters because in most cases, they aren't. Let's treat them as they are—aggressive, pushy, grouchy, unreasonable, unthinking, selfish—just like the rest of us.[1]

Where the woman is not free to be herself, neither is the man. Where the corporate wife seeks her identity through her attachment to her husband, the relationship becomes increasingly degrading for the woman and intolerable for the man. The pressures on most executives are enormous, and the emotional burden of a wife whose identity depends on him increases his already heavy load. I see an awful lot of marriages breaking up these days because of emotionally starved women grasping after emotionally drained men.

330

In the recent past corporations have experienced tremendous changes in their levels of social responsibility and their awareness of human feelings and emotions. The hold on the corporate wife may be one of the last "people expectations" to go, because of its economic consequences, as well as its perpetuation by both men and women; but individual couples are slowly forcing changes in the system. Even though none of us would suggest that an independent corporate wife is perfect bliss, we all benefit from a system where personhood is more important than one's sex. Men may live longer if they can learn from women how to show more emotion; and women may be happier if they can learn from men how to take more responsibility for their own lives. The life of the corporate wife, as well as her executive husband, is changing, and the number of options available to all of us is growing.

# References and Notes

Chapter 1
1. Norma Upson, *How to Survive as a Corporate Wife* (Garden City, N.Y.: Doubleday, 1974), p. 12.
2. Ibid., p. 17.
3. Ibid., p. 190.
4. Ninki Hart Burger, *The Executive's Wife* (New York: Macmillan, 1968), pp. 18–19.
5. Rosabeth Moss Kanter, *Men and Women of the Corporation* (New York: Basic Books, 1977), p. 108.
6. Ibid., p. 125.
7. Lois Wyse, *Mrs. Success* (New York: World, 1970), pp. 136–46.
8. Jane W. Torrey, "A Psychologist's Look at Women," in Robert A. Sutermeister, ed., *People and Productivity* (New York: McGraw-Hill, 1976), p. 156.
9. Gail Sheehy, *Passages: Predictable Crises of Adult Life* (New York: E. P. Dutton, 1976), p. 19.

Chapter 2
1. "For Married Couples, Two Careers Can Be Exercise in Frustration," *Wall Street Journal,* May 13, 1975, p. 1.
2. Hugh Davidson Spitzer, attorney, quoted in "Two Names," Seattle *Times,* September 29, 1975.

*Chapter 3*

1. Unpublished data from the U.S. Department of Health, Education, and Welfare, National Institute of Mental Health.
2. "Provisional data on federally funded community mental health centers, 1975–76," for administrative use only, DHEW, NIMH, April 1977.
3. "Feminist Psychotherapy: Seeking to Redefine 'Healthy' Woman," *New York Times*, March 5, 1974, p. 24.
4. Phyllis Chesler, *Women and Madness* (New York: Doubleday, 1972).
5. Walter R. Gove and Jeannette F. Tudor, "Adult sex roles and mental illness," *Journal of Sociology*, 78(4): 812–935, 1973.
6. Inge K. Broverman, Donald M. Broverman, Frank E. Clarkson, Paul S. Rosenkrantz, and Susan R. Vogel, "Sex-role stereotypes and clinical judgments of mental health," *Journal of Consulting and Clinical Psychology*, 34(1): 1–7, 1970.
7. Phyllis Chesler, "Women as psychiatric and psychotherapeutic patients," *Journal of Marriage and the Family*, 33(4): 746–59, 1971.
8. DHEW, NIMH, Mental Health Statistical Note No. 137, "Primary diagnosis of discharges from non-federal general hospital psychiatric inpatient units, United States, 1975," August 1977.
9. See Myra Weissman et al., "The educated housewife: mild depression and the search for work," *American Journal of Orthopsychiatry*, 43(4): 565–73, 1973. Also see E. Mostow and P. Newberry, "Work role and depression in women: a comparison of workers and housewives in treatment," *American Journal of Orthopsychiatry*, 45(4): 538–48, 1975.
10. Myrna Weissman and Eugene Paykel, "Moving and depression in women," *Transitions/Society*, 9(9): 24–28, 1972.
11. Josef E. Garai, "Sex differences in breakdown of mental health," *Genetic Psychology Monographs*, 81(2): 131–32, 1970.
12. *New York Times*, March 5, 1974, op. cit.

*Chapter 4*

1. William Bowen, "The Sex Life of American Executives," book review of *Executive Life Styles*, *Fortune*, November 1974, p. 242.
2. "Happy on High: Few Divorces for Chiefs," *Time*, June 19, 1978, p. 73.
3. Walt Menninger, "Kinsey Statistics on Men Who Cheat Are Confirmed," Seattle *Times*, April 30, 1978, p. B12.

*Chapter 5*

1. Ninki Hart Burger, *The Executive's Wife* (New York: Macmillan, 1968), p. 71.

2. Eleanor Maccoby and Carol Nagy Nacklin, *The Psychology of Sex Differences* (Stanford, Calif.: Stanford University Press, 1974), p. 160.
3. Ibid., p. 157.
4. Ibid., p. 157.
5. Margaret Hennig and Anne Jardim, *The Managerial Woman* (Garden City, N.Y.: Anchor Press/Doubleday, 1977).
6. Jane W. Torrey, "A Psychologist's Look at Women," in Robert A. Sutermeister, ed., *People and Productivity* (New York: McGraw-Hill, 1976), p. 152.
7. "Women Own Worst Enemies, Poll Reveals," Seattle *Times,* April 22, 1976, p. E1.
8. Hennig and Jardim, op. cit., p. 76.
9. Robert Seidenberg, *Corporate Wives—Corporate Casualties?* (New York: American Management Association, 1973), p. 97.
10. Ibid., p. 105.
11. Respectively the author of *The Total Woman,* and the organizer and writer against the Equal Rights Amendment.
12. Burger, op. cit., p. 9.
13. Seidenberg, op. cit., p. 152.

*Chapter 6*
1. Paula Costa Eastman, "Consciousness-raising as a resocialization process for women," *Smith College Studies in Social Work,* 43(3): 153–83, 1973.
2. A good description of assertiveness-training sessions was published in *New York* magazine, July 28, 1975: "Female Assertiveness: How a Pussycat Can Learn to Be a Panther," by Marsha Dubrow.
3. "Marriage Counseling," *Business Week,* May 1, 1978, pp. 108–110.
4. Myrna Weissman, "The depressed woman: recent research," *Social Work,* 17(5): 22, 1972.
5. "Feminist Psychotherapy: Seeking to Redefine 'Healthy' Woman," *New York Times,* March 5, 1974, p. 24.
6. Carol Wesley, "The Women's Movement and Psychotherapy," *Social Work,* 20(2): 120, 1975.
7. Ibid., p. 122.
8. Wilma Scott Heide, "Position paper on cultural and psychological impediments: are mental health practitioners contributing to the problem?" *The Impact of Fertility Limitation on Women's Life-Career and Personality,* Annals of the New York Academy of Sciences, Vol. 175, Article 3, 1970, p. 976.

*Chapter 8*
1. Rosabeth Moss Kanter, *Men and Women of the Corporation* (New York: Basic Books, 1977), pp. 112–22.

2. Ninki Hart Burger, *The Executive's Wife* (New York: Macmillan, 1968), p. 17.

## Chapter 9

1. "Life Gets Easier for Politicians' Wives," Seattle *Times*, July 21, 1975.
2. "How to Advance Your Husband's Career," two films from BNA Communications, Inc., 5615 Fishers Lane, Rockville, Maryland.
3. *Wall Street Journal*, October 21, 1977, p. 1.
4. Carole Combs quoted in "Moscow Is a Great Place to Study Slavic Languages," Seattle *Times*, July 6, 1977, p. F1.
5. James L. Collier, "Your Happiness and Your Husband's Ego," *Woman's Day*, October 1969, p. 12.
6. Robert Townsend, *Up the Organization* (New York: Knopf, 1970), p. 62.
7. Barry Kimmelman, "Executives' Wives—The Need for a Positive Company-Sponsored Approach," *California Management Review*, VI, Spring 1969, pp. 7–10.
8. Ninki Hart Burger, *The Executive's Wife* (New York: Macmillan, 1968), p. 11.
9. Myrna Weissman, "The depressed woman: recent research," *Social Work*, 17(5): 24, 1972.
10. Jonathan Miller, "The Power of Positive Moving," *Mainliner*, May 1977, pp. 40–43.
11. "Looking from the Inside Out," *Time*, October 3, 1977, p. 85.

## Chapter 10

1. Gloria Steinem quoted in Stephanie Harrington, "Two Faces of the Same Eve," *New York Times Magazine*, August 11, 1974, p. 76.
2. Jill Ruckelshaus quoted in "Different Roles for the Displaced," Seattle *Times*, February 2, 1977, p. H7.
3. Martha Patten, "Using Your Money," Seattle *Times*, October 10, 1977, p. H1.
4. "The Husbands Are Dynamic and So Are Wives," *New York Times*, August 18, 1975.
5. Robert Seidenberg, *Corporate Wives—Corporate Casualties?* (New York: American Management Association, 1973), p. 121.
6. Anne Taylor Fleming, "The Fear of Being Alone," *Newsweek*, December 13, 1976, p. 17.
7. E. Jerry Walker, " 'Til Business Us Do Part?" *Harvard Business Review*, January–February 1976, p. 98.
8. Matina S. Horner, "Toward an understanding of achievement-related conflicts in women," *Journal of Social Issues*, 28(2): 157–75, 1972.

336

9. "Husbands—They Make a Wife's Career Harder," Seattle *Times,* October 3, 1976, p. H7.

*Chapter 11*

1. "The Upward Mobility Two Incomes Can Buy," *Business Week,* February 20, 1978, p. 80.
2. Ibid., p. 86.
3. Sigmund Freud, *Civilization and Its Discontents* (New York: W. W. Norton, 1962), p. 27.
4. Lynn Caine, *Lifelines* (Garden City, N.Y.: Doubleday, 1978), p. 220.
5. "Women Still Denied Top Federal Jobs," Seattle *Times,* March 2, 1975.
6. "Half of Mothers with Young Children Work," Seattle *Times,* September 25, 1977, p. D11.
7. See articles in: *The Impact of Fertility Limitation on Women's Life-Career and Personality,* op. cit.
8. "Women's Jobs Lead to a Baby Bust," Seattle *Times,* October 16, 1977, p. E7.
9. "Gifted Women Who Followed Careers Happier, Study Finds," Seattle *Times,* November 10, 1975, p. E2.
10. Joyce Lain Kennedy, "Highly Paid Women Find Jobs Demanding," Seattle *Times,* September 25, 1977, p. B8.
11. *Wall Street Journal,* May 13, 1975, p. 1.
12. "When Mothers Are Also Managers," *Business Week,* April 18, 1977, p. 156.
13. "The Immobile Society," *Time,* November 28, 1977, p. 108.
14. "Wife-Career Factor Clouds Job Moves," Seattle *Times,* November 15, 1976, p. A18.
15. R. Paul Duncan and Carolyn Cummings Perrucci, "Dual occupation families and migration," *American Sociological Review,* 41 (April): 252–61, 1976.
16. Eleanor Johnson Tracy, "The Loneliness of the Master Turnaround Man," *Fortune,* February 1976, pp. 118–28.

*Chapter 13*

1. Robert Seidenberg, *Corporate Wives—Corporate Casualties?* (New York: American Management Association, 1973), p. 136.
2. Natalie Gittelson, *The Erotic Life of the American Wife* (New York: Dell, 1973).
3. "In Praise of Older Women," *Time,* April 24, 1978, pp. 99–100.
4. "How Men Are Changing," *Newsweek,* January 16, 1978, pp. 52–61.
5. John T. Molloy, "Bitter Plight of Women Executives' Husbands," Seattle *Times,* May 16, 1977, p. B3, and "Ideal Execu-

tive Husband: Plumber Need Not Apply," Seattle *Times*, May 23, 1977, p. D3.

6. Brian S. Moskal, "Executive Life-styles: Shifting Priorities," *Industry Week*, February 6, 1978, pp. 33–40.

7. "The '60s Kids as Managers: More Questions, Fewer Late Nights, and a Broader Concern for Society," *Time*, March 6, 1978, pp. 62–63.

8. "Mobile Society Puts Down Roots," *Time*, June 12, 1978, pp. 73–74.

9. "Firms Become Willing—or Eager—to Hire Divorced Executives," *Wall Street Journal*, May 18, 1978, p. 1.

10. Donald White, "Corporate Bigamists," San Francisco *Chronicle*, October 15, 1976.

11. Margery Williams, *The Velveteen Rabbit* (New York: Doubleday, 1971), pp. 16–18.

*Epilogue*

1. Bill Russell, "Self (n.) The Entire Person of an Individual," Seattle *Times*, March 12, 1978, p. A20.

# Appendix:

# Questionnaires Sent to Chief Executive Officers and Their Wives

THE CORPORATE WIFE: A SURVEY OF *FORTUNE* 500 COMPANY CHIEF EXECUTIVE OFFICERS

1. Please *circle* the qualities that you would consider most valuable in the "ideal" wife of a corporate executive.

| | | |
|---|---|---|
| Ability to entertain well | Enthusiasm | Punctuality |
| | Flexibility | Resourcefulness |
| Accomplishments of her own | Friendliness | Sense of humor |
| | Good health | Skilled conversationalist |
| Adaptability | Good manners | Unselfishness |
| Attractiveness | Graciousness | Versatility |
| Cooperativeness | Gregariousness | Other _____ |
| Creative thinking | Independence | _____ |
| Efficiency | Intelligence | _____ |

2. If you feel any of the above qualities would be detrimental to the functioning of a corporate wife, would you please *x* them out.

3. Please rank the following characteristics of a good corporation wife in order of importance, from 1 to 5.

_____ Able to communicate well with husband and others
_____ Able to entertain well
_____ Able to manage household smoothly
_____ Concerned about her own identity
_____ Devoted to husband and children

4. What would your attitude tend to be about the following situations:

| | Positive | Neutral | Negative |
|---|---|---|---|
| A male executive who is alcoholic | _____ | _____ | _____ |
| A corporate wife who is alcoholic | _____ | _____ | _____ |
| A male executive who has extramarital affairs | _____ | _____ | _____ |
| A corporate wife who has extramarital affairs | _____ | _____ | _____ |
| A male executive who is homosexual or bisexual | _____ | _____ | _____ |
| A corporate wife who is lesbian or bisexual | _____ | _____ | _____ |
| A male executive who seeks psychiatric treatment | _____ | _____ | _____ |
| A corporate wife who seeks psychiatric treatment | _____ | _____ | _____ |
| A corporate wife using a surname other than her husband's | _____ | _____ | _____ |
| A male executive living with a woman but choosing not to marry | _____ | _____ | _____ |
| A male executive occasionally taking time off to care for a sick child while his wife worked | _____ | _____ | _____ |
| A male executive planning his vacation time to coincide with his wife's vacation from her job | _____ | _____ | _____ |
| A corporate wife who is occasionally unavailable for entertaining because of career conflicts | _____ | _____ | _____ |
| A corporate wife who is often unavailable for entertaining because of career conflicts | _____ | _____ | _____ |

340

An executive and his wife who
    follow the principles of
    "open marriage" as you
    understand them          ____    ____    ____
Yourself having an extramarital
    sexual relationship      ____    ____    ____
Your wife having an extramarital
    sexual relationship      ____    ____    ____

5. If a man worked for your company from age 30 to 50, and
   rose to the rank of executive vice-president, approximately how
   many moves might he and his family be expected to make?
   Please circle:
                1  2  3  4  5  6  7  8  9  10  more than 10

6. Approximately how many business-social functions would *your
   wife* be expected to host in one year?
       0–5  6–10  11–15  16–20  21–25  26–30  more than 30
   Approximately how many additional business-social functions
   would she be expected to attend in one year?
       0–5  6–10  11–15  16–20  21–25  26–30  more than 30
   Approximately how many business-social functions would the
   *average corporate wife* in your company be expected to host
   in one year?
       0–5  6–10  11–15  16–20  21–25  26–30  more than 30
   Approximately how many additional business-social functions
   would she be expected to attend in one year?
       0–5  6–10  11–15  16–20  21–25  26–30  more than 30

7. In your company, would it help a male executive in gaining a
   promotion if he were married vs. single or divorced?
   Yes ____ No ____ If yes, why?

8. Would your attitudes as expressed thus far be approximately
   the same for the husband of a female executive?  Yes ____
   No ____ If no, how would they differ?

9. In the past few years, have your attitudes about corporate
   wives changed?  Yes ____  No ____  If yes, drastically
   ____ or slightly ____? In what ways?

10. Any other comments you would like to make would be ap-
    preciated.

11. What is your age?  Under 30____30 to 39____40 to 49
    ____50 to 59____60 or over____

**12.** What is your marital status?

| | |
|---|---|
| Single, never married | _____ |
| Living with someone, not legally married | _____ |
| Married, first marriage | _____ |
| Married, second marriage | _____ |
| Married, third or more marriage | _____ |
| Divorced | _____ |
| Widowed | _____ |

* Would you care to receive a summary of the survey results?
Yes ___ No ___
If yes, your name _____
company _____
address _____

* Would you be willing to meet with me personally to discuss some of your attitudes and experiences in more depth?
Yes ___ No ___
If yes, your name _____
company _____
address _____
phone no. _____

   * If you have identified yourself and wish to maintain complete anonymity for purposes of the survey, you might want to detach this part and return it in a separate envelope.

# THE CORPORATE WIFE: A SURVEY OF *FORTUNE* 500 CHIEF EXECUTIVE OFFICERS' WIVES

1. Please *circle* the qualities that you consider most valuable in the "ideal" wife of a corporate executive.

   | | | |
   |---|---|---|
   | Ability to entertain well | Enthusiasm | Punctuality |
   | Accomplishments of her own | Flexibility | Resourcefulness |
   | | Friendliness | Sense of humor |
   | | Good health | Skilled conversationalist |
   | Adaptability | Good manners | Unselfishness |
   | Attractiveness | Graciousness | Versatility |
   | Cooperativeness | Gregariousness | Other _____ |
   | Creative thinking | Independence | _____ |
   | Efficiency | Intelligence | _____ |

2. If you think any of the above qualities would be detrimental to the functioning of a corporate wife, would you please *cross* them *out.*

3. Please rank the following characteristics of a good corporate wife in order of importance, from 1 to 5.
   - _____ Able to communicate well with husband and others
   - _____ Able to entertain well
   - _____ Able to manage household smoothly
   - _____ Concerned about her own identity
   - _____ Devoted to husband and children

4. What would your attitude tend to be about the following situations in your husband's company:

   | | Positive | Neutral | Negative |
   |---|---|---|---|
   | A male executive who is alcoholic | ____ | ____ | ____ |
   | A corporate wife who is alcoholic | ____ | ____ | ____ |
   | A male executive who has extramarital affairs | ____ | ____ | ____ |
   | A corporate wife who has extramarital affairs | ____ | ____ | ____ |
   | A male executive who is homosexual or bisexual | ____ | ____ | ____ |
   | A corporate wife who is lesbian or bisexual | ____ | ____ | ____ |
   | A male executive who seeks psychiatric treatment | ____ | ____ | ____ |
   | A corporate wife who seeks psychiatric treatment | ____ | ____ | ____ |

| | | | |
|---|---|---|---|
| A corporate wife using a surname other than husband's | ___ | ___ | ___ |
| A male executive living with a woman but choosing not to marry | ___ | ___ | ___ |
| A male executive occasionally taking time off to care for a sick child while his wife works | ___ | ___ | ___ |
| A male executive planning his vacation time to coincide with his wife's vacation from her job | ___ | ___ | ___ |
| A corporate wife who is occasionally unavailable for entertaining because of career conflicts | ___ | ___ | ___ |
| A corporate wife who is often unavailable for entertaining because of career conflicts | ___ | ___ | ___ |
| An executive and his wife who follow the principles of "open marriage" as you understand them | ___ | ___ | ___ |
| Yourself having an extramarital sexual relationship | ___ | ___ | ___ |
| Your husband having an extramarital sexual relationship | ___ | ___ | ___ |

5. If a man worked for your husband's company from age 30 to 50, and rose to the rank of executive vice-president, approximately how many moves do you think he and his family would be expected to make? Please circle:

   1   2   3   4   5   6   7   8   9   10   more than 10

6. What word would most closely describe your attitude about company moves you have made?

   Enthusiastic _____        Resentful _____
   Accepting   _____        Other     _____

   What do you think the attitude of most other corporate wives is about company moves?

   Enthusiastic _____        Resentful _____
   Accepting   _____        Other     _____

7. Approximately how many business-social functions do *you* host in one year?

    0–5   6–10   11–15   16–20   21–25   26–30   more than 30

Approximately how many additional business-social functions do you attend in one year?

    0–5   6–10   11–15   16–20   21–25   26–30   more than 30

Approximately how many business-social functions would the *average corporate wife* in your husband's company host in one year?

    0–5   6–10   11–15   16–20   21–25   26–30   more than 30

Approximately how many additional functions would the average corporate wife attend in one year?

    0–5   6–10   11–15   16–20   21–25   26–30   more than 30

8. Do you think that expectations are approximately the same for the husbands of female executives as they are for corporate wives?

Yes _____ No _____ If no, how would they differ?

9. In the past few years, have your attitudes about corporate wives changed?

Yes _____ No _____ If yes, drastically _____ or slightly _____? In what ways?

10. Any other comments you would like to make would be appreciated.

11. What is your age? Under 30_____30 to 39_____40 to 49_____ 50 to 59_____60 or over _____

12. What is your marital status?   First marriage      _____
                                   Second marriage    _____
                                     Third or more marriage _____

\* Would you care to receive a summary of the survey results?

    Yes _____ No _____

    If yes, your name _____

    address _____

\* Would you be willing to meet with me personally to discuss some of your attitudes and experiences in more depth?

    Yes _____ No _____

    If yes, your name _____

address _____

phone no. _____

* If you have identified yourself and wish to maintain complete anonymity for purposes of the survey, you might want to detach this part and return it in a separate envelope.

# Index

347

351

# MORE BEST-SELLING BOOKS ON BUSINESS AND FINANCE FROM WARNER

**TOLL-FREE DIGEST '79**
*by Toll-Free Digest Co., Inc.*                    **(97-016, $4.95)**

Toll-Free Digest contains over 17,000 listings of numbers across the country that you can call at no charge. The money you save on your first toll-free call will pay for this directory — then it's welcome to the land of the free!

**YOUR CHECK IS IN THE MAIL**
*by Bruce Goldman, Robert Franklin &*
*Kenneth Pepper, Esq.*                    **(81-956, $2.50)**

Let three masters of the art of deferred payment show you how to lead a better life on other people's money, protect yourself from shoddy goods and service, and use business methods to keep businessmen from using your money interest-free.

**STOCK MARKET PRIMER**
*by Claude H. Rosenberg*                    **(91-168, $2.50)**

Here are all the fundamentals of how to increase your success in profit-making investing. This book takes the mystery out of the stock market and gives you valuable tools with which to pick the companies which will be tomorrow's big winners.